Reichskommissariat
Moskowien

Leningrad

W9-AAZ-572

Gorki

Kazan

Kuybyshev

Moscow

SLAV
LANDS

Tula

sk

Reichskommissariat
Ukraine

Kharkov

Stalingrad

Kiev

Rostov-on-Don

Reichskommissariat
Kaukasus

Odessa

Tblisi

harest

Black Sea

Burgas

Istanbul

GERMANY'S
SECRET
MASTERPLAN

GERMANY'S
SECRET
MASTERPLAN

WHAT WOULD HAVE HAPPENED
IF THE NAZIS HAD WON THE WAR

CHRIS McNAB

METRO BOOKS

New York

METRO BOOKS
New York

An Imprint of Sterling Publishing
1166 Avenue of the Americas
New York, NY 10036

Material in this book has been previously published under the title
World War II Data Book: Hitler's Masterplan, 1939–1945.

Additional text on pages 121–125 and 210–212 was taken from Michael Kerrigan's
World War II Plans That Never Happened.

Editorial and design by
Amber Books Ltd
74–77 White Lion Street
London
N1 9PF
United Kingdom

ISBN: 978-1-4351-5902-0

Project Editor: Michael Spilling
Designer: Colin Hawes
Picture Research: Terry Forshaw

For information about custom editions, special sales, and premium and corporate purchases,
please contact Sterling Special Sales at 800-805-5489 or specialsales@sterlingpublishing.com.

Manufactured in China

2 4 6 8 10 9 7 5 3 1

www.sterlingpublishing.com

Picture Credits
Alamy/World History Archive: 99
Art-Tech/Aerospace: 6, 42, 47, 51, 58, 210
Cody Images: 64, 73, 93, 94, 103, 105, 122 (top), 172, 175, 179, 193, 196, 212 (both)
Corbis/Bettmann: 108
Dreamstime/Gepapix: 17
Getty Images/Time & Life: 116
National Archives, UK: 76, 122 (bottom), 123–125 (all)
US Department of Defense: 24, 126, 132, 148

All profile artworks courtesy of Art-Tech except for centre and bottom 202 and 214 (all courtesy of Vincent Bourguignon)
All other images and illustrations © Amber Books

Contents

Absolute Power

Adolf Hitler's personality underpins almost every aspect of this book. His personal views on nationality, destiny, race, politics and war became the bedrock of the entire Nazi movement, and the galvanizing force for a world war.

Yet looking back on his life, Hitler's 'masterplan' was shaped not by a sharp and internally coherent political philosophy but by a conglomeration of often half-formed ideas and sentiments. Some of Hitler's most important decisions were made opportunistically, dictated by events rather than planning, and the design of his government was often chaotic and contradictory.

Yet from the mid-1920s, he had his eye firmly fixed on gaining power over Germany, and he skilfully attained that goal through a mixture of manipulation, threat and political aptitude.

Left: Adolf Hitler and other senior figures from the Nazi Party salute members of the *Sturmabteilung* (SA) in a parade in Nuremburg, before the outbreak of war.

Revenge and destiny

Born on 20 April 1889 in the village of Braunau, Austria, Adolf Hitler was raised between the poles of a serious, loving mother (Klara Poelzl Hitler) and a brutal, depressed father (Alois Schickelgruber Hitler), who often beat the young Adolf.

The friction between father and son developed into a battle of wills as the boy grew older, Adolf resisting his father's educational pressures by consistently underperforming – he left *Realschule* (a type of secondary school focusing on science) in 1905, at the age of 16, without graduating.

Several themes emerge from Hitler's first 16 years of life. First,

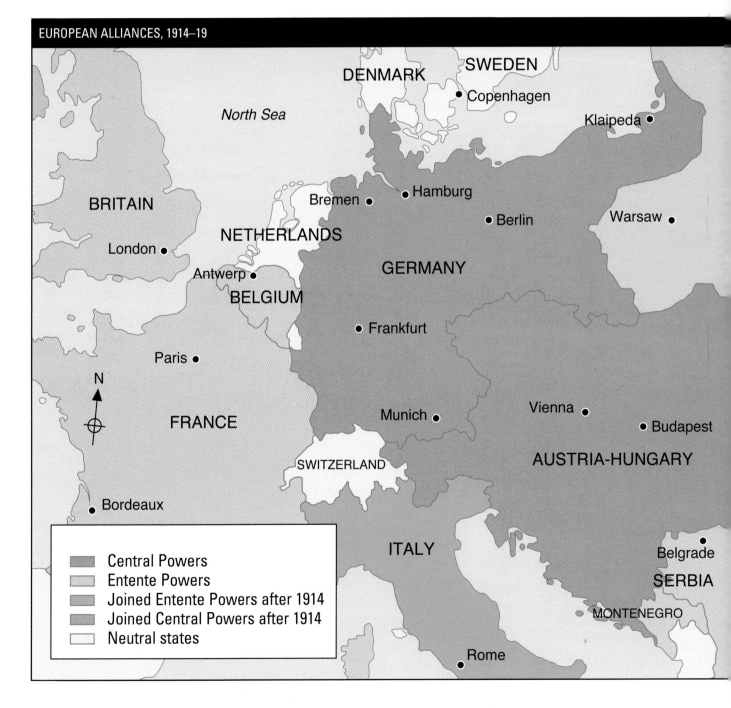

EUROPEAN ALLIANCES, 1914–19

North Sea

DENMARK
SWEDEN
● Copenhagen
Klaipeda ●

BRITAIN
Bremen ● ● Hamburg
Berlin ●
Warsaw ●

NETHERLANDS
London ●
GERMANY

Antwerp ●
BELGIUM

● Frankfurt

Paris ●

N

FRANCE
Munich ●
Vienna ●
● Budapest

SWITZERLAND
AUSTRIA-HUNGARY

● Bordeaux

ITALY
●
Belgrade

SERBIA

MONTENEGRO

Rome ●

Legend:
- Central Powers
- Entente Powers
- Joined Entente Powers after 1914
- Joined Central Powers after 1914
- Neutral states

by the time he left school he was familiar (through his father) with physical force as a way of imposing dominance. Second, one of the few enthusiasms Hitler demonstrated in school was for leadership games

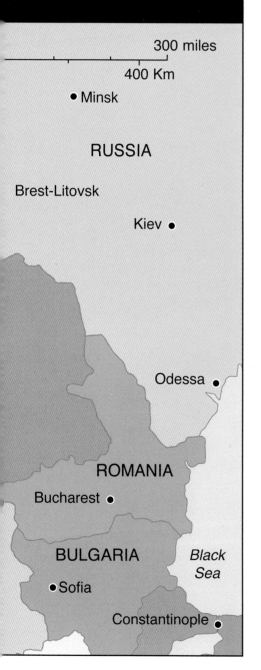

300 miles

400 Km

• Minsk

RUSSIA

Brest-Litovsk

Kiev •

Odessa •

ROMANIA

Bucharest •

BULGARIA   *Black Sea*

• Sofia

Constantinople •

such as 'Follow the Leader' – significantly, Hitler always took the role of chief in these activities. Third, Hitler went into the adult world deeply hostile to academia and academics, showing an inveterate distaste for bookish people. He also left education with a nascent nationalism, partly inspired by the beliefs of one of the few teachers he respected, Dr Leopold Poetsch.

Hitler's subsequent early adulthood showed a singular lack of promise or application. He aspired to be an artist – he was a reasonable sketch artist and painter – but spent the next two years of his life in frustrated indolence. His bitterness deepened in 1907, when he moved to Vienna and failed in his attempt to gain admission to the Vienna Academy of Fine Arts. Compounding his misery, his beloved mother died of cancer in 1908.

For five years, Hitler lived as a virtual vagrant in Vienna, scratching

Left: World War I developed from the political alliances between European states that took place following the unification of Germany in the aftermath of the Franco-Prussian War of 1870–71. One of the most significant alliances was between France and Russia, as this committed Germany to the possibility of a two-front war. For this reason, Hitler was later keen to ensure that he stayed on decent terms with the Soviet Union until the threat from Western Europe had been subdued. Only then could he turn to face Germany's traditional Russian foe.

out a subsistence living by selling sketches and taking odd jobs. Yet the frustration and sadness also found a harder expression in extreme nationalism and anti-Semitism, both of which were strong undercurrents in Europe during the early twentieth century.

Vienna was a city with a highly visible multiculturalism, and included a large Jewish community of 175,000 citizens, more than 17 per cent of the city's entire population. Hitler's nationalism, and probably a good deal of resentment towards Vienna's wealthier Jewish inhabitants, gathered into a hatred of the Jewish race *per se*. Hitler simultaneously fostered a loathing of Marxism, conflating Judaism and socialism in an angry political philosophy. Hitler's emerging world view was also fuelled by a new-found interest in academic study. By his own account in *Mein Kampf* (My Struggle), he studied history, politics and philosophy at every given opportunity, and began to exercise his political voice in workplace and café debates. He also developed an authoritarian model of politics, anti-democratic and anti-liberal:

The psyche of the broad masses is accessible only to what is strong and uncompromising. Like a woman whose inner sensibilities are not so much under the sway of abstract reasoning but are always subject to the influence of a vague emotional longing for the strength that completes her being, and who would rather bow to the strong man

CENTRAL POWERS MILITARY LOSSES, 1914–18

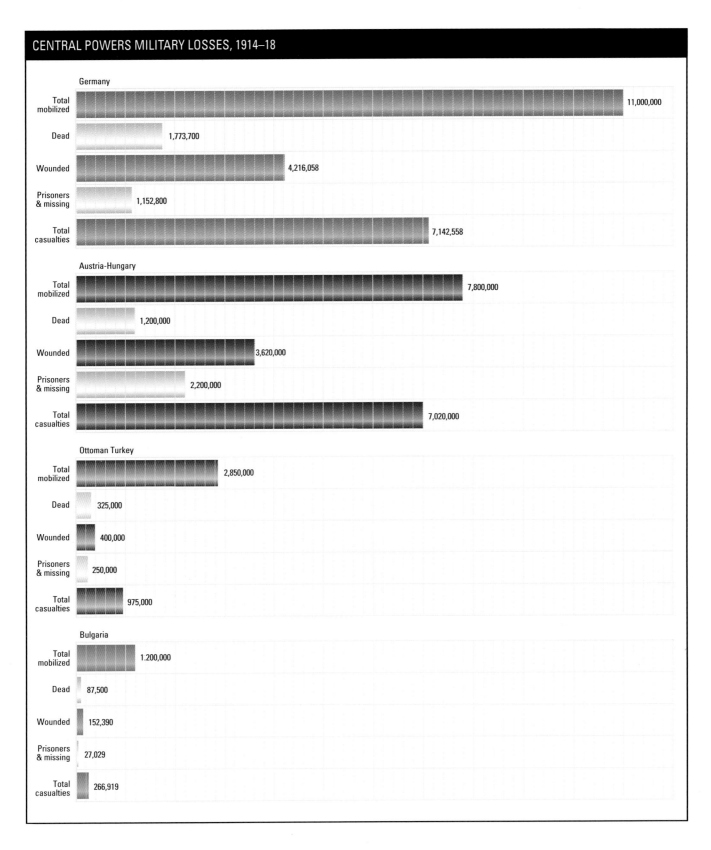

Germany

Total mobilized	11,000,000
Dead	1,773,700
Wounded	4,216,058
Prisoners & missing	1,152,800
Total casualties	7,142,558

Austria-Hungary

Total mobilized	7,800,000
Dead	1,200,000
Wounded	3,620,000
Prisoners & missing	2,200,000
Total casualties	7,020,000

Ottoman Turkey

Total mobilized	2,850,000
Dead	325,000
Wounded	400,000
Prisoners & missing	250,000
Total casualties	975,000

Bulgaria

Total mobilized	1.200,000
Dead	87,500
Wounded	152,390
Prisoners & missing	27,029
Total casualties	266,919

than dominate the weakling – in like manner the masses of the people prefer the ruler to the suppliant and are filled with a stronger sense of mental security by a teaching that brooks no rival than by a teaching which offers them a liberal choice.
— Hitler, *Mein Kampf*, p.45

Here Hitler saw society in terms of an unformed mass waiting to be led. As he strengthened his skills in political debate, he began to conceive of himself in such a role.

War and its aftermath

Vienna was the beginning of Hitler's political journey, but in 1914 began the event that would largely define the future direction of that journey. World War I saw Hitler join the 16th Bavarian Infantry, and he went on to serve with distinction, being awarded both the Iron Cross Second Class and First Class, the latter rarely given to someone of lowly NCO rank. (Hitler achieved only the rank of *Gefreiter* – the equivalent of a British Army lance-corporal – as the promotion boards did not think that he displayed the requisite leadership skills to go any higher.) Hitler experienced plenty of combat firsthand, and was wounded on two occasions, yet he seems to have been energized by the experience of war, finding a place and purpose after the wanderings of his Vienna years. He also saw the war as illustrating the primacy of 'will', something to which he would return in the dying days of

the Wehrmacht in 1944–45. In *Mein Kampf* he stated that:

Already in the winter of 1915–16 I had come through that inner struggle [between 'self-preservation' and duty]. The will had asserted its incontestable mastery. Whereas in the early days I went into the fight with a cheer and a laugh, I was now habitually calm and resolute.
— Hitler, *Mein Kampf*, p.137

The German defeat in 1918 and the subsequent Versailles Treaty settlement were amongst the events that truly radicalized the young Hitler, and stirred him to practical political action. It was a time of enormous upheaval and uncertainty in Germany. Following the Armistice in November 1918, left- and right-wing forces within Germany fought openly for supremacy, and for a time it looked as if revolutionary communism might take hold. In January 1919, however, a new, fragile democratic government was formed, based at Weimar. The Weimar Republic, as the state was known, would endure until 1933, but it was a deeply unpopular government with much of German society, its creation firmly identified with a humiliating military defeat. In 1919, the new government was obliged to sign the Versailles Treaty imposed by the Allies.

The terms of the treaty were tough in the extreme, clamping Germany under subjugating reparations payments, forcing it to admit to responsibility for starting

the war (the so-called 'War-Guilt Clause'), emasculating its armed forces and stripping Germany of its colonies and border territories.

Many in Germany came to subscribe to the *Dolchstoßtheorie* (stab-in-the-back theory). This theory held that the cause of the defeat in the war was not the German Army's battlefield performance, but its political betrayal by Jewish, liberal and socialist politicians at home. A *Reichstag* commission investigation into the basis of the theory produced a report by General Hermann von Kuhl, which summarized the commission's conclusions:

It is certain ... that a pacifistic, international, anti-military, and revolutionary undermining of the army took place which contributed in no small measure to the harm done and the disintegration of the army. It originated at home, but the blame does not attach to the entire population, which in the four and a half years of war endured superhuman sufferings; it attaches only to the agitators and corrupters of the people and of the army who for political reasons strove to poison the bravely-fighting forces.
— Quoted in Snyder, *Encyclopedia of the Third Reich*, p.72

The *Dolchstoßtheorie* was a particularly fiery torch carried by post-war nationalist far-right elements, and post-World War I Germany was virulently split between left and right, producing violence, attempted coups and political agitation. Paramilitary groups abounded, such as the *Freikorps* (Free Corps), a right-wing volunteer army of ex-soldiers and opportunistic radicals.

At first they were utilized by the Weimar Republic to quash revolutionary uprisings and provide security in the absence of a post-war army. Yet in sentiment the *Freikorps* were largely anti-Weimar, and following the formation of the

Reichswehr (Reich Defence – the new German armed forces) in 1920, elements of the *Freikorps* persisted as a violent thorn in the side of the Weimar government.

All of this political strife was compounded by Germany's severe economic problems. In 1923–24, a period of rapid hyperinflation rendered the *Reichsmark* (RM) virtually worthless – at its height it took millions of RM to buy a single loaf of bread. International reaction

eventually restored the value of the currency, but the effect was to devastate middle-class savings, creating a new seam of disgruntled German society, ripe for turning to nationalist politics.

NSDAP membership

So where was Hitler during this time of upheaval? He was a firm subscriber to the *Dolchstoßtheorie*, and sought out organizations that would give some structure to his

---

KEY TERRITORIAL AND POLITICAL CLAUSES OF THE VERSAILLES TREATY, AS PRESENTED FOR GERMAN SIGNATURE ON 28 JUNE 1919

■ ARTICLE 22.

Certain communities formerly belonging to the Turkish Empire have reached a stage of development where their existence as independent nations can be provisionally recognized subject to the rendering of administrative advice and assistance by a Mandatory [i.e., a Western power] until such time as they are able to stand alone. The wishes of these communities must be a principal consideration in the selection of the Mandatory.

■ ARTICLE 42.

Germany is forbidden to maintain or construct any fortifications either on the left bank of the Rhine or on the right bank to the west of a line drawn 50 kilometres to the east of the Rhine.

■ ARTICLE 45.

As compensation for the destruction of the coal mines in the north of France and as part payment towards the total reparation due from Germany for the damage resulting from the war, Germany cedes to France in full and absolute possession, with exclusive right of exploitation, unencumbered and free from all debts and charges of any kind, the coal mines situated in the Saar Basin....

■ ARTICLE 49.

Germany renounces in favour of the League of Nations, in the capacity of trustee, the government of the territory defined above.

At the end of fifteen years from the coming into force of the present Treaty the inhabitants of the said territory shall be called upon to indicate the sovereignty under which they desire to be placed.

Alsace-Lorraine. The High Contracting Parties, recognizing the moral obligation to redress the wrong done by Germany in 1871 both to the rights of France and to the wishes of the population of Alsace and Lorraine, which were separated from their country in spite of the solemn protest of their representatives at the Assembly of Bordeaux, agree upon the following....

■ ARTICLE 51.

The territories which were ceded to Germany in accordance with the Preliminaries of Peace signed at Versailles on February 26, 1871, and the Treaty of Frankfurt of May 10, 1871, are restored to French sovereignty as from the date of the Armistice of November 11, 1918.

The provisions of the Treaties establishing the delimitation of the frontiers before 1871 shall be restored.

right-wing political viewpoints. In September 1919 he joined the small, poorly funded *Deutsche Arbeiterpartei* (DAP; German Workers' Party), and through his talents in oratory and political manoeuvring became its leader within two years. In February 1920, Hitler issued his 'Twenty-five Points', a comprehensive programme of DAP policy and action. Each clause held ominous potential for the future, as can be seen from this selection:

3. We demand land and territory (colonies) for the nourishment of the [German] people and for settling our excess population.
4. Only members of the nation may be regarded as citizens of the state. None but those of German blood, whatever their creed, can be members of the nation. Therefore, no Jew can be a member of the nation.
6. The right to vote on leadership and legislation is to be held by the state alone. We therefore demand that all official positions, regardless of their kind, whether in the Reich, in the country, or in the smaller localities, shall be given to citizens of the state alone. We are against the corrupt practice of Parliament being filled with positions based on party considerations, and without reference to character or ability.

■ ARTICLE 119.
Germany renounces in favor of the Principal Allied and Associated Powers all her rights and titles over her overseas possessions.

■ ARTICLE 156.
Germany renounces, in favour of Japan, all her rights, title and privileges ... which she acquired in virtue of the Treaty concluded by her with China on March 6, 1898, and of all other arrangements relative to the Province of Shantung.

■ ARTICLE 159.
The German military forces shall be demobilized and reduced as prescribed hereinafter.

■ ARTICLE 160.
By a date which must not be later than 31 March 1920, the German Army must not comprise more than seven divisions of infantry and three divisions of cavalry.

After that date the total number of effectives in the Army of the States constituting Germany must not exceed 100,000 men, including officers and establishments of depots. The Army shall be devoted exclusively to the maintenance of order within the territory and to the control of the frontiers.

The total effective strength of officers, including the personnel of staffs, whatever their composition, must not exceed four thousand....

■ ARTICLE 231.
The Allied and Associated Governments affirm and Germany accepts the responsibility of Germany and her allies for causing all the loss and damage to which the Allied and Associated Governments and their nationals have been subjected as a consequence of the war imposed upon them by the aggression of Germany and her allies.

■ ARTICLE 232.
The Allied and Associated Governments recognize that the resources of Germany are not adequate, after taking into account permanent diminutions of such resources which will result from other provisions of the present Treaty, to make complete reparation for all such loss and damage.

The Allied and Associated Governments, however, require, and Germany undertakes, that she will make compensation for all damage done to the civilian population of the Allied and Associated Powers and to their property during the period of the belligerency of each as an Allied or Associated Power against Germany.

VERSAILLES TREATY, MAIN STRICTURES IMPOSED UPON GERMANY

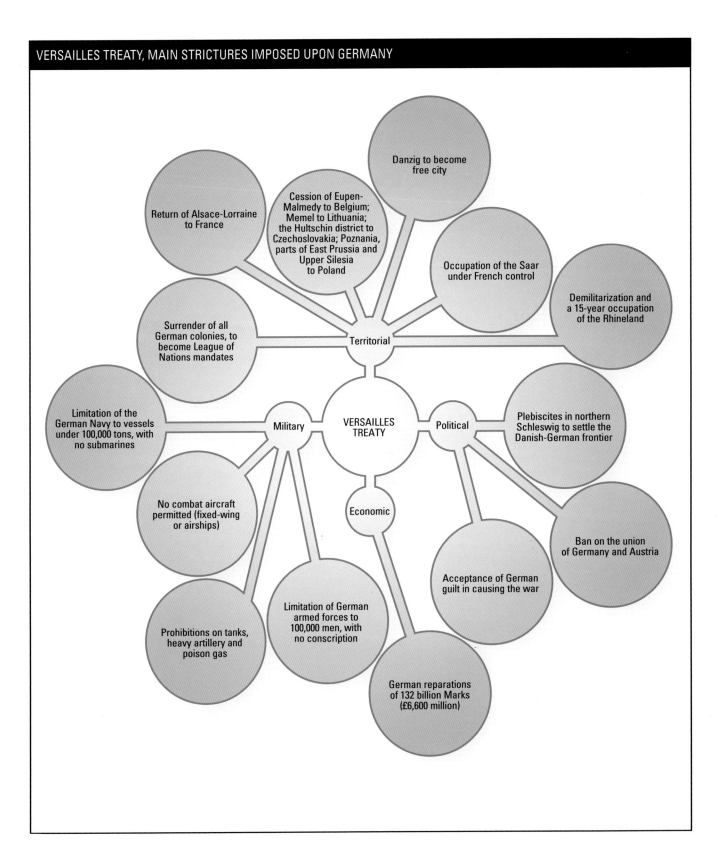

A further clause (24) also noted that 'We demand freedom for all religious denominations in the state, as long as they present no danger to the state and do not have a negative impact on the moral sentiments of the German race.' The clause naturally went on to state that Judaism was one of those threatening religions, and promised to fight 'the Jewish-materialist spirit both within and without'.

Two months after issuing the Twenty-five Points, Hitler changed the name of the DAP to the *Nationalsozialistische Deutsche Arbeiterpartei* (NSDAP; National Socialist German Workers' Party). From this point on, Hitler's power and popularity began to grow. His undoubted skill at public speaking and propaganda won many followers, particularly amongst working-class and middle-class nationalists. His publicity efforts were aided by a certain Joseph Goebbels, who joined the NSDAP in 1922 and subsequently became one of the most talented, and evil, propagandists in history.

Another early NSDAP luminary was World War I fighter ace Hermann Göring, who was to become Hitler's right-hand man during the formative years of the party. The NSDAP also developed its own paramilitary forces to act as muscle at political meetings, or to fight against left-wing equivalents. The *Sturmabteilung* (SA; Storm Detachment) was created out of *Freikorps* elements, while the seeds of the future *Schutzstaffel*

(SS; Security Unit) were sown in the formation of the *Stabswache* (Headquarters Guard) bodyguard unit in 1923; later in the year this was rebranded as the *Stoßtruppe Adolf Hitler* (Shock Troop Adolf Hitler), the name change a clear indication as to where its primary loyalties lay.

Revolution

The NSDAP's expanding powerbase was in Munich, and late in 1923 Hitler's sense of his own importance overreached itself. Believing that the Weimar Republic was exposed to a coup, Hitler and the NSDAP leadership attempted to launch a national revolution on 8 November 1923. Hitler, along with 600 supporters, invaded a meeting held by the Bavarian State Commissioner in the Bürgerbräu Keller, announcing that the governments in both Bavaria and Berlin were to be deposed. Hitler declared to the crowd: 'Tomorrow will find a national government in Germany, or you will find us dead.'

In reality, neither of these outcomes came about. Hitler was substantially heckled by other political figures, and the following day an NSDAP march into the centre of Munich was dispersed by police gunfire at the cost of 16 Nazis and three policemen dead. Göring was seriously injured, and Hitler was arrested, charged with high treason.

Trial and imprisonment

Hitler went to trial in February 1924, and was sentenced to five years'

imprisonment. Yet the 'Beer Hall Putsch' – as the November 1923 uprising in Munich became known – and the trial actually worked in Hitler's long-term favour. The episode raised Hitler to greater national prominence, and many saw him as a true man of the people, fighting for their cause. Hitler took advantage of the trial to deliver stirring political speeches, which were reported widely in the newspapers. He served only nine months of his prison sentence, during which time he began to write his awkward epic *Mein Kampf*, the central document of his political philosophy. Most important, when he emerged from prison he had adopted a new approach to politics. From now on he would turn away from the tools of revolution, and attempt to achieve power through legitimate means.

Mein Kampf

Mein Kampf is by no means a great literary work, even ignoring its frequently disturbing content. Its writing style is clumsy, distracted and frequently repetitive, Hitler often diverting into various rants about race and politics.

The grammar and spelling of his initial drafts required a great deal of editing to pull into shape, and even 'improved' subsequent editions could not mask the fact that the writer had little education behind him. Yet *Mein Kampf* is important, if only as a reference work for understanding Hitler's world view. The fact remains that the book was also highly influential in Germany and abroad – it was translated into nine languages, and sold 5.2 million copies by 1939.

Mein Kampf falls into two volumes. The first part was written during Hitler's incarceration in the Landsberg am Lech prison in Bavaria following the failed Beer Hall Putsch, Hitler dictating the content to fellow inmates Rudolf Hess and Emil Maurice. Hitler's life from childhood to the present state of National Socialism forms the essential core of this first volume, with hefty digressions about the political lessons gleaned during his development. The second part of the book – written between 1925 and 1927 – is more a section of pure political philosophy, dealing with issues such the nature of the state, the use of propaganda, trade unionism and Germany's relationship with Eastern Europe.

Altogether these two volumes form a work of more than 500 pages. The title itself is actually a compression of Hitler's original idea – *Four and a Half Years of Struggle against Lies, Stupidity and Cowardice*. Rightly sensing that the work needed a catchier title, Hitler's publisher, Max Amann, changed it to *Mein Kampf* (*My Struggle*).

Racial hierarchy

Mein Kampf covers a great deal of ideological territory, but some core ideas act as the cement of the entire work. The dominant theme concerns race. His model of race is strictly hierarchical, with the Indo-European 'Aryans' – and particularly the Teutonic Germans – occupying a noble and lofty summit, while those lower down the scale could corrupt this purity with their blood (by interbreeding) and ideas. At the very bottom were the Jews, whom Hitler presented in grotesque fashion as living in a purely parasitic relationship to society, as the following passage indicates:

Look at the ravages from which our people are suffering daily as a

---

KEY THEMATIC STATEMENTS FROM *MEIN KAMPF*

■ **JEWS**
From time immemorial, however, the Jews have known better than any others how falsehood and calumny can be exploited. Is not their very existence founded on one great lie, namely, that they are a religious community, whereas in reality they are a race? (Chapter X, p.185)

■ **MILITARIZATION**
After we had laid down our arms, in November 1918, a policy was adopted which in all human probability was bound to lead gradually to our complete subjugation. Analogous examples from history show that those nations which lay down their arms without being absolutely forced to do so subsequently prefer to submit to the greatest humiliations and exactions rather than try to change their fate by resorting to arms again. (Chapter XVI, p.510)

■ **WAR AND EXPANSIONISM**
When the territory of the Reich embraces all the Germans and finds itself unable to assure them a livelihood, only then can the moral right arise, from the need of the people to acquire foreign territory. The plough is then the sword; and the tears of war will produce the daily bread for the generations to come. (Chapter I, p.17)

■ **RACIAL PURITY**
In short, the results of miscegenation are always the following:
(a) The level of the superior race becomes lowered;
(b) physical and mental degeneration sets in, thus leading slowly but steadily towards a progressive drying up of the vital sap. (Chapter XI, p.224)

■ **PROPAGANDA**
The propagandist inculcates his doctrine among the masses, with the idea of preparing them for the time when this doctrine will triumph, through the body of combatant members which he has formed from those followers who have given proof of the necessary ability and will-power to carry the struggle to victory. (Chapter XI, p.444)

MEIN KAMPF – CHAPTER CONTENTS

result of being contaminated with Jewish blood. Bear in mind the fact that this poisonous contamination can be eliminated from the national body only after centuries, or perhaps never. Think further of how the process of racial decomposition is debasing and in some cases even destroying the fundamental Aryan qualities of our German people, so that our cultural creativeness as a nation is gradually becoming impotent and we are running the danger, at least in our great cities, of falling to the level where Southern Italy is today. This pestilential adulteration of the blood, of which hundreds of thousands of our people take no account, is being systematically practised by the Jew today. Systematically these negroid parasites in our national body corrupt our innocent fair-haired girls and thus destroy something which can no longer be replaced in this world.

– Hitler, *Mein Kampf*, p.429

In Hitler's world view, Germany's racial purity equates to national strength, and the Jewish people represent an almost predatory threat to that purity. Such views are appalling to modern eyes, with no basis in sociology, science, reason or morality, yet they were actually part of a broad anti-Semitism that thrived not only in Germany, but also across Europe and into the Americas.

In *Mein Kampf*, Hitler sees it as the business of the state to ensure racial purity as a priority, policing birth control and racial interbreeding, promoting 'racial knowledge', and at the same type promoting a fit and strong youth that would form the bedrock of future greatness. At the same time, the state had a responsibility for promoting a sense of 'national pride', an awareness of the greatness of the people.

A constant thread running through *Mein Kampf* is Hitler's contempt for the Jews; he also displays an equally sharp antipathy for Marxism – he believed that Marxism itself could also be traced back to a Jewish influence. Furthermore, in one of those implausible leaps made so frequently in the book, Hitler sees the principles and practices of parliamentary democracy as underpinning Marxist doctrine and ideology:

Democracy, as practised in Western Europe today, is the fore-runner of Marxism. In fact, the latter would not be conceivable without the former. Democracy is the breeding-ground in which the bacilli of the Marxist world pest can grow and spread. By the introduction of parliamentarianism, democracy produced an abortion of filth and fire, the creative fire of which, however, seems to have died out.

– Hitler, *Mein Kampf*, p.72

Hitler's parallel between Marxism and Judaism was a prevalent belief – the US industrialist Henry Ford held largely the same view. Later in *Mein Kampf*, Hitler also equates democracy with a form of 'cowardice', leaders hiding from their responsibility to take decisions behind the supposed will of the masses. In Marxism he saw only mental and political slavery, which had resulted in death and violence on a huge scale in the Soviet Union.

Hitler therefore guides the argument towards an authoritarian model of government: 'The best constitution and the best form of government is that which makes it quite natural for the best brains to reach a position of dominant importance and influence in the community.' The phrase 'dominant importance' would be one directly applicable to the next phase of Hitler's life.

Taking control

The years between Hitler's release from prison in December 1924 and his ascension to the chancellorship in January 1933 were ones of utter transformation for both Hitler and the German nation.

The 1920s continued Germany's economic hardship, as recession gave way to the financial devastation of the Great Depression in 1929, by which time some three million German people were unemployed. Such conditions provided Hitler with a crucial window of opportunity, as confidence in parliamentary democracy effectively collapsed, creating a surge in extremes of left-wing and right-wing views. Hitler, with the help of Goebbels, Göring and a swelling party membership, positioned himself cleverly within this

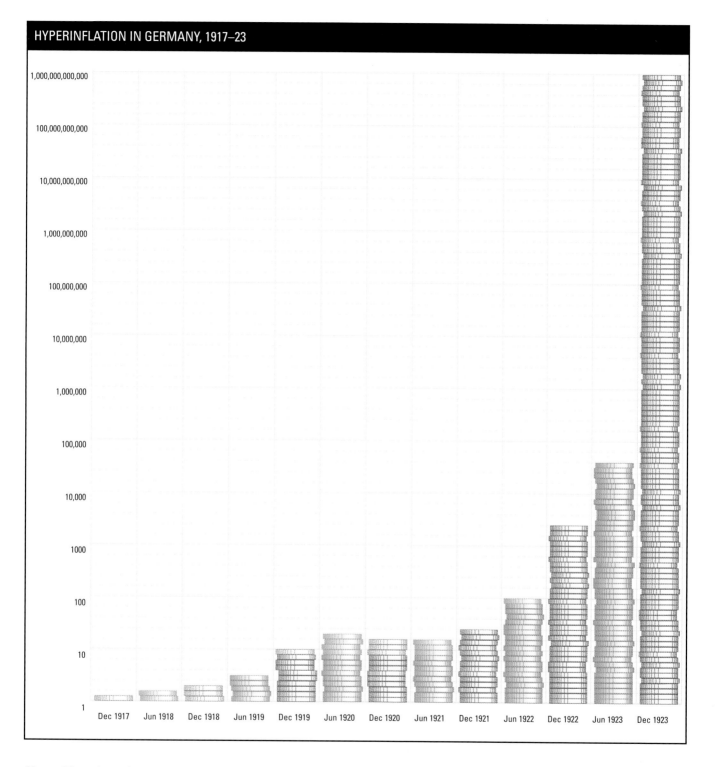

HYPERINFLATION IN GERMANY, 1917–23

Above: Plotted on a logarithmic scale (Dec 1917 = 1), the graph here shows how quickly hyperinflation spiralled out of control in Germany during the 1920s. The discontent these conditions bred amongst all classes of Germans made them more receptive to radical voices such as Hitler's.

turmoil. He managed to make the NSDAP appeal to conservative big business and the working classes, to the former by promising to protect enterprise from communism and unionism, and to the latter by appealing to national pride and the commitment to generating employment for the masses. The middle classes – who had borne the brunt of Germany's economic maladies – also found hope in the NSDAP with policies of financial reform. Furthermore, Hitler courted the military, presenting himself as an old soldier who wanted to restore the pride and power of the German forces, and free them from the shackles of Versailles.

It was a heady mix, but it worked, not least because of relentless

GERMAN DEBT COMPARED, 1931 (MILLIONS REICHSMARKS)

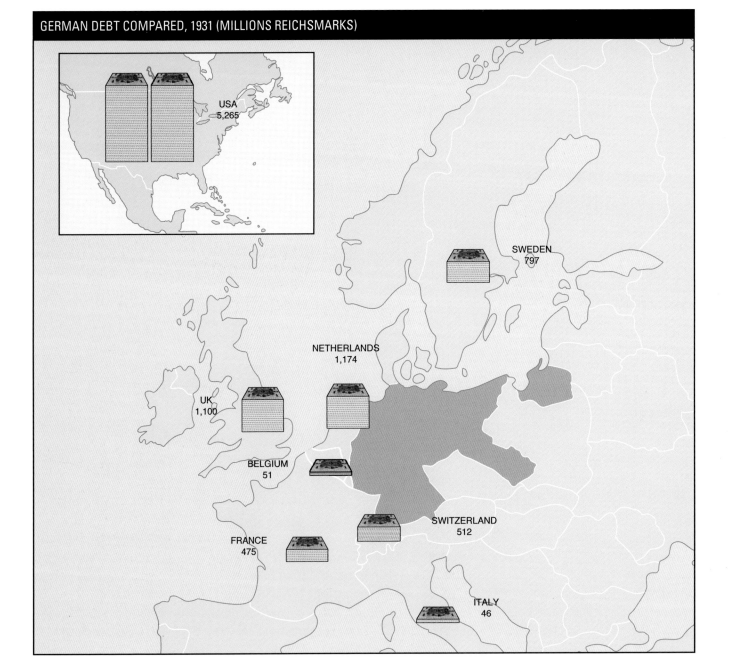

USA
5,265

SWEDEN
797

NETHERLANDS
1,174

UK
1,100

BELGIUM
51

SWITZERLAND
512

FRANCE
475

ITALY
46

MALE AND FEMALE COMPOSITION OF THE NSDAP

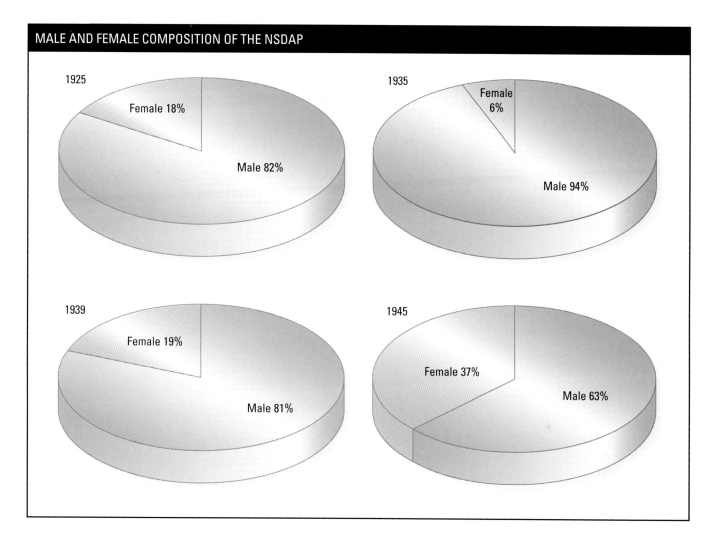

Nazi propaganda and a good eye for political theatrics that stirred a dispirited, vulnerable people. Hitler's oratorical skills (supported by Goebbels' persuasive speech-writing) went from strength to strength, and served him well. NSDAP membership rose significantly, from 27,000 in 1925 to 108,000 in 1928. In balance, however, membership of communist parties also grew impressively, and the NSDAP made little electoral progress during this time, many people still viewing the Nazis as little more than a highly vocal rabble. Hence in the 1929 *Reichstag* elections, the communists secured an impressive 54 seats, against the NSDAP's 12.

Opposite: Germany's debt to the victors of World War I was a deeply sore point for Adolf Hitler, who saw it as reducing Germany to a position of servitude. The contrast between Germany's appalling financial position during the 1920s and its apparent wealth in the 1930s became a cornerstone of Hitler's popularity.

Alliances

Yet from 1929, Hitler's political fortunes underwent a significant improvement. The Great Depression had filled Germans with an earnest desire for change. By allying himself with influential nationalists and industrialists, including Alfred Hugenberg – who controlled a powerful publishing and media empire – Hitler was able to drive home his message to a much wider audience, aided by large financial contributions from big business. Essentially, the Nazi Party thrived

MAJOR POLITICAL PARTIES OUTSIDE THE NSDAP

Orientation	Party	Translation	Policy notes
Nationalist	Deutschnationale Volkspartei (DNVP)	German National People's Party	Radical right agenda
			Rejected Weimar Republic and Versailles Settlement
			Strongly aligned with agrarian interests
	Deutsche Volkspartei (DVP)	German People's Party	Right-wing liberal party
			Anti-Republican/anti-Versailles
			Upper middle-class orientation
Catholic/Workers	Zentrum	Centre Party	Largely represented right-of-centre Catholic interests
			Initially pro-Republican, but became more right-wing after Depression
	Bayerische Volkspartei (BVP)	Bavarian People's Party	Similar to Zentrum, but representing Bavarian interests
			Anti-democratic
Liberal	Deutsche Demokratische Partei (DDP)	German Democratic Party	Social liberal agenda
			Emphasis on democratic, republican government
			Broad middle-class support
Socialist/communist	Sozialdemokratische Partei Deutschlands (SPD)	Social Democratic Party of Germany	Socialist agenda focused on working and low middle classes
			Supported the Weimar Republic
			Lost much support to communists during the Depression
	Kommunistische Partei Deutschlands (KPD)	Communist Party of Germany	Communist agenda Affiliated with the Comintern from 1919
			Attracted many disaffected socialists from other parties
			Resisted practical alliance with the SPD against the Nazis

under tough economic conditions, and this was reflected in voting figures. In the 1930 *Reichstag* elections, it took 107 seats, and in 1932 that figure rose to 230.

Just prior to the 1932 elections, Hitler had also run for the position of German president, although he was narrowly beaten by the elderly Paul von Hindenburg. Nazi votes actually contracted in a later election in 1932, but the NSDAP were now undeniably one of the dominant political forces in German life.

The muscular aspect of Nazi power – embodied in the expanding SA and SS – had also grown significantly by this time, and Hitler virtually had armies under his control to intimidate and fight his opponents, particularly communist groups. Yet Hitler would maintain his pursuit of legally acquired power. Since May 1932, when Hindenburg dismissed the incumbent chancellor, Heinrich Brüning, from office, the chancellorship had become the subject of intense political manoeuvring. Hindenburg came under pressure from a group of right-wing politicians and businessmen to appoint Hitler; they hoped to use Hitler's powerbase as a means of resisting communist influence and reshaping the Weimar Republic along their own lines. Under their influence, but also underestimating the man that he would elevate, Hindenburg relented. Adolf Hitler came to power as German chancellor on 30 January 1933. The first critical step in Hitler's 'masterplan' was now in place.

Authoritarian rule

As we have already seen, Hitler propounded an authoritarian model of government, with all decisions emanating from a single, dominant leader. Described by Hitler as the *Führerprinzip* (leadership principle), it was also allied to what was termed *Gleichschaltung* (coordination), a process of bringing all aspects of state life under the control of the National Socialist agenda and ideology. So it was that Hitler began working towards establishing Germany as his personal dictatorship.

On the night of 27 February 1933, the *Reichstag* was severely damaged in an arson attack. The Nazis blamed communist terrorists, although there is the equal possibility that the fire was started by the Nazis themselves as a convenient excuse for what followed. On 24 March 1933, in an act of emergency legislation, the *Reichstag* passed the *Gesetz zur Behebung der Not von Volk und Reich* (Law to Remove the Distress of People and State), also known as the Enabling Act. The law was meant to give Hitler emergency powers to fight communism, but in effect it buried the Weimar Republic and gave Hitler the powers of a dictator. All legislative authority, including domestic and foreign policy and budgetary decisions, was concentrated in the hands of the cabinet, not the *Reichstag*. In effect, Hitler now controlled the state.

Public opinion

Yet Hitler had more to do to consolidate his dictatorship. In May, just weeks after the Enabling Act, he pushed through laws banning trade unions, and took possession of their assets. Political parties (except, of course, the NSDAP) were then prohibited in July, effectively remodelling Germany as a one-party state. The concentration of power in his hands was truly completed in August 1934, when President Hindenburg died. Hitler was already chancellor; he now declared himself *Führer*. His power was supreme.

We must resist the sense that Hitler created his dictatorship with utter disregard for public opinion. His methods could certainly be brutal, as was proven when he crushed the leadership of the SA in the 'Blood Purge' of June 1934. His growing security service and concentration camp system also cast a dark shadow over all those with a mind to opposing him. Yet between 1933 and 1939 he revitalized Germany in such a way that cemented his popularity amongst the armed forces, big business and the people at large. The mechanisms by which he achieved this feat will be looked at in more detail in subsequent chapters, but they included:

■ Stabilizing the economy through a massive investment in public works projects and rearmament industries. The upshot of this investment was that from a figure of nearly eight million unemployed

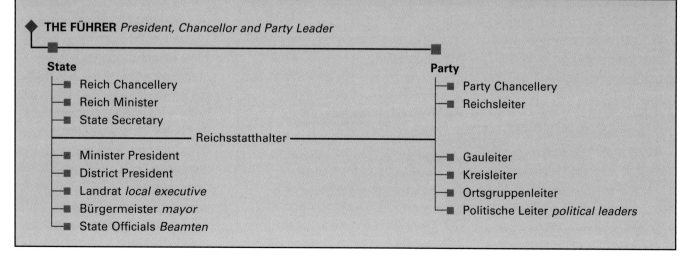

HITLER'S AUTHORITY OVER STATE AND PARTY

◆ **THE FÜHRER** *President, Chancellor and Party Leader*

State
- ■ Reich Chancellery
- ■ Reich Minister
- ■ State Secretary

——————— Reichsstatthalter ———————

- ■ Minister President
- ■ District President
- ■ Landrat *local executive*
- ■ Bürgermeister *mayor*
- ■ State Officials *Beamten*

Party
- ■ Party Chancellery
- ■ Reichsleiter

- ■ Gauleiter
- ■ Kreisleiter
- ■ Ortsgruppenleiter
- ■ Politische Leiter *political leaders*

Once established in Germany, his eyes fell on the wider world.

Gau divisions

Another element important to Hitler's control was the way he restructured the nature of the German state to centralize power upon himself. Hitler did not do away with all the existing mechanisms of state and local governance – these remained in place – but he effectively created a parallel party structure that sat alongside the civic offices and territorial divisions. Within Germany the primary Nazi territorial subdivision was the *Gau*, which mirrored the state *Land*. Each *Gau* was governed by a party *Gauleiter* (District Leader) and his ideologically faithful staff, and the *Gauleiter* was able to wield an onerous influence over the *Ministerpräsident* (Minister President) of the local *Land*. In fact, the independent authority of the *Länder* diminished considerably under Hitler, aided by the fact that thousands of civil servants were purged from their offices by the Nazis and replaced with party members. The *Gauleiter* had a range of important responsibilities within his territory, including overseeing economic and labour policy, as well as political and defence issues. As the political influence of the NSDAP stretched its roots deeper into state soil, party officials could also hold their equivalent state positions.

Opposite: The Nazi Party *Gaue* were essentially administrative districts that existed in parallel to the states and provinces of the civil government. They were headed by a *Gauleiter*, and these figures grew to have great local power, including a paramount influence over the civil authorities and their decision making. Such a system ensured that political control was overlaid on top of civil systems of governance. The number of *Gaue* increased over time with German territorial acquisitions, with 32 in 1934 reaching up to a total of 42 by the end of the war in 1945.

GAUE ESTABLISHED IN 1934		
English name	German name	Headquarters
Baden	Baden	Karlsruhe
Bayreuth	Bayerische Ostmark	Bayreuth
Düsseldorf	Düsseldorf	Düsseldorf
East Prussia	Ostpreußen	Königsberg
Eastern Hanover	Ost-Hannover	Lüneburg
Electoral Hesse	Kurhessen	Kassel
Cologne-Aix-la-Chapelle	Köln-Aachen	Cologne
Essen	Essen	Essen
Franconia	Franken	Nuremberg
Greater Berlin	Groß-Berlin	Berlin
Halle-Merseburg	Halle-Merseburg	Halle
Hamburg	Hamburg	Hamburg
Hesse-Nassau	Hessen-Nassau	Frankfurt am Main
Koblenz-Trier	Koblenz-Trier	Koblenz
Lower Silesia	Niederschlesien	Breslau
Magdeburg-Anhalt	Magdeburg-Anhalt	Dessau
Main-Franconia	Mainfranken	Würzburg
March of Brandenburg	Mark Brandenburg	Berlin
Mecklenburg	Mecklenburg	Schwerin
Munich-Upper Bavaria	München-Oberbayern	Munich
Pomerania	Pommern	Stettin
Saar-Palatinate	Saarpfalz	Neustadt an der Weinstraße
Saxony	Sachsen	Dresden
Schleswig-Holstein	Schleswig-Holstein	Kiel
Southern Hanover-Brunswick	Südhannover-Braunschweig	Hanover
Swabia	Schwaben	Augsburg
Thuringia	Thüringen	Weimar
Upper Silesia	Oberschlesien	Kattowitz (from 1939)
Weser-Ems	Weser-Ems	Oldenburg
Westphalia-North	Westfalen-Nord	Münster
Westphalia-South	Westfalen-Süd	Dortmund
Württemberg-Hohenzollern	Württemberg-Hohenzollern	Stuttgart

NAZI PARTY *GAUE*

Schleswig-Holstein

Danzig

Ostpreußen

Pommern

Hamburg

Mecklenburg

Ost- Hannover

Weser-Ems

Magdeburg-Anhalt

Berlin

Mark
Brandenburg

Südhannover-
Braunschweig

Westfalen-
Nord

Essen

Halle-Merseburg

Westfalen-
Süd

Düsseldorf

Sachsen

Schlesien

Köln-Aachen

Kurhessen

Thüringen

Hessen-Nassau

Koblenz-Trier

Mainfranken

Saarpfalz

Franken

Bayerische
Ostmark

Württemberg-
Hohenzollern

Baden

Schwaben

München-
Oberbayern

N

0   120 miles

0   200 Km

Destiny in War

There is only one word to express what
the German people owe to this army – Everything!
—*Hitler,* Mein Kampf

*With the clarity provided by hindsight, it now appears inevitable
that Adolf Hitler would eventually take his nation to war.
This martial destiny was the product of wide-ranging factors,
but at its heart it involved a man psychologically wedded to
the twin goals of militarism and expansionism.*

*Hitler committed his country to rapid and massive
military growth, while at the same time making demands
on the economy and on raw materials that he could not
sustain in the long term. In short, to fulfil what he saw as
Germany's imperial destiny, he had to take the country
down the road of violent acquisition.*

Left: Young German soldiers march across the plains of Western Russia during
the invasion of the Soviet Union, summer 1941.

Faith in the military

The German defeat in World War I in no way seemed to have shaken Hitler's faith in the nation's armed forces (or at least the German Army). Beyond the bitterness of his *Dolchstoßtheorie* stance, he viewed the humble German infantryman as the embodiment of responsibility, courage, order and organization.

For Hitler, military service was not just about mass obedience. It was also about the perfection of character:

The army trained what at that time was most surely needed: namely, real men. In a period when men were falling a prey to effeminacy and laxity, 350,000 vigorously trained young men went from the ranks of the army each year to mingle with their fellow-men. In the course of their two years' training they had lost the softness of their young days and had developed bodies as tough as steel. The young man who had been taught obedience for two years was now fitted to command. The trained soldier could be recognized already by his walk.

– Hitler, *Mein Kampf*, pp.219–20

Throughout his political career, Hitler had a fondness for likening soldiers to steel, seeing the processes of military training and combat experience as a form of psychological tempering. He was also deeply inspired by the idea that it was will-power which made the difference between the victor and the vanquished. Tactical skill, good equipment and seasoned leaders were all well and good, but if they were not fortified by a fanatical (and ideologically pure) will to triumph and fight, then soldiers would crumble under adversity.

Hitler's insistence upon the supremacy of will became a near-mystical incantation, and it led to his general wartime aversion to anything that could be construed as retreat.

When, in the winter of 1942, it was tentatively suggested that German forces retreat from Stalingrad, Hitler reportedly grew furious and shouted 'Where the German soldier sets foot, there he remains!' The consequence was that the German Sixth Army did indeed remain in the city – to be killed or captured by the triumphant Red Army.

Future threat

Looking back to the 1920s, we see clear signs that Hitler believed Germany's armed forces would have to experience rebirth to help the nation shake off the military subjugation and economic humiliation placed upon it by the Versailles Treaty. In *Mein Kampf* Hitler sharply worked up an impression of French persecution, eternally committed to reducing Germany's martial and financial stature in the world:

Persistently and on every opportunity that arose, the effort to dislocate the framework of the Reich was to have been carried on. By perpetually sending new notes that demanded disarmament, on the one hand, and by the imposition of economic levies which, on the other hand, could be carried out as the process of disarmament progressed, it was hoped in Paris that the framework of the Reich would gradually fall to pieces.

– Hitler, *Mein Kampf*, pp.513–14

Hitler was able to find a ready audience in the German public

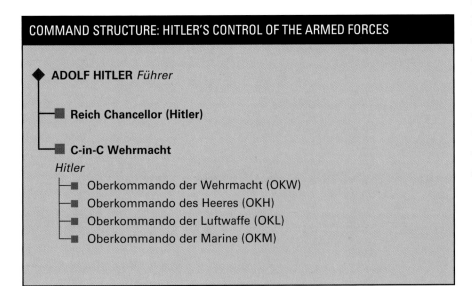

COMMAND STRUCTURE: HITLER'S CONTROL OF THE ARMED FORCES

◆ **ADOLF HITLER** *Führer*

■ **Reich Chancellor (Hitler)**

■ **C-in-C Wehrmacht**
Hitler
  ■ Oberkommando der Wehrmacht (OKW)
  ■ Oberkommando des Heeres (OKH)
  ■ Oberkommando der Luftwaffe (OKL)
  ■ Oberkommando der Marine (OKM)

for such views. The French were singularly hard-minded when it came to enforcing the articles of the Versailles Treaty, and their leadership seemed as intent on completely debasing German power as on extracting reparations. The French occupation of the Rhineland and acquisition of Alsace-Lorraine were bad enough, from the German perspective, but in 1923 Germany's default on reparations payments led French and Belgian troops to occupy the Ruhr, the industrial heart of the German state.

Hitler railed against what he saw as French aggression, and warned that the days of French 'attack' and passive German 'defence' could not continue indefinitely without dire results. For this reason, Hitler wrote both a warning and rallying cry:

Only when the Germans have taken all this fully into account will they cease from allowing the national will-to-life to wear itself out in merely passive defence, but they will rally together for a last decisive contest with France. And in this contest the essential objective of the German nation will be fought for. Only then will it be possible to put an end to the eternal Franco-German conflict which has hitherto proved so sterile.

– Hitler, *Mein Kampf*, pp.514–15

Hitler's language is that of eschatology – the philosophy of final things. He sees France and Germany locked in an 'eternal' conflict, which threatens to wear down the people's will-power. Only if the Germans rise up to fight the last battle will they finally be free.

Such language, read today, can seem hyperbolic, alarming and idealistic, but it doubtless resonated with many in the German population dispirited by the post-war humiliation of their country. Yet as the French occupation of the Ruhr proved, Germany was still powerless to resist its neighbours in the 1920s. That situation would change entirely in the 1930s, once Hitler was in power. Rearmament became an overarching priority – rebuilding the military services of the Third Reich so the nation could no longer be intimidated. To succeed, this strand of Hitler's 'masterplan' had to manoeuvre its way through the restrictions of the Versailles Treaty. That it did so in just a few years was arguably Hitler's greatest pre-war achievement as a statesman, although it also set the world on course for another war.

Versailles limitations

The Military, Naval and Air Clauses of the Versailles Treaty (Nos 159–213) laid down a list of serious proscriptions on the German armed forces.

In essence, the treaty aimed to leave Germany with the barest means of providing internal security, with no ability to wage offensive war in the future. German Army personnel numbers were capped at 100,000 men. Aware that police

COMPARATIVE MILITARY MANPOWER (INCLUDING RESERVES), SEPTEMBER 1939

Country	Manpower
Germany	3,180,000
Soviet Union	9,000,000
France	900,000
UK	681,000
Poland	1,200,000
Belgium	600,000
Italy	1,899,600
Japan	1,700,000
Netherlands	270,000
Australia	13,000
Canada	63,100

and other security forces might be re-employed in paramilitary roles to circumvent the treaty, its writers also noted that:

The number of employees or officials of the German States, such as customs officers, forest guards and coastguards, shall not exceed that of the employees or officials functioning in these capacities in 1913. The number of gendarmes and employees or officials of the local or municipal police may only be increased to an extent corresponding to the increase of population since 1913 in the districts or municipalities in which they are employed. These employees and officials may not be assembled for military training.

– Article 162

In a similar vein, the numbers of artillery pieces, machine guns, mortars, rifles and rounds of ammunition were also restricted, and the treaty governments had to be informed of the locations, activities and outputs of any factories engaged in armament production. Imports or exports of military equipment were strictly forbidden, and production of armoured cars or tanks was prohibited.

In an attempt to restrict future military growth, the Versailles Treaty also hobbled Germany's military training and recruitment system. Conscription was banned – the German Army now had to be a volunteer-only force. Military schools were to be reduced in both number and the volume of students they could take, and non-military educational establishments were forbidden from providing any sort of military instruction, such as running shooting clubs. Article 180 stated that 'All fortified works, fortresses and field works situated in German territory to the west of a line drawn fifty kilometres to the east of the Rhine shall be disarmed and dismantled.'

Navy

For the German Navy, the Versailles Treaty was equally stern. Within two months of the treaty coming into force, the navy had to reduce itself to a total of six battleships, six light cruisers, 12 destroyers and 12

Left: At the end of World War I, the bulk the German High Seas Fleet was interned by the Allies at Scapa Flow, but most of the vessels were eventually scuttled on the orders of the fleet's commanding officer on 21 June 1919.

CRUISERS INTERNED AT SCAPA FLOW

Name	Sunk/beached	Time	Fate
Bremse	Sunk	1430 GMT	Salvaged November 1929
Brummer	Sunk	1305 GMT	Unsalvaged
Dresden	Sunk	1350 GMT	Unsalvaged
Köln	Sunk	1350 GMT	Unsalvaged
Karlsruhe	Sunk	1550 GMT	Unsalvaged
Nürnberg	Beached		To Britain, sunk as target 1922
Emden	Beached		To France, scrapped 1926
Frankfurt	Beached		To USA, sunk as target 1921

BATTLESHIPS INTERNED AT SCAPA FLOW

Name	Sunk/beached	Time	Fate
Kaiser	Sunk	1315 GMT	Salvaged March 1929
Prinzregent Luitpold	Sunk	1315 GMT	Salvaged March 1929
Kaiserin	Sunk	1400 GMT	Salvaged May 1936
König Albert	Sunk	1254 GMT	Salvaged July 1935
Friedrich der Grosse	Sunk	1216 GMT	Salvaged 1937
König	Sunk	1400 GMT	Unsalvaged
Grosser Kurfürst	Sunk	1330 GMT	Salvaged April 1933
Kronprinz Wilhelm	Sunk	1315 GMT	Unsalvaged
Markgraf	Sunk	1645 GMT	Unsalvaged
Baden	Beached		To Britain, sunk as target 1921
Bayern	Sunk	1430 GMT	Salvaged September 1933

torpedo boats – submarines were not allowed in any shape or form. (Some 58 major warships were also allocated for surrender to the Allies, as well as 50 torpedo boats.) Any vessels built to replace these units had their tonnages capped at the following stipulated levels:

- Armoured ships (essentially battleships and heavy cruisers) – 10,000 tons
- Light cruisers – 6000 tons
- Destroyers – 800 tons
- Torpedo boats – 200 tons

As the pre-World War I arms race had been primarily conducted through naval systems, the personnel cuts imposed on the German Navy were also scything – a permitted maximum of 15,000 personnel, including officers of all grades and even administrative staff.

Air force

Regarding German air power, the Versailles Treaty took an even harder line than that adopted for ground and sea forces. Effective immediately, Germany was banned

from having military aviation. Given restrictions upon pilot training and the manufacture or importation of aircraft parts, Germany was also going to struggle to sustain convincing civil aviation.

The Versailles Treaty contained many more prohibitions and limitations on Germany's military development. Just from those outlined above, however, it was clear that the new Germany Army and Navy – to be known as the *Reichsheer* and *Reichsmarine* respectively – were to be slender

DESTROYERS INTERNED AT SCAPA FLOW

Name	Sunk/beached	Fate	Name	Sunk/beached	Fate
S32	Sunk	Salvaged June 1925	V83	Sunk	Salvaged 1923
S36	Sunk	Salvaged April 1925	G86	Sunk	Salvaged July 1925
G38	Sunk	Salvaged September 1924	G89	Sunk	Salvaged December 1922
G39	Sunk	Salvaged July 1925	G91	Sunk	Salvaged September 1924
G40	Sunk	Salvaged July 1925	G92	Beached	To Britain, scrapped 1922
V43	Beached	To USA, sunk as target 1921	G101	Sunk	Salvaged April 1926
V44	Beached	To Britain, scrapped 1922	G102	Beached	To USA, sunk as target 1921
V45	Sunk	Salvaged 1922	G103	Sunk	Salvaged September 1925
V46	Beached	To France, scrapped 1924	G104	Sunk	Salvaged April 1926
S49	Sunk	Salvaged December 1924	B109	Sunk	Salvaged March 1926
S50	Sunk	Salvaged October 1924	B110	Sunk	Salvaged December 1925
S51	Beached	To Britain, scrapped 1922	B111	Sunk	Salvaged March 1926
S52	Sunk	Salvaged October 1924	B112	Sunk	Salvaged February 1926
S53	Sunk	Salvaged August 1924	V125	Beached	To Britain, scrapped 1922
S54	Sunk	Salvaged September 1921	V126	Beached	To France, scrapped 1925
S55	Sunk	Salvaged August 1924	V127	Beached	To Japan, scrapped 1922
S56	Sunk	Salvaged June 1925	V128	Beached	To Britain, scrapped 1922
S60	Beached	To Japan, scrapped 1922	S132	Beached	To USA, sunk 1921
S65	Sunk	Salvaged May 1922	S136	Sunk	Salvaged April 1925
V70	Sunk	Salvaged August 1924	S137	Beached	To Britain, scrapped 1922
V73	Beached	To Britain, scrapped 1922	S138	Sunk	Salvaged May 1925
V78	Sunk	Salvaged September 1925	H145	Sunk	Salvaged March 1925
V80	Beached	To Japan, scrapped 1922	V100	Beached	To France, scrapped 1921

CHAPTER 1 OF THE MILITARY, NAVAL AND AIR CLAUSES OF THE VERSAILLES TREATY: EFFECTIVES AND CADRES OF THE GERMAN ARMY

■ ARTICLE 159.

The German military forces shall be demobilized and reduced as prescribed hereinafter.

■ ARTICLE 160.

(1) By a date which must not be later than March 31, 1920, the German Army must not comprize more than seven divisions of infantry and three divisions of cavalry.

After that date the total number of effectives in the Army of the States constituting Germany must not exceed one hundred thousand men, including officers and establishments of depots. The Army shall be devoted exclusively to the maintenance of order within the territory and to the control of the frontiers.

The total effective strength of officers, including the personnel of staffs, whatever their composition, must not exceed four thousand.

(2) Divisions and Army Corps headquarters staffs shall be organized in accordance with Table No. 1 annexed to this Section.

The number and strengths of the units of infantry, artillery, engineers, technical services and troops laid down in the aforesaid Table constitute maxima which must not be exceeded.

The following units may each have their own depot: An Infantry regiment; A Cavalry regiment; A regiment of Field Artillery; A battalion of Pioneers.

(3) The divisions must not be grouped under more than two army corps headquarters staffs.

The maintenance or formation of forces differently grouped or of other organisations for the command of troops or for preparation for war is forbidden.

The Great German General Staff and all similar organisations shall be dissolved and may not be reconstituted in any form.

The officers, or persons in the position of officers, in the Ministries of War in the different States in Germany and in the Administrations attached to them, must not exceed three hundred in number and are included in the maximum strength

of four thousand laid down in the third sub-paragraph of paragraph (1) of this Article.

■ ARTICLE 161.

Army administrative services consisting of civilian personnel not included in the number of effectives prescribed by the present Treaty will have such personnel reduced in each class to one-tenth of that laid down in the Budget of 1913.

■ ARTICLE 162.

The number of employees or officials of the German States such as customs officers, forest guards and coastguards, shall not exceed that of the employees or officials functioning in these capacities in 1913.

The number of gendarmes and employees or officials of the local or municipal police may only be increased to an extent corresponding to the increase of population since 1913 in the districts or municipalities in which they are employed.

These employees and officials may not be assembled for military training.

■ ARTICLE 163.

The reduction of the strength of the German military forces as provided for in Article 160 may be effected gradually in the following manner:

Within three months from the coming into force of the present Treaty the total number of effectives must be reduced to 200,000 and the number of units must not exceed twice the number of those laid down in Article 160.

At the expiration of this period, and at the end of each subsequent period of three months, a Conference of military experts of the Principal Allied and Associated Powers will fix the reductions to be made in the ensuing three months, so that by March 31, 1920, at the latest the total number of German effectives does not exceed the maximum number of l00,000 men laid down in Article 160. In these successive reductions the same ratio between the number of officers and of men, and between the various kinds of units, shall be maintained as is laid down in that Article.

GERMAN AND ALLIED CAPITAL SHIPS COMPARED

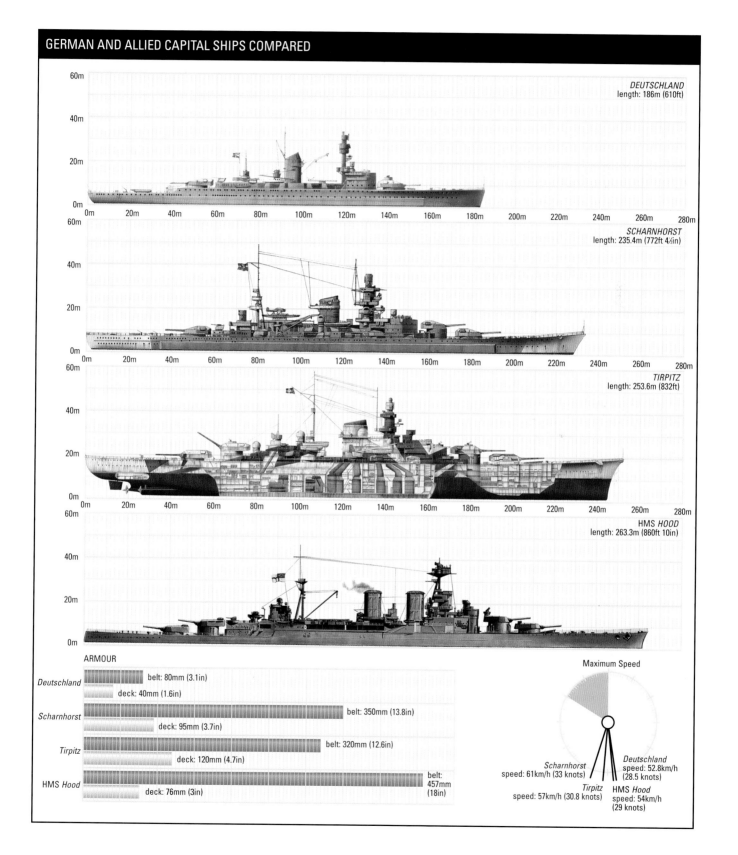

DEUTSCHLAND
length: 186m (610ft)

SCHARNHORST
length: 235.4m (772ft 4⅛in)

TIRPITZ
length: 253.6m (832ft)

HMS *HOOD*
length: 263.3m (860ft 10in)

ARMOUR

Deutschland
belt: 80mm (3.1in)
deck: 40mm (1.6in)

Scharnhorst
belt: 350mm (13.8in)
deck: 95mm (3.7in)

Tirpitz
belt: 320mm (12.6in)
deck: 120mm (4.7in)

HMS *Hood*
belt: 457mm (18in)
deck: 76mm (3in)

Maximum Speed

Scharnhorst
speed: 61km/h (33 knots)

Tirpitz
speed: 57km/h (30.8 knots)

Deutschland
speed: 52.8km/h (28.5 knots)

HMS *Hood*
speed: 54km/h (29 knots)

AIR CLAUSES OF THE VERSAILLES TREATY

■ ARTICLE 198.

The armed forces of Germany must not include any military or naval air forces.

Germany may, during a period not extending beyond October 1, 1919, maintain a maximum number of one hundred seaplanes or flying boats, which shall be exclusively employed in searching for submarine mines, shall be furnished with the necessary equipment for this purpose, and shall in no case carry arms, munitions or bombs of any nature whatever.

In addition to the engines installed in the seaplanes or flying boats above mentioned, one spare engine may be provided for each engine of each of these craft.
No dirigible shall be kept.

■ ARTICLE 199.

Within two months from the coming into force of the present Treaty the personnel of air forces on the rolls of the German land and sea forces shall be demobilised. Up to October 1, 1919, however, Germany may keep and maintain a total number of one thousand men, including officers, for the whole of the cadres and personnel, flying and non-flying, of all formations and establishments.

■ ARTICLE 200.

Until the complete evacuation of German territory by the Allied and Associated troops, the aircraft of the Allied and Associated Powers shall enjoy in Germany freedom of passage through the air, freedom of transit and of landing.

■ ARTICLE 201.

During the six months following the coming into force of the present Treaty, the manufacture and importation of aircraft, parts of aircraft, engines for aircraft, and parts of engines for aircraft, shall be forbidden in all German territory.

■ ARTICLE 202.

On the coming into force of the present Treaty, all military and naval aeronautical material, except the machines mentioned in the second and third paragraphs of Article 198, must be delivered to the Governments of the Principal Allied and Associated Powers.

Delivery must be effected at such places as the said Governments may select, and must be completed within three months.

In particular, this material will include all items under the following heads which are or have been in use or were designed for warlike purposes:

Complete aeroplanes and seaplanes, as well as those being manufactured, repaired or assembled.

Dirigibles able to take the air, being manufactured, repaired or assembled.

Plant for the manufacture of hydrogen.

Dirigible sheds and shelters of every kind for aircraft.

Pending their delivery, dirigibles will, at the expense of Germany, be maintained inflated with hydrogen; the plant for the manufacture of hydrogen, as well as the sheds for dirigibles, may at the discretion of the said Powers, be left to Germany until the time when the dirigibles are handed over.

Engines for aircraft.

Nacelles and fuselages.

Armament (guns, machine guns, light machine guns, bomb-dropping apparatus, torpedo-dropping apparatus, synchronisation apparatus, aiming apparatus).

Munitions (cartridges, shells, bombs loaded or unloaded, stocks of explosives or of material for their manufacture).

Instruments for use on aircraft.

Wireless apparatus and photographic or cinematograph apparatus for use on aircraft.

Component parts of any of the items under the preceding heads.

The material referred to above shall not be removed without special permission from the said Governments.

shadows of their former selves. Just to be clear about the limits of future German military power, the treaty also laid down some ground rules about the extent to which Germany could embroil itself in other people's wars:

Germany agrees, from the coming into force of the present Treaty, not to accredit nor to send to any foreign country any military, naval or air mission, nor to allow any such mission to leave her territory, and Germany further agrees to take appropriate measures to prevent German nationals from leaving her territory to become enrolled in the Army, Navy or Air service of any foreign Power, or to be attached to such Army, Navy or Air service for the purpose of assisting in the military, naval or air training thereof, or otherwise for the purpose of giving military, naval or air instruction in any foreign country.

– Article 179

Essentially, this article prevented Germany from bolstering its strength through military alliances, or attempting to expand its interests in foreign climes through military 'missions'. It also cleverly put the responsibility on Germany to police its nationals abroad, thereby removing the possibility of excuses based on deniability.

All told, the Versailles Treaty appeared to do a comprehensive job of shackling Germany's military rebirth. Yet within 15 years, Germany was openly moving beyond the Versailles Treaty and remodelling itself, with an army, navy and air force, each of which would prove to be among the most powerful in history. How it did so was in many ways due to the diplomatic skill of Adolf Hitler, and the political weaknesses of the former Allies.

Diplomatic victories

Hitler cannot be fully credited for putting Germany on the road to rearmament – many of Germany's nationalists sought an armed resurgence even as the gunfire from World War I died away.

Throughout the 1920s, German military commanders and industrialists found ways to develop weapons and train men secretly, usually by basing their operations in foreign countries (such as Russia), or masking the real activities through civilian front companies. (The civilian Lufthansa airline, for example, was used to train military aviators and develop combat aircraft types.)

Yet furtive rearmament was not an answer to comprehensive rearmament, and so from the time that Hitler came to power in 1933 Germany began to adopt a more defiant posture.

Hitler's first year in office as chancellor was a critical test of the international community's strength of resolve over Versailles. Almost immediately, militarization became one of Hitler's priorities, and he ordered a significant increase in rearmament efforts, including instructions to create an air force and to expand the manpower levels of the army to three times greater than that permitted by Versailles (Hitler wanted 300,000 men in 21 divisions by 1937). In what would become a familiar routine over the next few years, Hitler contravened the terms of the treaty (although at this point in time he was still doing so secretly) and then waited to see how the international community would react.

Within that community, times had changed since the days when the treaty was drafted. Political and strategic tensions between the former Allies meant that unified responses to German rearmament were difficult to achieve. Furthermore, the continuing economic and social fallout from World War I meant that Britain, France and other nations were understandably reluctant to commit themselves to any course of action that might precipitate a costly occupation at best, or outright war at worst. Many statesmen also felt that it was time to allow Germany to enter the international community once again, and that such a policy would actually be the best method of preventing another global conflict in the future.

Hitler preyed on such sentiments by continually and publicly committing himself to the path of peace while simultaneously rearming and becoming more militarily aggressive. It was clever positioning, which kept Britain and France anxious but not so unsettled that they took positive action.

Later in 1933, Hitler upped the ante when he pulled Germany out of an international disarmament conference in Geneva. He had argued that Germany should be allowed to rearm itself to the levels of France, but when he found resistance to the idea he simply withdrew Germany from the conference, and also from the League of Nations. Efforts towards rearmament subsequently increased, but France and Britain made no determined steps to prevent it. Britain was dealing with its own crises, and France preferred to concentrate its efforts on defensive expenditure, including sinking millions of francs into the Maginot Line defences on the Franco-German border (fortifications that the Germans would simply bypass in 1940).

Open rearmament

German rearmament was now essentially an ill-kept secret. Military expenditure grew in Hitler's first two fiscal years from 0.75 billion RM to 1.95 billion RM, a total increase of 160 per cent in just a year. Moreover, in March 1935 Germany evidently felt strong enough to tell the world about its plans.

On 10 March, Hermann Göring declared to the British air attaché that Germany now had an air force, stating that it had some 1500 combat aircraft (the reality

---

ORGANIZATION OF THE *REICHSWEHR*, 1933

◆ **REICH PRESIDENT** *Gen FM Paul von Hindenburg*

Chancellor *Gen-Lt Kurt von Schleicher*
└ Minister of Defence *Gen-Maj Ferdinand von Bredow*
  └ Chef der Heeresleitung *Gen der Inf Kurt Freiherr von Hammerstein-Equord*

  ├ Gruppenkommando 1 *(Berlin) Gen der Inf Gerd von Rundstedt*
  │ ├ 1 Division/Wehrkreiskommando I *(Königsberg) Gen der Inf Werner von Blomberg*
  │ ├ 2 Division/Wehrkreiskommando II *(Stettin) Gen-Lt Fedor von Bock*
  │ ├ 3 Division/Wehrkreiskommando III *(Berlin) Gen-Lt Werner Freiherr von Fritsch*
  │ ├ 4 Division/Wehrkreiskommando IV *(Dresden) Gen-Lt Curt Freiherr von Gienanth*
  │ ├ 1 Kavallerie-Division *(Stettin) Gen-Lt Ludwig Beck*
  │ └ 2 Kavallerie-Division *(Berlin) Gen-Maj Ewald von Kleist*

  └ Gruppenkommando 2 *(Kassel) Gen der Inf Hans Freiherr Seutter von Lötzen*
    ├ 5 Division/Wehrkreiskommando V *(Stuttgart) Gen-Lt Curt Liebmann*
    ├ 6 Division/Wehrkreiskommando VI *(Münster) Gen-Lt Wolfgang Fleck*
    ├ 7 Division/Wehrkreiskommando VII *(Munich) Gen-Lt Wilhelm Ritter von Leeb*
    └ 3 Kavallerie-Division *(Münster) Gen-Maj Wilhelm Knochenhauer*

A Wehrkreis is a German military district. Seven were established in 1919 when the Reichswehr was established as the Armed Forces Command of the Weimar Republic. The Wehrkreis had responsibility for recruiting, drafting and training German soldiers for the division of the Reichsheer that was established at the same location. It also had responsibility for the mobilization of divisions, training them and providing them with trained replacements.

was closer to 800). Even more shockingly, on 16 March Hitler announced to a gathering of foreign ambassadors that he had now authorized the creation of a new *Wehrmacht* (armed forces) of 550,000 men in 36 divisions, aided by the re-introduction of military conscription.

Breaking the treaty

Hitler's plans, which effectively demolished the Versailles Treaty, were greeted with a mix of incredulity and reticence abroad, and enthusiasm and worry at home. As events played out, however, there were no serious repercussions for Germany. Indeed Britain, beginning its role as a dedicated appeaser of Hitler's ambitions, even signed the Anglo-German Naval Agreement with Germany in the following June. This treaty not only granted Germany permission to build a surface fleet 35 per cent of the size of the Royal Navy, but it also allowed the creation of a submarine fleet the same size as Britain's. Here was a green light for Germany's rearmament, and one that the British would subsequently come to regret significantly.

This breakaway from the terms of the Versailles Treaty opened the floodgates to an accelerating programme of German rearmament. In 1932, German Army strength (excluding reserves) had sat at 100,000 men, yet by 1939 that number had climbed to 730,000. Aircraft figures had risen from just 36 to an astonishing 8295 during

GERMAN MILITARY EXPENDITURE, 1925–44 (MILLION RM)

Year	Expenditure
1925	2312
1930	3933
1932	2494
1933	2772
1934	6134
1935	8017
1936	12,325
1937	13,360
1938	22,000
1939	37,340
1940	66,445
1941	86,500
1942	110,400
1943	110,400
1944	132,800

the same period, and the number of major warships from 26 to 88.

Crude expenditure on armaments had gone from 0.75 billion RM to 1939's figure of 17.24 billion RM – in rough terms an increase of more than 2000 per cent. Hitler steered Germany's rearmament through the international community even when there were clear indicators of an expansionist mentality – as evidenced by the remilitarization of the Rhineland in March 1936, the *Anschluss* with Austria in March 1938 and the annexation of the Sudetenland of Czechoslovakia in September 1938.

Furthermore, from 1936 to 1939, Germany also tested out its new weapons and tactics in the Spanish Civil War, supporting General Francisco Franco's rightist Nationalists in the fight against the Republicans, and learning invaluable lessons about combined arms operations for the future. Germany's armed forces were clearly sharpening themselves for war. Other forces, however, were also driving Germany to conflict.

Autarky and the need for war

A critical year in both Germany's rearmament and its move towards an eventual war was 1936. In that year, Hitler announced the launch of his 'Four-Year Plan', a blueprint for the economic remodelling of the German state. The proclamation's opening statement contained a clear outline of Germany's new economic aims:

In four years Germany must be wholly independent of foreign areas in those materials which can be produced in any way through German ability, through our chemical and machine industry, as well as through our mining industry. The re-building of this great German raw material industry will serve to give employment to the masses. The implementation of the plan will take place with National Socialist energy and vigour. But in addition, Germany cannot relinquish the solution of its colonial demands. The right of the German people to live is surely as great as that of other nations …
 – Quoted in Snyder, *Third Reich*

This paragraph expresses a clear desire for Germany to take more control of its raw materials destiny. Hitler was all too aware of how the Allied naval blockade of Germany during World War I had starved the country of natural resources, and he was keen to avoid a similar situation playing itself out in the future. He therefore subscribed to a policy of national self-sufficiency, called *Autarkie* (autarky).

Under the charge of Hermann Göring rather than the Minister of Economics, Hjalmar Schacht (who was opposed to the overriding focus on rearmament amongst the Nazi hierarchy), the Four-Year Plan was itself an expression of autarky, and Göring focused the efforts of industrialists on internal production or sourcing of substances such as fuel oil, synthetic rubber, iron ore and aluminium. At the same time,

German farmers were subsidized to produce more food, and imports of foreign food were reduced.

The efforts towards autarky were never entirely successful. Germany's dependence on foreign natural resources remained high, despite a major reduction in imports. At the same time, the stern focus on rearmament was significantly distorting the German economy. Availability of consumer goods and certain food types dropped, prompting Göring to deliver his famous 'butter-or-guns' speech in 1936. In this speech, he rhetorically asked the German people whether they would prefer to have guns (shorthand for all armaments), which would give Germany 'freedom', or butter (luxury goods), which would simply serve to make the German people 'fat'.

Economic limits

Yet ultimately, rearmament was adversely affecting the Germany economy, raising the spectre of high inflation and generating problems in foreign exchange to purchase the shortfalls in raw materials. The problem reached critical levels in 1938–39. In November 1938, the *Oberkommando der Wehrmacht* (OKW; Supreme Command of the Armed Forces) announced broad reductions in the amounts of raw materials available for armaments production, a situation that only worsened in 1939.

In short, war was probably the only practical solution by which Hitler could prevent his plans for

German greatness unravelling financially. Not that this forced situation was out of kilter with Hitler's general sense of destiny. He had issued a memorandum alongside the Four-Year Plan in 1936, in which he outlined in almost mystical terms the inevitability of future conflict:

Since the French Revolution, the world has been accelerating towards a new conflict, which in its most extreme shape is named Bolshevism, but whose nature and objective is to remove those levels of society that provide leadership to humanity up to the present, replacing them with international

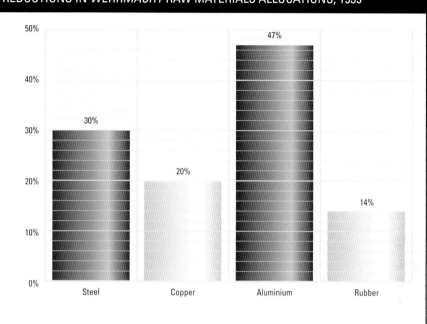

REDUCTIONS IN *WEHRMACHT* RAW MATERIALS ALLOCATIONS, 1939

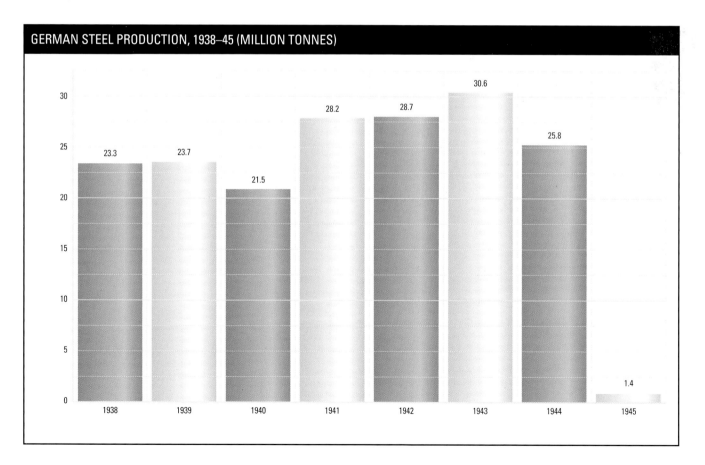

GERMAN STEEL PRODUCTION, 1938–45 (MILLION TONNES)

HITLER'S DECREE ON TAKING COMMAND OF THE *WEHRMACHT*, 4 FEBRUARY 1938

As of now, I am personally assuming direct command of the entire Wehrmacht. The former Department of the Wehrmacht in the Reich Ministry of War, with all its assignments, comes directly under my command as the High Command of the Wehrmacht and as my military staff. The former Chief of the Department of the Wehrmacht becomes Chief of Staff of the High Command of the Wehrmacht with the title 'Chief of the High Command of the Wehrmacht'. His rank is equivalent to that of a Reich Minister. The High Command of the Wehrmacht assumes control of the affairs of the Reich Ministry of War, the Chief of the Wehrmacht exercises, in my name, the authority hitherto vested in the Reich Minister of War. The obligation of the High Command of the Wehrmacht in time of peace is the unified preparation in all spheres of the defence of the Reich according to my directives.

Berlin, 4 February 1938

The Führer and Reich Chancellor: ADOLF HITLER

Jewry. … The gravity of such a disaster cannot be predicted … Faced with the need to fight off this threat, all other considerations must be placed in the background as totally without significance.

Amongst his generals and party leaders, Hitler spoke of 1940 being the likely beginning of this global conflict. As the last sentence of the quotation implies, rearmament in this context took on unprecedented importance if Germany was to survive the inevitable clash of nations.

Designing the *Wehrmacht*

Another key incentive for Hitler to launch a war in the late 1930s and early 1940s was that his potential opponents were getting stronger the more time passed.

At the beginning of his rule, Hitler faced three principal opponents in the event of another global conflict: Britain, France and the Soviet Union. All three, however, had been seriously militarily weakened by the experience of World War I.

Both France and Britain were suffering economically and had implemented broad cuts across the armed forces following the Armistice. The Soviet Union had huge amounts of manpower and armaments, but politically and industrially it was in turmoil, and between 1936 and 1938 Stalin's paranoia got the better of him when he purged the officer corps of thousands of its most talented commanders. Then, in 1939, the Soviet Union was, temporarily, taken out of the threat equation for Germany, when Hitler signed the Nazi-Soviet Non-Aggression Pact.

One consequence of Germany's open rearmament from 1935 was that it triggered a new arms race amongst the former combatants. Yet military expansion in France and Britain was never embraced as wholeheartedly as in Nazi Germany, and both nations would enter the war with serious structural and materiel weaknesses. The fact remained that Hitler's potential enemies were to some degree rearming. Individually he could fight them, but together they presented a formidable force. In essence, Hitler had to take his country to war before his enemies became too strong.

Tactical force

So what sort of *Wehrmacht* did Hitler create? The question is an important one, as it not only reveals Hitler's military thinking, but it also to some extent shows the type of war that he intended to fight.

Hitler had never been a military commander, but his understanding of tactics and weapons systems impressed many of those around him. He had an exceptionally retentive mind for facts and data, a talent that enabled him to pick holes in seemingly watertight reports, and to spot flaws in thinking. It has become historical shorthand to present Hitler as a military meddler, someone who interfered in areas he did not fully grasp and in so doing led the country to certain destruction. Such was indeed the case during the later years of

the war, when the overwhelming pressures of a disintegrating Reich unhinged Hitler through fatigue, illness and unrealistic expectations. Yet during the early years of the conflict, Hitler made some judicious decisions, and approved plans that brought him the conquest of Europe.

Looking back into the pre-war rearmament period, we see fascinating evidence of the type of armed services Hitler was trying to create. Between 1934 and 1939, the *Heer* (Army) always retained the largest proportion of annual expenditure compared with the other services. It accounted for an average of 41 per cent of the total military spend between 1934

and 1938, but then leapt to an impressive 54.8 per cent in the fiscal year 1938–39, as the Third Reich geared itself up for war.

Within the *Heer* spending, Hitler came to focus much of his attention upon the development of the new Panzer arm. The tactical

INCREASES IN MILITARY EXPENDITURE OF THE GREAT EUROPEAN POWERS

	1931–32	1938–39
Great Britain	£107.5m	£397.4m
France	13.8bn francs	29.1bn francs
USSR	1.4m roubles	27m roubles
Germany	0.61bn RM	17.24bn RM
Italy	5.01bn lire	15.02bn lire

MILITARY CAPABILITY, 1932 AND 1939

1932

Britain: 284; 445; 192,000

France: 175; 400; 350,000

Soviet Union: 89; 2595; 562,000

Italy: 150; unknown; 234,000

1939

Britain: Warships 290; Aircraft 7940; Men 237,000

France: Warships 161; Aircraft 3163; Men 500,000

Soviet Union: Warships 101; Aircraft 10,382; Men 1.9m

Italy: Warships 240; Aircraft 3296; Men 400,000

use of armour had been a hot topic of debate amongst the German military leadership since the end of the World War I. Some saw it as nothing more than a support arm for the infantry, while others (fewer in number) believed it to be a war-winning force. One of the latter was Heinz Guderian.

A communications specialist and a veteran of World War I, Guderian developed a special interest in the use of armour and mechanization as methods of rapidly overwhelming a defensively positioned enemy. In 1922 he became Inspector of Motorized Troops, and commander of a motorized battalion in 1930. Utilizing the ideas of British military theorists such as Basil Liddell Hart and John Fuller, Guderian now laid the technological and tactical groundwork for the future *Blitzkrieg* ('Lightning War') tactics.

In terms of composition, he saw German offensive forces consisting

Below: The *Wehrkreis* system geographically streamlined the process of recruiting, training and assigning soldiers. By 1943 there were 19 *Wehrkreise*, and they corresponded with the peacetime corps areas, designated by Roman numerals. The headquarters of each *Wehrkreis* had an active field component and also a deputy component that remained in the home territory and was responsible for administering new intakes of soldiers and controlling the application of reserves.

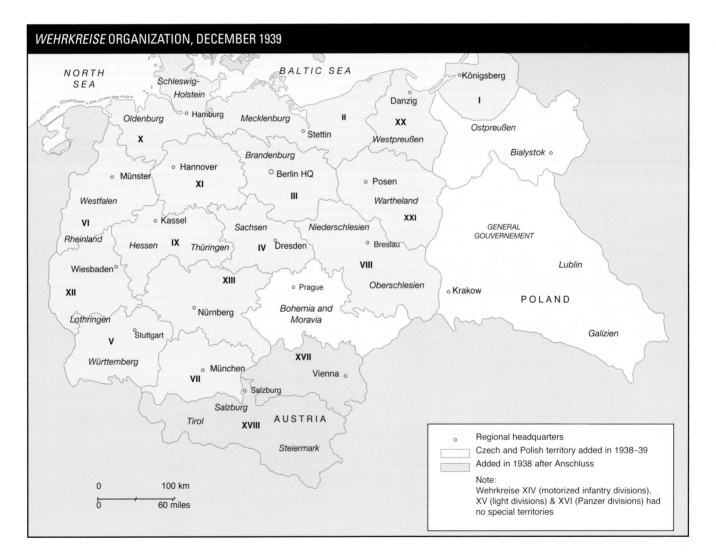

WEHRKREISE ORGANIZATION, DECEMBER 1939

of four principal elements. First, there were armoured and motorized reconnaissance forces, mainly consisting of fast, wheeled vehicles that reported back from the front edge of the battlefield, utilizing radio communications to provide real-time information. (Guderian was a practical pioneer of combat radio

PERCENTAGE ALLOCATIONS OF FUNDING TO THE THREE ARMED SERVICES, 1934–39

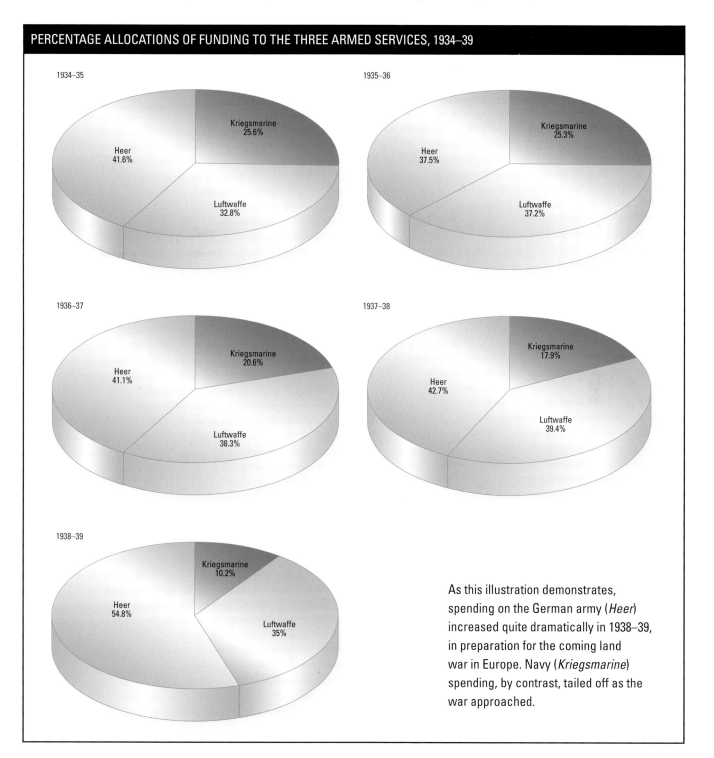

As this illustration demonstrates, spending on the German army (*Heer*) increased quite dramatically in 1938–39, in preparation for the coming land war in Europe. Navy (*Kriegsmarine*) spending, by contrast, tailed off as the war approached.

communications.) Second came the Panzer forces themselves. Guderian condemned the idea that the Panzers should be mixed in with infantry units, as he explained in his influential 1937 work, *Achtung – Panzer!*:

Tanks will lose the capacity to concentrate on the decisive spot if they are incorporated as organic elements of all infantry divisions. Many of the machines will end up in terrain that stops them or slows them down, exposing them to heavy losses, and they will be forced to accord with the slow-moving tactics of horse-drawn artillery and marching infantry.

– Guderian, *Achtung – Panzer!*, p.169

Guderian feared that armoured forces could be squandered through treating them as nothing more than rolling infantry fire support. Instead, his tactical vision for the Panzers was of their working *en masse*, attacking in a concentrated force and utilizing the shock value of fast movement (which required suitable terrain), rapid penetration and overwhelming punch at key points. These armoured spearheads would also work in tandem with tactical air power.

Guderian recognized that one of the greatest threats to his new Panzer arm was from enemy tanks, so anti-tank detachments were the third integral part of his mechanized forces. These motorized units 'have the responsibility for providing protection for the parent formations whether they are at rest, or on the move or in action'. If handled intelligently, they would have the capacity to break up enemy counterattacks and prevent flanking movements, or simply inflict a steady attrition upon opposing armour. A final level of offensive power came from units of motorized infantry. By being deployed to the front line in trucks, rather than on foot, infantry units, Guderian believed, could follow just behind the armoured advanced, consolidating ground as the tanks pushed forward. To make this a workable synergy, Guderian argued strongly for regular training between infantry and armour, to produce the necessary cooperation.

Hitler's support

Guderian effectively created the practical workings of the modern *Blitzkrieg* tactics (although the Germans themselves are unlikely to have used the word as a tactical concept). While he often struggled to get his ideas accepted by many military commanders, Guderian experienced no such trouble with the *Führer*. In 1934, at Kummersdorf, Hitler spent half an hour watching Guderian demonstrate the principles of his armoured warfare with a small number of vehicles. At the end of the demonstration, Hitler was ebullient, and declared 'That's what I need! That's what I have to have!'

With Hitler's backing of the Panzer arm, the *Heer* began to build itself a core armoured force. In 1935 alone, three Panzer divisions were formed – 1, 2 and 3 – and two more followed in 1938 – numbers 4 and 5. The year 1935 also saw the appointment of the first *General der Panzertruppe*, in the form of Oswald Lutz. NSDAP support for the growing Panzer arm was provided in the form of the *Nationalsozialistisches Kraftfahrerkorps* (NSKK; National Socialist Motor Corps), which provided substantial training facilities to instruct the new generation of Panzer crews and military drivers.

There remained resistance in many traditionalist quarters to the mechanization of the German Army. Partly for this reason, Hitler was never quite able to achieve the armoured fighting vehicle (AFV) production figures he aspired to during the pre-war period. Production improved somewhat in 1938–39, once Hitler had taken over as commander-in-chief of the *Wehrmacht*, and Guderian was given a new position – *Chef der Schnellen Truppen* (Chief of Mobile Troops). Since he reported directly to Hitler, this enabled him to bypass many of the political logjams that hampered production.

By such means Hitler was largely able to craft the army of his choice, reflecting a new approach to warfare and military technology that he personally found exciting. Note, however, that a huge percentage of the German Army remained as traditional foot-slogging, horse-drawn infantry of the type that trudged into action in World War

GERMAN SOLDIER'S TEN COMMANDMENTS (PRINTED IN PAY BOOK)

1. *While fighting for victory, the German soldier will observe the rules of chivalrous warfare. Cruelties and needless destruction are below his values.*

2. *Combatants will be wearing uniform or will wear specially introduced and clearly identifiable badges. Fighting in civilian clothes or without such badges is prohibited.*

3. *No enemy who has surrendered will be executed, including partisans and spies. They will be duly punished by courts.*

4. *POWs will not be ill-treated or mocked. Arms, maps and records will be taken away from them, but their personal belongings will not be touched.*

5. *Dum-Dum bullets are prohibited; also no other bullets may be transformed into Dum-Dums.*

6. *Red Cross institutions are sacrosanct. Injured enemies are to be treated humanely. Medical personnel and army chaplains should not be hindered in performing their medical or clerical activities.*

7. *The civilian population is sacrosanct. No looting nor egregious destruction is permitted by the soldier. Landmarks of historical value or buildings serving religious purposes, art, science, or charity are to be especially respected. Deliveries in kind made, as well as services rendered by the population, may only be claimed if ordered by superiors and only against compensation.*

8. *Neutral territory will never be entered nor passed over by aircraft, nor shot at; it will not be the focus of warmaking of any kind.*

9. *If a German soldier is made a POW he will give his name and rank if he is asked for them. Under no*

Above: A young German soldier poses for the camera during the invasion of France, May 1940. He is armed with a Kar 98 rifle and has a stick grenade tucked in his belt.

circumstances will he reveal the unit to which he belongs, nor will he give any information about German military, political and economic conditions. Neither promises nor threats may induce him to do so.

10. *Offences against the a/m matters of duty will be punished. Enemy offences against the principles under 1 to 8 are to be reported. Reprisals are only permissible on order of higher commands.*

KEY TANKS OF THE *WEHRMACHT*, 1933–39

PzKpfw 38(t) Ausf A

Type: Light tank
Crew: 4
Powerplant: 6-cylinder Praga EPA
Speed: 42km/h (26mph)
Weight: 9.4 tonnes (10.4 tons)
Length: 4.6 (15ft 1in)
Width: 2.14m (7ft)
Height: 2.25m (7ft 4.6in)
Armament: 1 x 3.7cm (1.5in) KwK 38(t) cannon; 2 x 7.92mm (0.31in) MG34s

PzKpfw II

Type: Light tank
Crew: 3
Powerplant: 105kW (140hp) 6-cylinder Maybach HL
Speed: 40km/h (25mph)
Weight: 7.2 tonnes (7.9 tons)
Length: 4.8m (15ft 9in)
Width: 2.2m (7ft 3in)
Height: 2.0m (6ft 7in)
Armament: (Ausf A–F) 1 x 2cm (0.78in) KwK 30 cannon;
    1 x 7.92mm (0.31in) MG34

PzKpfw III

Type: Medium tank
Crew: 5
Powerplant: 220kW (296hp) 12-cylinder Maybach HL 120 TRM 300 PS
Speed: 40km/h (25mph)
Weight: 23 tonnes (24.4 tons)
Length: 6.41m (21ft)
Width: 2.9m (8ft 6in)
Height: 2.5m (8ft 2.4in)
Armament: (Ausf A–F) 1 x 3.7cm (1.5in) KwK 36 cannon;
    2–3 x 7.92mm (0.31in) MG34s

PzKpfw IV Ausf C

Type: Medium tank
Crew: 5
Powerplant: 220kW (296hp) 12-cylinder Maybach HL 120 TR & TRM
Speed: 40km/h (25mph)
Weight: 19 tonnes (21 tons)
Length: 5.92m (19ft 5in)
Width: 2.83m (9ft 3.4in)
Height: 2.68m (8ft 9.5in)
Armament: 1 x 7.5cm (3in) KwK 37 L/24; 1 x 7.92mm (0.31in) MG34

l. Given the size of the *Heer*, mechanization was always a partial achievement, but at least in the early years of the war it gave the Germans a critical edge over less modern rivals.

Air power

Between 1933 and 1939, spending on developing an air force was only just below that on building up the land forces. Hitler's commitment to creating a powerful combat aviation element to his *Wehrmacht* was unwavering, as indicated by the fact that his right-hand man, Hermann Göring, held the positions of supreme influence over the *Luftwaffe* (Air Force). These positions included the post of *Reichsluftfahrtminister* (Reich Minister of Aviation) at the *Reichsluftfahrtministerium* (RLM; Reich Ministry of Aviation) and, from February 1935, that of the *Oberbefehlshaber der Luftwaffe* (Commander-in-Chief of the *Luftwaffe*).

Tactical air force

In the short term, Göring's appointments worked to the advantage of the nascent air force. He brought political muscle to aviation rearmament, which meant that the Luftwaffe was able to build itself up from a skeleton arm up to a world-class service. In the long term, however, Göring was a disastrous choice. Although a former fighter pilot himself, he had little understanding of the capabilities or technologies of modern aircraft, and therefore either left big decisions (or big arguments) to subordinates or periodically waded into the fray with ill-informed expectations and judgements.

For Hitler's part, his main interest in the *Luftwaffe* was largely in sheer numbers of aircraft – his grasp of aviation at a strategic and tactical level was sketchy. And here lay the seeds of a serious future problem. During the 1930s, and indeed throughout World War II, Germany largely developed a *tactical* air force without a *strategic* component capable of long-range industrial warfare against distant targets. Despite the advocacy of strategic bombing by judicious individuals such as *Generalleutnant* Walther

Wever, Chief of the *Luftwaffe* General Staff until his death in 1936, Germany never seriously engaged with building a powerful four-engine bomber type, such as the US B-17 or the British Lancaster. The reasons were both strategic in nature and practical. In essence, Hitler and many high-ranking leaders saw the main threats to Germany as cross-border ones – that is, France, Poland and Czechoslovakia; therefore shorter-range air power was more suited to the challenges of supporting ground forces.

Long-range air power was deemed as less relevant to Germany's immediate needs, despite the fact that long-range heavy bombers would give Germany the ability to make major strikes at Britain from Germany were a blockade situation imposed. Consequently, at the outbreak of war the *Luftwaffe's* bomber force was primarily composed of Ju 87 dive-bombers (dive-bombing was a particular obsession of the *Luftwaffe* during the 1930s) and twin-engine medium bombers such as the Dornier Do 17 and the Heinkel He 111.

Naval investment

The *Kriegsmarine* (Navy) came a poor third in the race to secure rearmament investment. Maritime matters were something Hitler neither understood nor, at least until the onset of hostilities, was largely interested in. In consequence, investment in building up Germany's naval force went from about 25 per

cent of total military investment in 1932–33, down to 10.2 per cent in 1938–39.

Although some of this late slump represented the realities of general cuts in raw materials allocations, there were several other reasons for the underinvestment. First, Germany was largely landlocked as a nation, so the military and political leaders naturally felt that most of the nation's future fighting would be done on land, not at sea. They were also realistic about the possibilities of competing effectively with the combined might of the Royal Navy (then the most powerful navy in the world) and the French Navy. Much of Germany's *Hochseeflotte* (High Seas Fleet) had been scuttled at Scapa Flow on 21 June 1919, and what was left was heavily constrained by the terms of the Versailles Treaty.

As with the other branches of service, the *Reichsmarine* (the predecessor of the *Kriegsmarine*) engaged in secret contra-Versailles activities during the 1920s, including the pursuit of new submarine designs through a Dutch company established in The Hague in 1922. Internationally approved warship types also emerged, mainly light vessels such as torpedo boats. In the early 1930s, however, the *Oberbefehlshaber der Reichsmarine* (Commander-in-Chief Reich Navy), *Admiral* Erich Raeder, pushed German warship production on with greater, more controversial projects. Between 19 May 1931 and 30 June 1934, three new major

GERMAN COMBAT AIRCRAFT, 1939–40

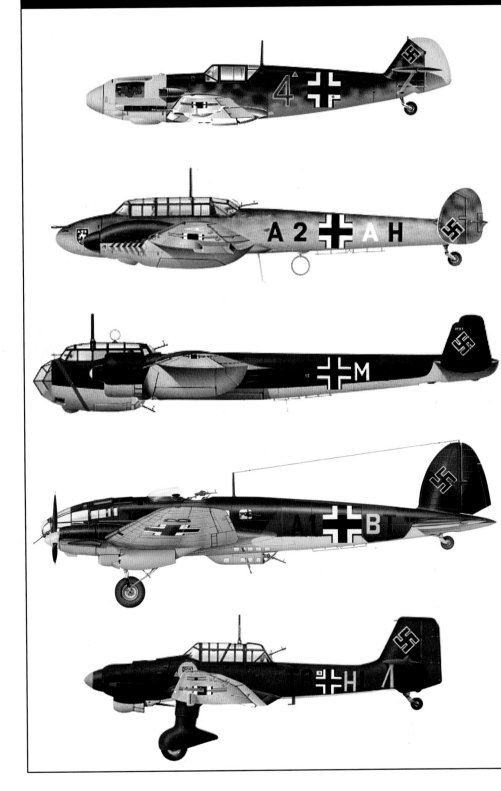

Bf 109E-3

Crew: 1
Powerplant: 895kW (1200hp) DB 601N
  12-cylinder inverted V
Maximum speed: 570km/h (354mph)
Range: 700km (435 miles)
Service ceiling: 10,500m (34,450ft)
Dimensions: span 9.87m (32ft 4in);
  length 8.64m (28ft 4in); height 2.28m (7ft 5.5in)
Weight: 2505kg (5523lb) max loaded
Armament: 2 x wing 20mm (0.78in) cannon;
  2 x 7.92mm (0.31in) MGs

Bf 110C-2

Crew: 2
Powerplant: 2 x 820kW (1100hp) DB 601A
  12-cylinder inverted V
Maximum speed: 560km/h (349mph)
Range: 775km (482 miles)
Dimensions: span 16.27m (50ft 3in);
  length 12.65m (41ft 6in); height 3.5m (11ft 6in)
Weight: 6750kg (14,881lb) max take-off
Armament: 2 x 20mm (0.78in) and 4 x 7.92mm
  (0.31in); plus twin 7.92mm (0.31in) in rear

Do 17Z-2

Crew: 4
Powerplant: 2 x 746kW (1000hp) BMW Bramo
  323P Fafnir nine-cylinder radials
Maximum speed: 425km/h (263mph)
Range: 1160km (721 miles) with light load
Service ceiling: 8150m (26,740ft)
Dimensions: span 18m (59ft); length 15.79m
  (51ft 9in); height 4.56m (14ft 11.5in)
Weight: 9000kg (19,841lb) loaded
Armament: 6 x 7.92mm (0.31in) MGs; 1000kg
  (2205lb) bombload

He 111H

Crew: 4/5
Powerplant: 2 x 895kW (1200hp) Junkers Jumo
  211D 12-cylinder
Maximum speed: 415km/h (258mph)
Range: 1200km (745 miles) with max load
Service ceiling: 7800m (25,590ft)
Dimensions: span 22.6m (74ft 2in);
  length 16.4m (53ft 9.5in); height 4m (13ft 1.5in)
Weight: 14,000kg (30,864lb) max loaded
Armament: up to 7 x MG; 1 x 20mm (0.78in)
  cannon; up to 2000kg (4410lb) bombload

Ju 87B-2

Crew: 2
Powerplant: 895kW (1200hp) Junkers Jumo 211
Maximum speed: 350km/h (217mph)
Range: 600km (373 miles)
Dimensions: span 13.2m (43ft 4in);
  length 11m (36ft 1.1in); height 3.77m (12ft 4in)
Weight: 4400kg (9700lb) max take-off
Armament: 3 x 7.92mm (0.31in) MGs;
  single 1000kg (2205lb) bomb

ships were commissioned in the navy – *Deutschland*, *Admiral Scheer* and *Admiral Graf Spee*. Classified as *Panzerschiffe* (armoured ships), they were fast, powerful warships designed principally as commerce raiders to strike at enemy merchant shipping; and along with other signs they indicated that Germany was pushing the boundaries of the Versailles Treaty.

Unfulfilled potential

As we have seen, 1935 transformed the fortunes of the German armed forces. At last free from the Versailles Treaty, the newly named *Kriegsmarine* could now plan to

return to strength. Yet in reality, underinvestment and dated thinking always held it back from its full potential. For example, five light battleships and five heavy cruisers were planned, but only two of the former and three of the latter were completed. Nevertheless in 1936 two new large battleships – *Bismarck* and *Tirpitz* – were laid down, and by the time they were commissioned in the early 1940s this pair did indeed represent some of the finest warships of any surface navy.

The vessels that would subsequently prove to be the most important types – submarines

and aircraft carriers – were negligently treated. Germany never developed any aircraft carriers within its fleet, and by August 1939 the *Kriegsmarine* had only 56 submarines on its establishment, of which fewer than than half were capable of ocean-going operations. Given the effectiveness of U-boats during World War I, this neglect of the submarine arm was unconscionable. Once the lethality of U-boats was proven in the critical battle of the Atlantic from 1940, Germany attempted to drive ahead with U-boat production, but the numbers never grew high enough to be decisive.

ERICH JOHANN ALBERT RAEDER

Above: Grand Admiral Raeder, photographed for *Signal* propaganda magazine.

Raeder was steeped in the traditions of the Imperial German Navy in which he served with distinction. After the German defeat in 1918, his exceptional administrative skills ensured his rapid promotion in the post-war Reichsmarine.

Birth:	*24 April 1876*
Death:	*6 November 1960*
Place of birth:	*Wandsbek, Schleswig-Holstein*
Father:	*Hans Raeder*
Mother:	*Gertraudt (née Hartmann)*
Siblings:	*n/k*
Personal relationships:	*One son, Hans*
Naval service:	*Officer Cadet: 1894*
	Chief of Staff to Admiral Franz von Hipper: 1912–17
	Rear-Admiral: 1922
	Vice-Admiral: 1925
	Admiral: 1928
	Reichsmarine Chief of Staff: 1928
	General-Admiral: 1936
	Grand-Admiral: 1939
	Admiral Inspector: January 1943
	Retired: May 1943

Z-Plan

Interestingly enough, despite his apparent lack of practical commitment to naval matters, Hitler did approve the *Kriegsmarine*'s 'Z-Plan' in 1938. This ambitious shipbuilding programme was designed to give Germany the capability of taking on the Royal Navy in realistic terms. During the 1930s, there were two different threads of argument about how the navy should be developed. There were those who advocated building large numbers of capital vessels to fight against the French and British navies directly, while others argued for large contingents of U-boats and commerce-raiding light warships better suited to preying on enemy merchant shipping.

The Z-Plan aimed to give Germany the capability to do both by 1944, with a programme that included building an extensive mixed force of battleships, aircraft carriers, heavy and light cruisers, destroyers and submarines. The level of commitment Hitler had to this idea is uncertain, but the Z-Plan never came to fruition. Perhaps he felt that victories on land would give the *Kriegsmarine* time, space and resources to create such a force. The reality is that the German Navy would always play second fiddle to the nation's army and air force.

Looking over the totality of German rearmament during the 1930s, Hitler's goal of having world-class armed services by the early 1940s was largely fulfilled. The *Wehrmacht* was truly formidable technologically, and its training doctrines produced an excellent generation of warriors. The weaknesses of the armed services would take time to reveal themselves, but for a period of roughly three years, the *Wehrmacht* would appear almost unbeatable. Ultimately, decisions made by Hitler about what to do with this force would be its undoing.

Ships that never were

In 1937, the *Oberkommando der Kriegsmarine* (OKM) ordered a design study of new battleships to succeed the *Bismarck* class. Initial proposals were for enlarged and more powerfully armed developments of the basic *Bismarck* design which could be completed to meet the schedule imposed by the Z-Plan.

The schedule soon slipped due to Hitler's love of super-heavy artillery, which caused problems early in the design process. He was adamant that the ships should have 508mm (20in) main armament, rather than the 406mm (16in) guns proposed by the naval design teams. He reluctantly authorized the smaller weapons after it was explained that any battleship with 508mm (20in) guns would be between 81,280 and 121,920 tonnes (80,000–120,000 tons) with an overall length of roughly 300m (984ft). Vessels of this size would need new, greatly enlarged harbour facilities and would take far longer to design and build than more conventional capital ships.

H-39

As finally approved, the H-39 design was basically an enlarged version of the *Bismarck* class. The most prominent recognition feature of the new design was its twin-funnel layout, in contrast to the single funnels of all the *Kriegsmarine*'s earlier capital ships. Internally, the H-39 was very different to *Bismarck* and *Tirpitz* because it was to be powered by 12 MAN diesel engines instead of the earlier vessels' steam turbines. It was calculated that the adoption of diesel engines would increase the H-39s' range by 60 per cent and give a top speed of 55.5km/h (30 knots), comparable to that of the battleships entering service in foreign navies.

The increased proportion of space occupied by the engines and funnels forced a redesign of the aircraft handling arrangements, which on the *Bismarck* concentrated the hangars and catapult amidships. The chosen solution was to site hangars for four Arado Ar 196 seaplanes in the aft superstructure with rails running either side of the after turrets to allow the aircraft to be easily moved to a centreline catapult on the quarterdeck. A total of six H-39-class battleships were ordered under the Z-Plan as follows:

- *Schlachtschiff* H to Blohm & Voss, Hamburg
- *Schlachtschiff* J to Deutsche Schiff- und Maschinenbau AG, Bremen
- *Schlachtschiff* K to Deutsche Werke, Kiel

Z-PLAN FLEET, 1939

C-IN-C NAVY *Gr-Adm Raeder*

Battleships

Schlachtschiff H

Schlachtschiff J

Schlachtschiff K

Schlachtschiff L

Schlachtschiff M

Schlachtschiff N

Battlecruisers

Schlachtkreuzer O

Schlachtkreuzer P

Schlachtkreuzer Q

Flugzeugträger

*Kleiner
Flugzeugträger*

*De Grasse
(Hilfsflugzeugträger II)*

Europa

Gneisenau

Potsdam

Seydlitz

A picture of what might have been. Here we see the principal vessels envisaged in the German 'Z-Plan' of the mid- to late 1930s. This was a serious attempt to provide Germany with a surface vessel fleet capable of taking on Allied navies. Note the major emphasis on maritime aviation in the form of Flugzeugträger (aircraft carriers) and the aircraft-capable Flugdeckkreuzer (flight-deck-equipped cruisers). Most of the aircraft carriers that were actually commissioned ultimately served as passenger ships, and none of the Flugdeckkreuzer were built.

Flugdeckkreuzer

*Grossflugzeugkreuzer
A II*

*Grossflugzeugkreuzer
A III*

*Grossflugzeugkreuzer
A IV*

*Grossflugzeugkreuzer
A IIa*

Flugdeckkreuzer E IV

Flugdeckkreuzer E V

Light Cruisers

Kreuzer M

Kreuzer N

Kreuzer O

Kreuzer P

Kreuzer Q

Kreuzer R

Heavy Cruiser

Kreuzer P1

Kreuzer P2

Kreuzer P3

Kreuzer P4

Kreuzer P5

Kreuzer P6

Kreuzer P7

Kreuzer P8

Kreuzer P9

Kreuzer P10

Kreuzer P11

Kreuzer P12

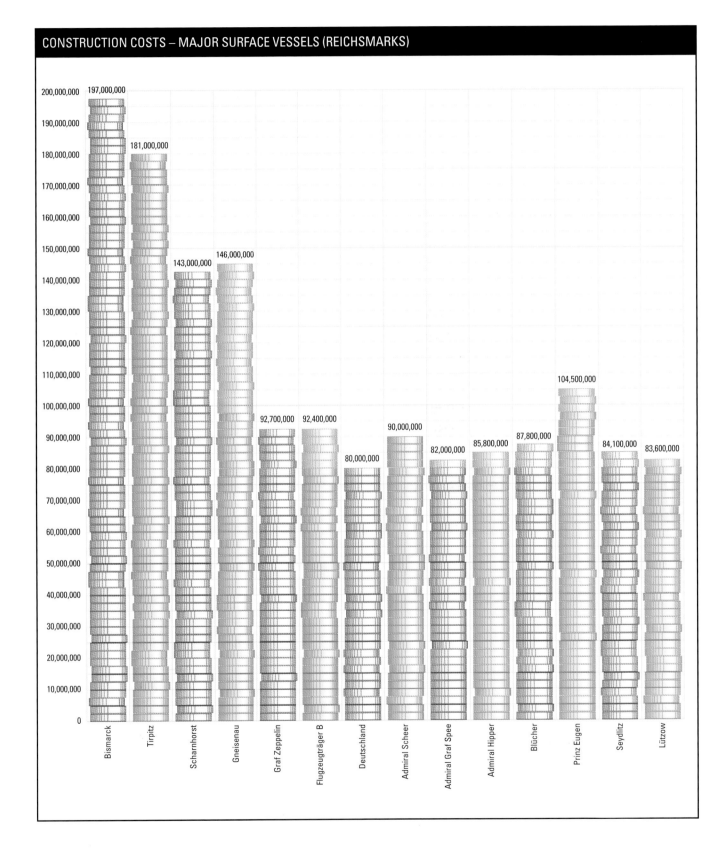

CONSTRUCTION COSTS – MAJOR SURFACE VESSELS (REICHSMARKS)

197,000,000 — Bismarck
181,000,000 — Tirpitz
143,000,000 — Scharnhorst
146,000,000 — Gneisenau
92,700,000 — Graf Zeppelin
92,400,000 — Flugzeugträger B
80,000,000 — Deutschland
90,000,000 — Admiral Scheer
82,000,000 — Admiral Graf Spee
85,800,000 — Admiral Hipper
87,800,000 — Blücher
104,500,000 — Prinz Eugen
84,100,000 — Seydlitz
83,600,000 — Lützow

- *Schlachtschiff* L to the Kriegsmarinewerft, Wilhelmshaven
- *Schlachtschiff* M to Blohm & Voss, Hamburg
- *Schlachtschiff* N to Deutsche Schiff- und Maschinenbau AG, Bremen

'H' was laid down on 15 July 1939 and 'J' on 1 September 1939. 'K' was scheduled to be laid down on 15 September, but work was postponed because of the outbreak of war. (Work on 'H' and 'J' was also suspended at about this time.) When construction was frozen, 'H' had 14,280 tonnes (14,055 tons) of material ordered, of which 5893 tonnes (5800 tons) had been delivered but only 778 tonnes (766 tons) worked into the keel. Less work had been carried out on 'J', for which 3587 tonnes (3531 tons) of material had been ordered but only 40.6 tonnes (40 tons) put into the keel. In 1940, it was decided to cancel the H-39 programme to free resources for U-boat construction – 'H' and 'J' were duly scrapped, but studies into improved battleships continued.

H-40

The first of these design studies began in 1940, with an examination of potential improvements to the armour protection of the original H-39 design. Two solutions were considered, which were unofficially referred to as H-40A and H-40B. H-40A shipped a reduced main armament of three twin 406mm (16in) turrets to permit much thicker armour without greatly increasing displacement, whilst H-40B retained the original four twin 406mm (16in) turrets but was substantially enlarged to provide increased protection. As the increased weight required greater power to maintain the design speed of 59km/h (32 knots), it was decided to switch to a mixed powerplant of marine diesels supplemented by steam turbines, now driving four shafts instead of three. (These were unofficial studies, and did not significantly influence later designs from H-41 onwards.)

H-41

In 1941, OKM authorized a further study of future battleships, specifying a speed of at least 55.5km/h (30 knots) with armour and firepower to match those of the latest foreign capital ships. This resulted in the H-41 design, which featured increased horizontal armour and deeper torpedo bulkhead protection, together with the mixed propulsion system of the 1940 designs but retaining a three-shaft layout. The H-41 design was slightly larger than the Japanese *Yamato* class, displacing nearly 77,216 tonnes (76,000 tons) full load with an overall length of just over 300m (984ft).

H-42

The loss of the *Bismarck* in May 1941 focused attention on the problem of vulnerability to air attack. A new series of modifications to H-41 was drafted, which attempted to reduce the vulnerability of propellers and rudders to torpedo attack. The proposals also reflected the lessons learned from the damage inflicted on *Scharnhorst* by RAF bombing during 1941. Initially, amendments were worked into the existing plans for the H-41, but it soon became clear that a fresh start was required and a new design, designated H-42, was developed instead. It now used four shafts, with shrouding to protect the propeller skegs, and multiple rudders aligned with the shafts to provide manoeuvring redundancy in the event of damage to the steering gear. The construction and operation of these vessels would have stretched 1940s technologies to their limits, as H-42 had become far larger than its predecessors. Improved armour and anti-torpedo protection resulted in a vessel 305m (1000ft) long with a beam of nearly 43m (141ft) and a full-load displacement of 99,600 tonnes (98,000 tons) – the size of a modern nuclear-powered supercarrier.

H-43 and H-44

After the H-42, the designs became increasingly unrealistic – in order to defeat all possible opponents, the main armament was increased to eight 508mm (20in) guns, one of the largest calibres ever considered for naval use. However, there was no significant improvement to the secondary and heavy AA armament that had proved inadequate on *Bismarck's* sole operational voyage. Only 37mm (1.45in) and 20mm (0.79in) weapons were augmented, but they offered only limited improvements to the ship's air defence. The H-43 was impractical – German yards would have been extremely hard-pressed to build the class, and the ships' sheer size would have made operations hazardous in any confined waters. The design merely illustrated the possibilities, given no constraints – rather like the US Navy's Tillman 'maximum battleship' studies of 1916.

The H-44 was the last serious large battleship study and incorporated elaborate protection, including multiple armoured decks that were intended to resist all but the heaviest armour-piercing bombs. The multiple anti-torpedo bulkheads had a total transverse depth of 11m (36ft) (twice that on the *Bismarck*), and a triple bottom was proposed to minimize mine damage. The four-shaft mixed-propulsion system was similar to those designed for the H-42 and H-43, but the increased size of the H-44 caused a slight reduction in speed, although endurance remained the same: 37,000km (20,000 nautical miles) at 35km/h (19 knots).

H-44's main armament was identical to that of the H-43: eight 508mm (20in) guns in four twin turrets. Given the increasingly serious air threat, it is surprising that the heavy AA armament was unchanged from that of the *Bismarck* and *Tirpitz*. Smaller AA guns were more numerous – a total of 28 37mm (1.45in) weapons in twin mounts plus 10 20mm (0.79in) quadruple *Flakvierling* mounts

were to be carried. The increased tonnage of the H-44 allowed a larger hangar, with room for up to nine seaplanes.

The last word – 'H-45'

Although H-44 was the last proper battleship design study, there is a final twist to the story. In the aftermath of the loss of the *Bismarck*, Hitler pressed for the H-class designs to be enlarged to allow the fitting of a main armament of eight 800mm (31.5in) guns derived from the 'Gustav'/'Dora' railway guns. 'H-45' would have exceeded the displacement of the 656,988-tonne (646,642-ton) former supertanker *Knock Nevis*, widely regarded as the largest ship ever built.

O-class battlecruisers

The O-class battlecruisers formed a key part of the Z-Plan, being intended to operate against Allied convoys in conjunction with two task forces, each of which would be built around three H-class battleships and an aircraft carrier. Operational planning envisaged that the task forces would attack the convoy escorts, whilst the battlecruisers went for the merchant vessels. Although orders for three vessels were placed in 1939, none were completed as U-boat construction took priority.

Aircraft carriers

Under the terms of the 1935 Anglo-German Naval Agreement, the *Kriegsmarine* was allowed a total

carrier tonnage of about 42,672 tonnes (42,000 tons). Design studies had begun the previous year and two vessels, nominally of 20,320 tonnes (20,000 tons) each, were authorized. German shipbuilders had no practical experience of aircraft carriers and a delegation visited Japan in the autumn of 1935 to study the carrier *Akagi*, which was undergoing modernization. They returned with over 100 blueprints of *Akagi* and the new carrier *Soryu*, which was then under construction.

Work on the first German carrier, '*Flugzeugträger* A', began on 26 December 1936 at Deutsche Werke in Kiel. Construction work progressed well and it was launched as the *Graf Zeppelin* on 8 December 1938. The vessel was 85 per cent complete at the outbreak of war, but there were severe problems in finalizing the design of the catapults and arrester gear. The order was given to suspend all further work on the vessel in April 1940 and it was moved to Götenhafen, where the guns were removed for use in Norwegian coastal defences.

The second carrier, '*Flugzeugträger* B', was laid down at Germaniawerft, Kiel, in autumn 1938 and the pace of work was deliberately slow to allow time for lessons from the construction of *Graf Zeppelin* to be incorporated in the new vessel. By February 1940 the hull had been completed up to the level of the armoured deck, but at this point the project was cancelled and the vessel was scrapped.

By mid-1942, the British, American and Japanese navies had demonstrated the value of aircraft carriers, and work on *Graf Zeppelin* resumed. The planned base for the carrier was Drontheim, at the south end of the Faettenfjord. At the same time, an auxiliary carrier programme was drawn up for the conversion of the liners *Potsdam*, *Gneisenau* and *Europa* together with the Hipper-class heavy cruiser *Seydlitz*. The *Graf Zeppelin* was again transferred to Kiel for completion, but the poor showing of the *Lützow* and *Hipper* in the Battle of the Barents Sea on 31 December 1942 led Hitler to abandon work on all major surface vessels in order to free resources for U-boat construction. The auxiliary carrier programme was cancelled and the *Graf Zeppelin* was moved Stettin in April 1943, where it languished until scuttled on 23 April 1945 as the Red Army overran the area. The carrier was refloated in March 1946 and underwent limited repairs before being used to transport captured German weaponry and factory equipment to the Soviet Union. In August 1947 it was finally sunk by the Soviets as a target ship.

H-39, H-44, 'H-45', ROYAL NAVY *LION* CLASS, US *MONTANA* CLASS: ARMAMENTS COMPARED

Ship	Main	Secondary	AA	Torpedo tubes
H-39 battleship	8 x 406mm (16in) Schnelladekanone C/34	12 x 150mm (5.9in)	16 x 105mm (4.1in) 16 x 37mm (1.45in) 24 x 20mm (0.79in)	6 x 533mm (21in)
H-44 battleship	8 x 508mm (20in)	12 x 150mm (5.9in)	16 x 105mm (4.1in) 28 x 37mm (1.45in) 40 x 20mm (0.79in)	6 x 533mm (21in)
'H-45' battleship	8 x 800mm (31.5in)	12 x 240mm (9.5in) DP	24 x 128mm (5.04in) u/k number of 55mm (2.17in) u/k number of 30mm (1.18in)	–
Lion class	9 x 406mm (16in)	16 x 133mm (5.25in) DP	48 x 40mm (1.57in) 2pdr	–
Montana class	12 x 406mm (16in)	20 x 127mm (5in) DP	40 x 40mm (1.57in) Bofors 56 x 20mm (0.79in) Oerlikon	–

O-CLASS BATTLECRUISER

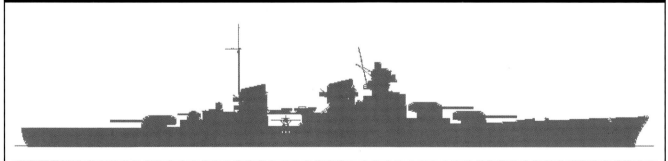

Specifications

Displacement: 32,818 tonnes (32,300 tons) standard; 38,813 tonnes (38,200 tons) full load
Length: 256m (840ft)
Beam: 30m (98ft)
Draught: 8.02m (26ft 3.5in)
Engines: 8 x 24-cylinder diesel engines, plus Brown Boveri turbines totalling 131,243kW (176,000hp)

Speed: 65km/h (35 knots)
Range: 26,000km (14,000 nautical miles) at 35km/h (19 knots)
Complement: 1965
Armour: 190mm (7.5in) belt, 210mm (8.3in) turrets
Aircraft: 4

Armament (Main): 6 x 380mm (15in)
(Secondary): 6 x 150mm (5.9in)
(AA): 8 x 105mm (4.1in), 8 x 37mm (1.45in), 20 x 20mm (0.79in)
(Torpedo): 6 x 533mm (21in) torpedo tubes
No. Completed: None

Creating the German Empire

Hitler was ultimately never satisfied with the territory he inherited when he came to power in 1933. Land lost in the Versailles Treaty was one source of annoyance, but he also felt the drive to expand German space much further, particularly into the east.

What amounted to naked imperial ambitions were bound up with the concept of Lebensraum *(living space), the idea that only territorial expansion would provide Germany with the requisite natural resources and space to foster its growing population.*

He stated this principle bluntly in Mein Kampf: Only a sufficiently large space on this earth can assure the independent existence of a people.

Left: German Panzers role through Wenceslas Square, Prague, during the German occupation of Czechoslovakia, 1938.

The Concept of *Lebensraum*

Lebensraum is one of the most persistent themes running through Hitler's writings. The idea was by no means original to Hitler, and had even been used as a term favouring the unification of the German states in 1871.

It was philosophically sharpened by German geographer Friedrich Ratzel (1844–1904), who postulated that to remain 'healthy' any people had to embark on migration and territorial expansion. The drive to acquire new space in which to live would inevitably bring conflict, but once a territory was acquired the colonizers would be able to settle on the new land and turn it to their own productive needs. (At heart, the key theme of Ratzel's *Lebensraum* was agrarian, with expansionism mainly focusing on grabbing, settling and developing new farmland.)

The interpretation of *Lebensraum* in Germany changed over time to suit the prevailing mood and political circumstances. During the late 1800s it was thought of primarily in terms of simple colonization, developing new colonies in Africa and the Pacific, whereas in the early twentieth century it became more

KEY ARTICLES OF THE TREATY OF BREST-LITOVSK, 1918

■ ARTICLE 1.

Germany, Austria-Hungary, Bulgaria and Turkey on the one hand and Russia on the other declare that the condition of war between them has ceased. They have decided to live in peace and accord in the future.

■ ARTICLE 2.

The contracting parties will refrain from all agitation or propaganda against the governments or all state and military institutions of the other side. Inasmuch as this obligation affects Russia, it affects also the territories occupied by the powers of the Quadruple Alliance.

■ ARTICLE 3.

The territories lying to the west of the line determined by the contracting powers and which formerly belonged to Russia will no longer be under her sovereignty. The line determined upon is marked on [a] map, which is an important part of the present treaty of peace. The precise location of this line will be worked out by a German–Russian commission.

In respect to the mentioned territories no obligations towards Russia are to be considered as issuing from their formerly having belonged to that country.

Russia gives up all interference in the internal affairs of the said territories, Germany and Austria-Hungary intend to determine the future fate of the said territories with the consent of their inhabitants.

■ ARTICLE 4.

Germany is ready, as soon as general peace is established and Russian demobilization will have completely taken place, to vacate the territories lying east of the line mentioned in part 1 of Article 3, insomuch as Article 6 does not rule otherwise.

Russia will do all in her power to have the provinces of eastern Anatolia promptly evacuated and returned to Turkey.

The territories of Ardakhan, Kars and Batum will also be cleared without delay of Russian troops. Russia will not interfere in the new organization of internal juridical and international juridical relations of such territories, but will allow the populations of these territories to establish new governments in agreement with neighbouring states, especially with Turkey.

■ ARTICLE 5.

Russia will, without delay, proceed to demobilize her army, including those army units newly formed by her present government.

Moreover Russia will either bring her warships into Russian ports and keep them there until general peace is concluded, or will disarm them at once. The warships of the countries continuing in a state of war with the Quadruple Alliance, in so far as such warships are within the sphere of Russian sovereignty, must be treated as Russian warships.

The prohibition zone of the Arctic Ocean remains in force until the conclusion of general peace in the Baltic Sea and those parts of the Black Sea under Russia's supremacy;

militarily charged, with pan-German nationalists arguing for an expansion into eastern territories – particularly western Russia and the Ukraine – by force. The popularity of such views intensified during World War I, and indeed came close to being practically realized.

At the Treaty of Brest-Litovsk in March 1918, Russia effectively ceded Poland, Estonia, Latvia, Lithuania, Belorussia and Ukraine to the German Empire. These were short-lived acquisitions, and a mixed blessing for the Germans – the new territory soaked up thousands of occupying soldiers who could be better used elsewhere, and the countries provided less than expected in terms of food output. The defeat in the war just a few months later, furthermore, meant that Germany did not hang onto its gains for long.

After World War I, *Lebensraum* hung about as a concept amongst nationalists and pan-Germans. It began to be associated with the desire to reclaim territory lost to the Versailles Treaty, and as such it found ready reception in the mind of a young Adolf Hitler. It was an idea to which he would

the clearing away of mine defences must be begun at once. Merchant navigation in those sea regions is free and is to recommence at once. Mixed commissions are to be formed for the purpose of framing more concise regulations and especially for the purpose of publication of general information as to safe courses of sailing for trading vessels. Such courses must always be free of floating mines.

■ *ARTICLE 6.*
Russia undertakes to conclude peace at once with the Ukrainian people's republic and to recognize the treaty of peace between the state and the powers of the Quadruple Alliance. The territory of the Ukraine must be, at once, cleared of Russian troops and of the Russian Red Guard. Russia ceases all agitation or propaganda against the government or the public institutions of the Ukrainian people's republic.

Esthonia and Livonia must be also immediately cleared of Russian troops and the Russian Red Guard. The eastern boundary of Esthonia passes in general along the River Narova. The eastern boundary of Livonia, in general, crosses the Lakes Chud [Peipus] and Pskov up to the southwestern corner of the latter, thence it runs across Lake Luban in the direction of Lievenhof on the Western Dvina. Esthonia and Livonia will be occupied by German police forces until public safety is secured by proper institutions of the country and until governmental order is reestablished. Russia will at once liberate all the inhabitants of Esthonia and Livonia who have been arrested or deported and will secure a safe return of all deported Esthonians and Livonians.

Finland and the Åland Islands will be also, without delay, cleared of Russian troops and the Russian Red Guard and Finnish ports of the Russian fleet and of Russian naval forces. While ice renders impossible the conveying of warships to Russian ports there must remain on board only a limited crew. Russia ceases all agitation or propaganda against the government or public institutions of Finland.

The fortifications constructed on the Åland Islands must be razed at the first opportunity. As regards the prohibition to erect fortifications on these islands in the future, as well as the question of their future in general in a military respect and in respect to the technical side of navigation, a special agreement must be concluded between Germany, Finland, Russia and Sweden; the parties consent that at Germany's desire other countries bordering the Baltic Sea may be called upon to take part in the above agreement.

■ *ARTICLE 7.*
Considering the fact that Persia and Afghanistan are free and independent countries, the contracting parties bind themselves to respect the political and economic independence and the territorial inviolability of Persia and Afghanistan.

become firmly wedded, and it would form a bedrock for future military and political policy. Before we look specifically at how, some words of caution. Historians have often treated Hitler's notion of *Lebensraum* as an obsessive engine at the heart of all his strategic decisions. Yet as with so much of Hitler's frequently confused and ill-formed world view, *Lebensraum* appears in many ways to be a loose theory or aspiration to which circumstances and opportunities were fitted, rather than a drumbeat policy directive. *Lebensraum* advances and recedes in Hitler's thinking over time. It was most prominent in his speeches in the late 1920s and late 1930s, but the emphasis changed according to his mood and the political moment. During times of severe economic problems, the idea temporarily receded into the background, to be replaced by more practical proposals about creating German-

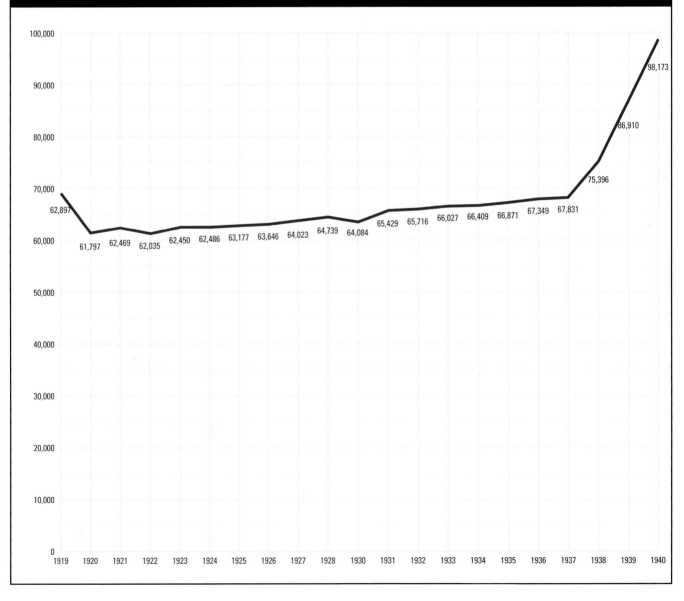

GERMAN POPULATION (THOUSANDS), 1919–40

led trading markets within Europe. What cannot be doubted, however, is that Hitler did conceive of Germany's future as a great world power, and that to do so would implicitly involve expansionism by military means.

Taking a closer look at the content of Hitler's *Lebensraum*, the core view was that Germany offered insufficient space for its growing population. As with all industrialized European nations, Germany had experienced population increases from the late nineteenth century. At the time of German unification in 1871, the population had been in the order of 41 million, whereas by the mid-1920s the nation contained more than 70 million souls.

The population density for every square kilometre of German territory had tightened from 76 people in 1871 to 120 in 1910, and reached 133 by 1925. Furthermore, the population kept increasing by about 900,000 people a year. For Hitler,

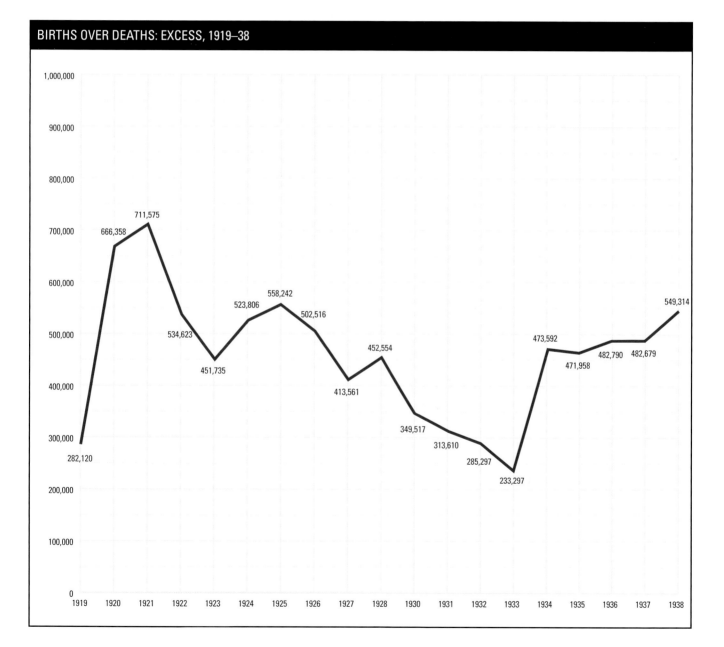

BIRTHS OVER DEATHS: EXCESS, 1919–38

this matter was of grave concern. In his view, expressed repeatedly in *Mein Kampf*, the nation was in danger of becoming sickly and weak through its overcrowding:

The foreign policy of a People's State must first of all bear in mind the duty of securing the existence of the race which is incorporated in this State. And this must be done by establishing a healthy and natural proportion between the number and growth of the population on the one hand and the extent and resources of the territory they inhabit, on the other. That balance must be such that it accords with the vital necessities of the people.

What I call a healthy proportion is that in which the support of a people is guaranteed by the resources of its own soil and sub-soil. Any situation which falls short of this condition is none the less unhealthy even though it may endure for centuries or even a thousand years. Sooner or later, this lack of proportion must of necessity lead to the decline or even annihilation of the people concerned.
– Hitler, *Mein Kampf*, p.491

True to form, Hitler conceives of territorial claustrophobia in apocalyptic terms – if the German

POPULATIONS OF MAJOR GERMAN CITIES, 1938

City	Number	City	Number
Berlin	4.2m	Wuppertal	409,000
Hamburg	1.1m	Chemnitz	351,000
Cologne	757,000	Gelsenkirchen	333,000
Munich	735,000	Bremen	323,000
Leipzig	714,000	Königsberg	316,000
Essen	654,000	Bochum	315,000
Dresden	642,000	Magdeburg	307,000
Breslau	625,000	Mannheim	275,000
Frankfurt/Main	556,000	Stettin	271,000
Dortmund	541,000	Altona	242,000
Düsseldorf	499,000	Kiel	218,000
Hanover	444,000	Halle	209,000
Duisburg	440,000	Oberhausen	192,000
Stuttgart	415,000	Augsburg	177,000
Nuremberg	410,000	Kassel	175,000

people don't get the 'healthy proportion' of territory to people, then they will become 'unhealthy' and eventually wither on their increasingly crowded vine. Nor did he see solutions through the traditional routes of coping with population growth. Increasing imports would simply chain Germany to dependence on foreign markets and nations, and emigration would rob Germany of some of its best and brightest people.

East and west

For Hitler, there were two main practical themes for his *Lebensraum* – the retaking of territories lost to the Versailles Treaty and, more grandly, the seizing of large expanses of territory in the east, from Russia, as a zone in which to resettle millions of Germans. Hitler's obsession with the east was abiding.

Since its takeover by 'Jewish Bolshevism' (in Hitler's warped view), he felt that the entire Soviet empire was ripe to crumble, while at the same time it posed a proximate threat to German nationhood and racial health. For these reasons, Hitler stated in *Mein Kampf* that in terms of future expansion, the German people had to begin looking eastwards.

In 1939, for example, Hitler authorized the signing of the Nazi–Soviet Pact, a cynical treaty that effectively made Germany and the Soviet Union temporary allies and partners in the invasion and occupation of Poland. Yet there seems no denying, based on

what was to come, that Hitler was repeatedly inspired by thoughts of acquiring large expanses of territory in the east.

Lebensraum for Hitler had a rather mystical element to it. It connected to his belief in *Blut und Boden* (Blood and Soil), a nostalgic sense that the German people were bonded to the nation literally through its land, agrarian living bringing out the true identity of the individual and state. The mysticism became practical, however, during the late 1930s, when Hitler put Germany on the path to expansion, empire and war.

Reclaiming the *Reich*

From the mid-1930s, the first stage in Hitler's desire to expand Germany's borders took place with his successful efforts to unstitch the geographical threads of the Versailles Treaty.

An initial minor success came on 13 January 1935, when a plebiscite held in the Saarland – a German territory occupied and governed by the French and the British since 1920 – voted 90 per cent in favour of a return to German rule, a vote that was approved by the League of Nations. Hitler's next objective, however, was riskier – the Rhineland. The Rhineland had been declared a demilitarized zone by the Versailles Treaty, acting as a barrier between France and a potentially belligerent future Germany. On 7 March 1936, however, in a high-risk gamble, Hitler sent more than 30,000 troops and police into the

region. (Hitler was politically bouyed by the fact that Britain was already secretly discussing the possibility of remilitarization of the Rhineland in return for other diplomatic assurances.) Faced with arguably the world's last great chance to stop Hitler, France did nothing to overturn the action, even though Hitler himself later said: 'If the French had then marched into the Rhineland we would have had to withdraw with our tails between our legs, for the military resources at our disposal would have been wholly inadequate for even a moderate resistance.'

The Rhineland was a crucial testing of the waters. It revealed that the international community was largely impotent, at least psychologically, and further bold action would likely be rewarded, if Hitler proceeded carefully. The next objective for incorporation into the Third Reich was Austria.

Austria and Czechoslovakia

Union between Austria and Germany – forbidden under the Versailles Treaty – remained on the table during the 1920s and 1930s, courtesy of a large pro-German, then pro-Nazi element in the Austrian population. A suggested customs union was refused by the Permanent Court of International Justice in The Hague in 1931. From 1933, with Hitler in power, political unrest within Austria created the conditions for a Nazi takeover. In July 1934 Nazi sympathizers murdered the Austrian chancellor Engelbert Dollfuss, and in 1938 Hitler reneged on an earlier recognition of Austria's independence and began to lean on the new chancellor, Kurt von Schuschnigg.

France and Britain were at this time distracted by other foreign policy issues, and Hitler's demands that Austria align itself economically with Germany left Schuschnigg unsure of which way to turn. In the end, he opted for a referendum on the issue of national independence, but before the referendum could be held, Hitler sent Schuschnigg an order to resign in favour of the pro-Nazi Artur von Seyss-Inquart, then deployed troops into Austria on 12 March 1938. Schuschnigg was therefore forced out, and Seyss-Inquart was directed into

HITLER'S ANNEXATIONS, 1936–39

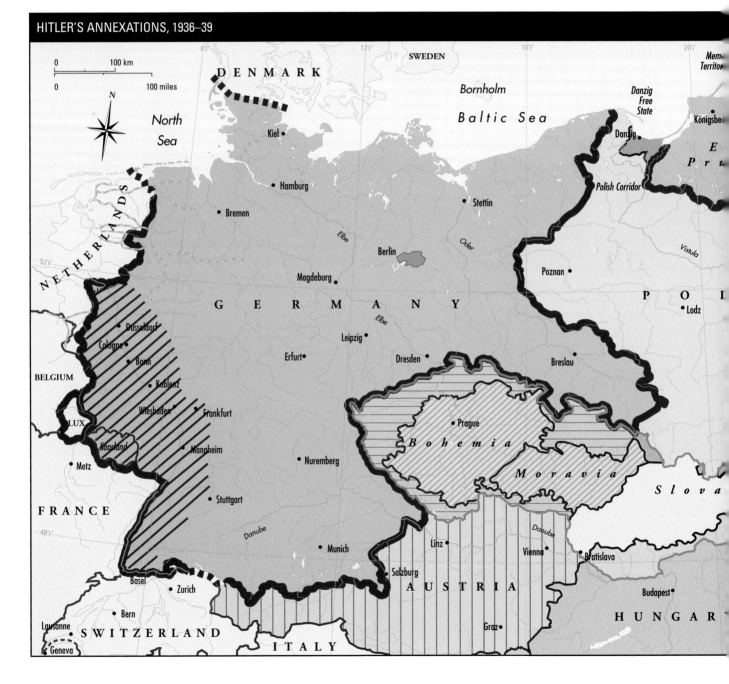

the full *Anschluss* of Austria with Germany.

With Hitler riding the wave of his growing power, the next domino to fall to Germany was Czechoslovakia, on the other side of Germany's southeastern border. To support the 'rights' of the German minority in Czechoslovakia, Hitler was building up to direct military invasion and occupation – war, in effect. Duly alarmed, the British prime minister, Neville Chamberlain, flew out to see Hitler on 15 September 1938. Hitler was made aware that both Britain and France stood by ready to defend Czechoslovakia if necessary, but in the subsequent negotiations Hitler was granted annexation of the Sudetenland. This infamous act of appeasement was seen by Chamberlain as placating Germany's expansionism and guarding against a future war, but the British had been fooled. Having taken the Sudetenland, Hitler then simply ordered his troops into Bohemia and Moravia in March 1939. With Slovakia to the east now little more than a Nazi puppet state, Hitler had taken over Czechoslovakia.

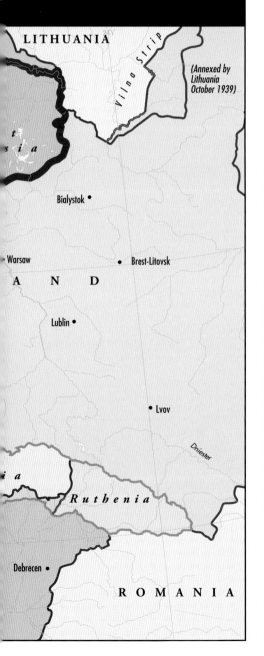

Left: This map graphically illustrates how important territorial expansion became to Hitler as he sought to exorcize the ghosts of defeat during the late 1930s. The remilitarization of the Rhineland, in particular, beginning in March 1936, sent a message to the world that Germany would no longer be subservient to conditions imposed by foreign powers.

Hitler's Annexations
1936–39

	Germany after 1919
	Troops into demilitarized Rhineland March 1936
	Anschluss (union with Austria) March 1938
	Occupation of Sudetenland October 1938
	Original Czechoslovak border
	Formerly Czechoslovakia occupied March 1939
	Moravian territory to Poland October 1938
	Memel territory to Germany March 1939
	Protectorate of Slovakia territory to Hungary Nov 1938
	Czechoslovak territory to Hungary March 1939

AREA OF THE GERMAN FEDERAL STATES/REICHSGAUE, 1941 (IN KM²)

State	km²
Anhalt	2315
Baden	15,069
Bavaria	77,785
Bremen	324
Brunswick	3570
Carinthia	11,553
Danzig-West Prussia	26,057
Hamburg	746
Hesse	7690
Lippe	1215
Lower Danube	23,502
Mecklenburg	5721
Oldenburg	5396
Prussia	321,788
Saarland	1924
Salzburg	7152
Saxony	14,994
Schaumburg-Lippe	340
Styria	17,383
Thuringia	11,760
Tyrol	13,126
Upper Danube	14,216
Vienna	1215
Wartheland	43,905
Württemberg	19,507

Below: The once great empire of Austria-Hungary was dissolved in the aftermath of World War I, split into the multi-ethnic parts that the emperors had not been able to hold together. Austria-Hungary's performance in World War I had largely been disappointing. As with the Italians in the following global conflict, the Austro-Hungarian armed forces frequently found themselves in trouble when they acted unilaterally, and required the help of the more proficient Germans to avoid disaster. Austria's union with Germany itself was forbidden by the terms of the Versailles Treaty.

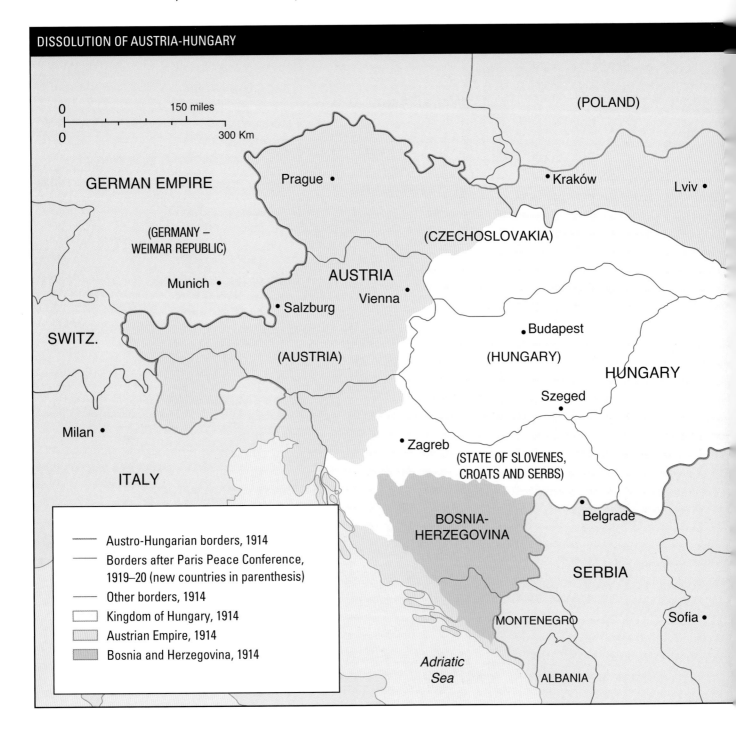

DISSOLUTION OF AUSTRIA-HUNGARY

0   150 miles
0   300 Km

GERMAN EMPIRE

(GERMANY – WEIMAR REPUBLIC)

Munich

SWITZ.

Milan

ITALY

Prague

AUSTRIA

Vienna

Salzburg

(AUSTRIA)

(POLAND)

Kraków

Lviv

(CZECHOSLOVAKIA)

Budapest

(HUNGARY)

HUNGARY

Szeged

Zagreb

(STATE OF SLOVENES, CROATS AND SERBS)

BOSNIA-HERZEGOVINA

Belgrade

SERBIA

Sofia

MONTENEGRO

Adriatic Sea

ALBANIA

Legend:
- Austro-Hungarian borders, 1914
- Borders after Paris Peace Conference, 1919–20 (new countries in parenthesis)
- Other borders, 1914
- Kingdom of Hungary, 1914
- Austrian Empire, 1914
- Bosnia and Herzegovina, 1914

Within five years of coming to power, therefore, Adolf Hitler had achieved some of the conditions of *Lebensraum* in a series of conquests that required nothing more than

RUSSIAN EMPIRE

RUSSIAN SOVIET
FEDERATIVE
SOCIALIST REPUBLIC
(SOVIET UNION)

N

(ROMANIA)

ROMANIA

•Bucharest

BULGARIA   Black Sea

TURKEY

strong nerves and intense political manipulation of weaker enemies. The German Reich had expanded significantly in its territorial scope. Yet for Hitler, whose martial confidence was growing along with his ever-expanding armed forces, it was now the moment to build the Greater German Empire further.

War and conquest

Space does not allow for a detailed description of the war that began in September 1939, when the German armed forces were unleashed on Poland.

Our main concern here, in any case, is to assess what Hitler achieved through bloody conquest between 1939 and 1945, and how far those achievements (at their peak, at least) matched his ultimate ambitions to transform Germany into a great world power.

First, a brief run through the German war campaign will anchor our understanding of what followed. On 1 September 1939, Germany invaded Poland in force from the west, the Soviets also surging across the Polish border from the east. Hitler had previously leaned on Poland to cede the 'Danzig Corridor', a passage of Polish territory created by the Versailles Treaty that separated Germany from its territory of East Prussia. It was actually quite late in the year before the decision was taken to invade, beginning what became World War II (within days of the invasion, Britain and France had declared war on Germany).

Poland was not to be an isolated conquest. After a six-month period of relatively little fighting between the combatants, Hitler then launched one of the most successful military campaigns in all history. Denmark and Norway were invaded on 9 April 1940, then the offensive into France, the Netherlands and Belgium began on 10 May.

Despite the combined strength of Britain and France against the German onslaught, all the countries invaded eventually fell to the Germans, whose military services demonstrated a form of combined arms warfare that completely outclassed and outmanoeuvred their opponents.

Factoring in Germany's alliance with Mussolini's fascist Italy, most of Europe from Poland to the French coast lay directly under Axis control by the end of June 1940. On 22 June, in a moment of supreme symbolism, France signed a capitulation in the actual railway carriage in which Germany had signed its own surrender in 1918.

The Balkans and the USSR

Now Hitler suffered his first setback of the war. A planned invasion of Britain, *Unternehmen Seelöwe* (Operation *Sealion*), was postponed by September 1940, after the *Luftwaffe* was unable to defeat the RAF in the Battle of Britain. By this time, anyway, Hitler was switching the focus of his attentions to the east, beginning the huge preparations for the invasion of Soviet Russia.

NATURAL RESOURCES: GERMANY AND AXIS-OCCUPIED TERRITORIES, 1940–45

NORWAY
1,278
951.8

SWEDEN
(Neutral)

FINLAND
126

NORTH
SEA

DENMARK
488.1

BALTIC
SEA

Königsberg

USSR
8,883
10.6

HOLLAND
7,716
417.2

Hamburg

EAST
PRUSSIA

Smolensk

GREAT
BRITAIN
99.9

Amsterdam

Berlin

POLAND

Poznan

London

BELGIUM
4,517
75.8

Brussels

Leipzig

Warsaw

Lille

Frankfurt am Main

GERMANY

Prague

BOHEMIA-MORAVIA

Cracow

Rouen

Paris

SLOVAKIA

Krivoi Rog

Munich

Vienna

FRANCE
25,848
1047.7

SWITZ.
(Neutral)

AUSTRIA

Budapest

HUNGARY
51

ROMANIA
12

Lyon

Padua

Bologna

YUGOSLAVIA
678
46.1

Bucharest

SPAIN

MEDITERRANEAN
SEA

Rome

ITALY
1,432

BULGARIA
27

Sofia

BLACK
SEA

ALBANIA
29

TURKEY
(Neutral)

GREECE
3,758
170

Athens

Axis and Axis-occupied areas (1942)

Coalfields and industrial regions

Other industrial regions

Crude oil plants

Synthetic oil plants

Cost of German war effort borne by occupied
2,173   or allied states (in RM million)

Tonnage of merchant shipping seized
10.4   (in thousand tons)

Mineral resources

Lead

Chrome

Zinc

Iron Ore

Bauxite

Magnesite

Zinc

Oil

Copper

Manganese

0   400 km

0   200 mls

His focus was momentarily diverted, however, when his Italian allies, eager to make some conquests of their own, fell into severe trouble fighting the Greeks, Yugoslavs, British and other Commonwealth nations in the Balkans and North Africa. German forces were diverted south, conquering both Yugoslavia and Greece, and beginning two years of fighting in North Africa (followed by two further years in Italy).

Finally, on 22 June 1941, Hitler launched *Unternehmen Barbarossa* (Operation *Barbarossa*), the invasion of the Soviet Union. It was a vast undertaking, and at first it appeared as if Hitler would repeat the great victories of 1940. It was not to be. Fanatical Soviet resistance, and the eventual onset of the Russian winter, stopped the German offensive just short of Moscow.

Fighting on the Eastern Front reached unimaginable intensity over the four years of the German–Soviet War, and the Eastern Front became a huge grinding mill of German men

Opposite: The Germans accessed a broad spectrum of raw materials through their conquests, in addition to the manpower derived from occupied populations, although acquiring enough oil always presented a challenge. European countries made a sizeable financial contribution to the German war effort, either directly through liquidated financial assets or through labour costs, contributions of raw materials and the German use of industrial plants and machinery.

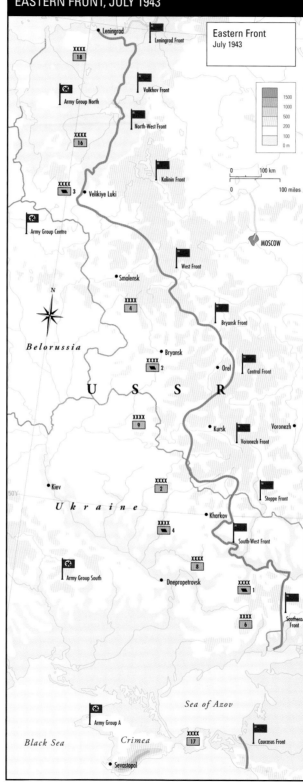

EASTERN FRONT, JULY 1943

Eastern Front
July 1943

Left: Kursk was such an obvious objective that the Soviets began fortifying it almost as soon as the Germans decided to attack it. As early as March, Marshal Georgi Zhukhov and his front commanders were presenting Stalin with their expectations on likely German plans for the coming campaigning season. Their predictions proved to be remarkably accurate when the battle started in July. In addition, the Red Army planned new offensives of its own, scheduled to open the moment the German attack stalled. Stalin and his most senior commanders gambled that they could hold Kursk against the elite Panzer divisions, absorb the full strength of the German blow, and then unleash a multi-front offensive that would liberate the Ukraine.

there were moments when his dream of Germany's great imperial destiny seemed to have come true, particularly after the fall of France in 1940.

At this point, it is interesting to speculate about what would have happened had Hitler been content with these conquests alone, and turned his back on the invasion of the east. If Hitler had let the dust settle, put in place efficient national administrations that did not alienate the local population, then there is the alarming possibility that he could have held on to his Western European possessions indefinitely. Although Britain remained free, it was not unilaterally capable of taking back the continent of Europe, and with some less defiant diplomacy Hitler could well have prevented Germany's eventual war with the United States.

Another possibility, of course, was that Germany could have launched a victorious invasion of Britain in 1940, depriving the future Allies of their base for launching the Second Front in 1944. Britain in general forms an interesting possibility for Hitler's creation of his *Großdeutsches Reich* (Greater German Reich). The fact was that Hitler had a fundamental respect for the British and their empire.

Below: At the time when Adolf Hitler came to power in 1933, the British Empire was the greatest imperial power on the planet. Its possessions stretched from Canada in the west across to Australia in the east, with major colonies in between in Africa, the Middle East and India. Hitler appears to have had an ideological fondness for the British (at least before 1940), and he saw the possibility of allying a new German Empire to the British Empire, together dominating most of the globe. The dogged resistance of Winston Churchill, however, ensured that there would be no alliance between Germany and Britain, and Hitler's Anglo-German dreams faded.

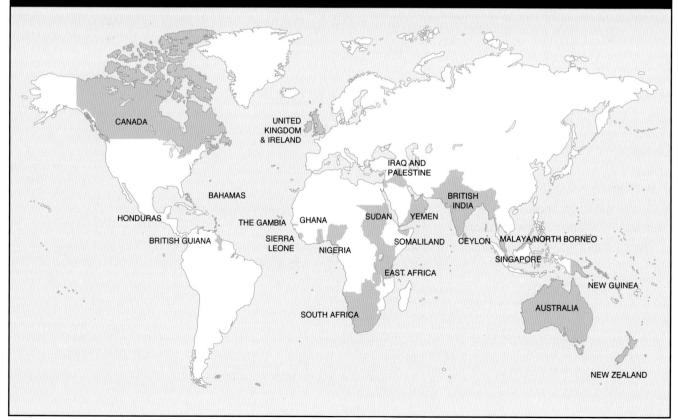

EXTENT OF BRITISH EMPIRE, 1930s

CANADA

UNITED KINGDOM & IRELAND

IRAQ AND PALESTINE

BAHAMAS

BRITISH INDIA

HONDURAS

THE GAMBIA GHANA SUDAN YEMEN

BRITISH GUIANA

SIERRA LEONE NIGERIA SOMALILAND CEYLON MALAYA/NORTH BORNEO

SINGAPORE

EAST AFRICA

NEW GUINEA

AUSTRALIA

SOUTH AFRICA

NEW ZEALAND

To expand on this theme, one of the great debates of World War II concerns the reasons for Hitler's famous 'halt order' of 1940. With the British Expeditionary Force (BEF) crammed onto the beaches of Dunkirk, Hitler stopped his Panzer forces just 19km (12 miles) from the coastline, on 24 May. That decision, and the failure of the *Luftwaffe* to stop the Allied escape, has been described as one of Hitler's greatest blunders. It effectively allowed the British to get away and fight another day, and also ensured that the island nation would receive the largesse of American Lend-Lease supplies.

Why did Hitler stop?

Reasons for the halt order are hotly debated, and include practical possibilities such as Hitler wanting to preserve his exhausted Panzer forces. Another intriguing possibility was that Hitler did not want to crush Britain, with whom he could build an international alliance, the German and British empires combining their influence around the globe. A fascinating insight into this possibility comes from General Günther Blumentritt, one of the key planning figures behind the invasion of France. Talking to Basil Liddell Hart after the war, Blumentritt noted his surprise at a speech given by Hitler following the halt order:

[Hitler] then astonished us by speaking with admiration of the British Empire, of the necessity for its existence, and of the civilization that Britain had brought into the world. He remarked, with a shrug of the shoulders, that the creation of its Empire had been achieved by means that were often harsh, but where there is planing, there are shavings flying. He compared the British Empire with the Catholic Church, saying they were both essential elements of stability in the world. He said that all he wanted

THE *SONDERFAHNDUNGSLISTE* G.B. (SPECIAL SEARCH LIST GB)

Individual	Position/Status
Sir Norman Angell	Labour MP who had been awarded the Nobel Peace Prize in 1933
Robert Baden-Powell	Head of the Scout Movement
Edvard Benes	President of the Czech government-in-exile
Violet Bonham Carter	Anti-fascist liberal politician
Vera Brittain	Feminist writer and pacifist
Neville Chamberlain	Former British Prime Minister
Winston Churchill	British Prime Minister
Duff Cooper	Minister of Information
Noël Coward	Actor and playwright
Anthony Eden	Secretary of State for War
E.M. Forster	Author
Sigmund Freud	Founder of psychoanalysis (Jew)
Sir Philip Gibbs	Journalist and novelist
J.B.S. Haldane	Geneticist and evolutionary biologist
Ernst Hanfstaengl	German refugee, and former supporter of Hitler
Aldous Huxley	Author
Harold Laski	Political theorist, economist and author
David Low	Political cartoonist
F.L. Lucas	Literary critic, writer and anti-fascist campaigner
Jan Masaryk	Foreign Minister of the Czech government-in-exile
Gilbert Murray	Classical scholar and activist for the League of Nations
Ignacy Jan Paderewski	Former Prime Minister of Poland
J.B. Priestley	Author and anti-fascist campaigner
Hermann Rauschning	German refugee and former friend of Hitler
Bertrand Russell	Philosopher, historian and pacifist
C.P. Snow	Physicist and novelist
Stephen Spender	Poet, novelist and essayist
Gottfried Treviranus	Former German minister
Beatrice Webb	Socialist and economist
Chaim Weizmann	Zionist leader
H.G. Wells	Author and socialist
Rebecca West	Suffragist and writer
Virginia Woolf	Author

The Nazis created a list of British public figures to be arrested following the successful invasion of the country.

from Britain was that she should acknowledge Germany's position on the Continent. The return of Germany's colonies would be desirable but not essential, and he would even offer to support Britain with troops if she should be involved in difficulties anywhere ...

– Liddell Hart,
The Other Side of the Hill, p.200

Had Hitler achieved any sort of alliance with Britain, the international ramifications would have been profound. As history now knows, however, Churchill was resolutely opposed to making any deal, a fact that infuriated Hitler. Yet the belief that Germany and Britain would eventually come to some rapprochement was durable in

Hitler's mind. On occasions, Hitler apparently even spoke of the possibility of Britain and Germany one day fighting together against America (although he admitted he would no longer be alive to see it), and felt that Britain had much to teach Germany about the installation and running of an empire. The idea of Hitler wanting to build a lasting

OPERATION SEALION: PLANNED INVASION OF BRITAIN

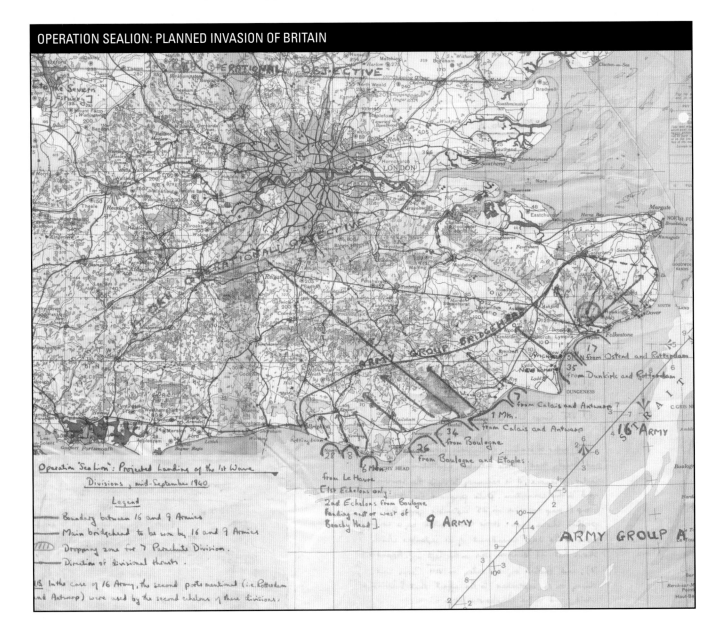

global alliance with Britain is even given some support by Germany's preparations for the invasion of Britain, Operation *Sealion*. Extensive planning for the invasion was conducted from June 1940 (although the outline of the operation had been sketched out back in 1939), including a detailed invasion document prepared by the OKW and post-invasion security planning by the *Gestapo* and other security services.

Wavering commitment

Hitler's commitment to the practical planning phases of *Sealion*, however, was less than total. Many of his top commanders found Hitler indecisive and distracted on the topic, and some (such as General Hans Jeschonnek, Chief of Staff of the *Luftwaffe*) even refused to assist the German Army in invasion-planning on the basis that it would never actually happen. Issues about the practicality of the operation also existed – there was the danger that the invasion fleet could be massacred in the English Channel by the Royal Navy and the undefeated RAF – and Hitler

Opposite: Operation *Sealion*, the proposed German invasion of Britain, envisaged a major amphibious landing around Britain's southeastern corner, driving quickly inland to isolate and then secure the capital. The failure to subdue the Royal Air Force, however, and the threat to amphibious forces from the Royal Navy meant the plan was not viable.

TABLE OF COMPARATIVE DISTANCES PROVIDED IN OKW STUDY OF OPERATION *SEALION*:

UK	Germany
London–Edinburgh 460km (285 miles)	Berlin–Essen 460km (285 miles)
London–Dublin 430km (267 miles)	Berlin–Frankfurt am Main 425km (264 miles)
London–Dover 100km (62 miles)	Berlin–Cottbus 100km (62 miles)
London–Paris 350km (217 miles)	Berlin–Nuremberg 370km (229 miles)
London–Brussels 310km (192 miles)	Berlin–Breslau 290km (180 miles)
London–Manchester 260km (160 miles)	Berlin–Hamburg 255km (155 miles)
London–Brighton 75km (46 miles)	Berlin–Frankfurt an de Oder 80km (50 miles)

OKW DATA ON ROAD CONDITIONS IN GREAT BRITAIN

■ TOTAL LENGTH OF GB ROAD NETWORK:
287,000km

■ TOTAL LENGTH OF URBAN ROADS:
66,080km

■ ROAD CLASSIFICATIONS:
– *Class A roads (main roads): 36,000km (22,370 miles)*
– *Class B roads (roads connecting small towns): 27,100km (16,840 miles)*
– *Unclassified roads: 215,730km (133,600 miles)*

■ TYPES OF SURFACING MATERIAL:
1. Tarmacadam surface
2. Various kinds of asphalt surface, particularly rolled asphalt
3. Concrete surface
4. Stone paving surfaces (large and small blocks)
5. Wooden surface
6. Water-bound tarmacadam surface
7. Gravel surface produced by treatment of top layer

■ PERCENTAGES OF SURFACES COMPRISING THE BRITISH ROAD NETWORK:
1. Tarmacadam – 50–55 per cent
2. Rolled asphalt – 30–33 per cent
3. Concrete – 6–8 per cent
4. Other types – 8–10 per cent

IMPORTANT PHRASES PROVIDED IN OKW REPORT ON OPERATION *SEALION*:

German	English
Welches ist der kürzeste Weg nach X?	Which is the shortest way to X?
Gehen Sie geradeaus und biegen Sie dann nach links (rechts)	Go straight down and then turn to the left (right)
Wie heißt diese Stadt?	What is the name of this town?
Wohin führt dieser Weg?	Where does this way lead?
Wo ist der nächste Brücke?	Where is the next bridge?
Wo ist das nächste Postamt?	Where is the next post office?
Wo sind die Kasernen?	Where are the barracks?
Wo kann ich etwas zu essen bekommen?	Where can I get something to eat?
Wo können wir schlafen?	Where can we sleep?
Können Sie mir den Weg nach Y zeigen?	Can you show me the way to Y?

eventually suggested that *Sealion* would be more feasible in 1941, but during that year his attention switched wholeheartedly to the invasion of the Soviet Union.

Plans for the invasion of Britain would never be revived in any substantial form for the rest of the war. Hitler did occasionally, however, flirt with ways to subvert Britain's colonies. The British Empire encompassed a huge diversity of peoples, not all of whom were enamoured with British rule. India was a case in point. On 3 April 1941, Subhas Chandra Bose – an Indian revolutionary and nationalist who had been arrested by the British no fewer than 11 times – visited Berlin with a proposition for Hitler. In essence, he wanted Germany's help in forming a 100,000-strong Indian national army that would rise up against the British and overthrow their rule. Bose certainly found interest in his plans

amongst the Nazi high command, particularly once Japan entered the war in December 1941 and put Britain on the back foot in Southeast Asia. The new army would be known as the 'Free India Legion', and raised substantially from Indian POWs captured in North Africa by Rommel's forces. Recruitment began in earnest in August 1942, but only 3000 men signed up to the cause.

Furthermore, Bose increasingly found that his relationship with Germany was less than supportive. Bose had a left-wing political orientation, which didn't sit well with Germany's invasion and exploitation of the Soviet Union from June 1941. More practically, with Germany's defeat at Stalingrad, the prospect of direct German military assistance in India vanished.

Consequently, Bose returned to India in February 1943 to focus on working more with the Japanese.

Back in Germany, his demoralized newly recruited army was eventually absorbed by the German armed services, particularly the *Waffen-SS*.

The new order
Hitler's military adventure would eventually lead to defeat, but by the winter of 1941 it looked as if Germany was about to become one of the largest empires on earth. Such acquisitions raised the question of how they would be politically, socially and economically managed. The *Neuordnung* (New Order) was the term the Nazis used for the empire that they would create from the conquered or subjugated lands. In its ideal state, the *Großdeutsches Reich* would stretch from Great Britain in the west across to the Ural mountains and the Caucasus in the east, and from Scandinavia down to Greece and Italy in the south.

The political status of the territories within this huge area

Opposite: A governmental issue for any empire is how to control far-flung territories from the centre. In the Third Reich, this was achieved through a mixture of policies. Some states or regions were managed simply via military occupation, while others were directly incorporated into Germany, principally the German-speaking territories (indigenous or settled) that became *Reichsgaue*. Note also how the alliances that Germany made created important security buffer zones around the Reich in the south, southeast and north.

NAZI-OCCUPIED EUROPE AND ITS ALLIES, 1942

0 ——— 400 km

0 ——— 200 mls

Iceland

NORTH SEA

BALTIC SEA

Finland

Norway

Soviet Union

Occupied Soviet Union

United Kingdom

German Reich

Poland

France

Hungary

Romania

BLACK SEA

Vichy France

Italy

Bulgaria

Turkey

Spain

Greece

Tunisia

MEDITERRANEAN SEA

Libya

Axis territories
Greater Germany
Incorporated by Germany
Occupied by Germany
Allied territories
Neutral territories
Vichy Line

would vary considerably. Above all came Greater Germany itself, formed from Germany plus the regions annexed during the 1930s. This core would be enlarged by direct annexations from conquered regions of Poland and the far western reaches of the Soviet Union. Much of Western and Northern Europe and the Balkans would constitute satellite or allied states, given some freedom of rule but with their foreign policies and economies centred upon Berlin.

Then there was the vast expanse of the east. Here would be a land for German resettlement and exploitation, providing the *Großdeutsches Reich* with raw materials, manpower and *Lebensraum*. Those Soviets who remained outside German control would live beyond the Urals in the eastern Slav Lands, a region whose basic agricultural lifestyle would ensure that it never again threatened German interests. The proposed eastern border of the new German Empire was known as the A–A line, so called because it ran from Arkhangelsk in northwestern Russia down to Astrakhan in the southwest. It was predicted that this line would be permanently militarized, and be a zone of constant, bubbling warfare between the German Empire and the remaining, disaffected Soviets further out to the east.

Although there were some arguments over the fine details, this imperial end state was deemed to satisfy the conditions of German security and *Lebensraum*. It was also intended to act as a powerful counterbalance to the growing industrial might of the United States, pulling the world's economic centre to the east, focused on Berlin and Vienna. At the same time, this shift in gravity would also break the power of London and Paris, and make them dependent upon the conditions and favours of the Reich.

Below: From the end of 1941, Germany had an ally in the war against Britain and the United States in the form of Japan, although these two Axis powers fought in completely separate theatres of operations. There lay the future possibility, however, of the Japanese and German empires meeting, and potentially clashing, in Russia and Central Asia. A meeting between the two powers in January 1942, therefore, set a demarcation line. As history was to show, such plans would be nothing but wishful thinking for both parties.

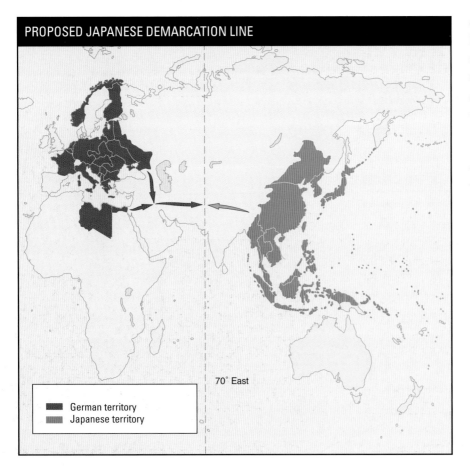

PROPOSED JAPANESE DEMARCATION LINE

70° East

German territory
Japanese territory

Reality of rule: Western Europe

It should be emphasized that the German vision of the *Neuordnung* was very much an ill-formed ideal. In reality, German occupation policy was far more haphazard and thuggish. The brutal realities of the emerging German Empire ensured that there were few bridges built between Germany and the conquered populations – and the opportunity to build a stable, consensual Reich was therefore lost.

In terms of political order, Western Europe was subject to a wide variety of arrangements. To ensure the continued smooth running of the European economies, Hitler largely left the countries' civil services and much of the government intact, although these systems gave only a veneer of independence – there was no doubt that Germany was now in charge.

The nature of German authority over Western Europe varied on a country-by-country basis. In Scandinavia, Denmark was governed by a Nazi-approved coalition government, overseen by a *Reichsbevollmächtiger* (Reich Plenipotentiary), even though King Christian X remained on the throne. Norway's government had fled to Britain, so was replaced by a new administration under local Nazi Vidkun Quisling, although he in turn was watched over by the *Reichskommissar* (Reich Commissioner) to Norway, Josef Terboven.

Further south, the Netherlands became the *Reichskommissariat Niederlande* (Reich Commission Netherlands), under military occupation and governed by a civilian Nazi administrator in the form of Arthur Seyss-Inquart. France was a special case. Alsace-Lorraine was incorporated into Germany, while northern and western France were

under direct military occupation, with a military governor headquartered in Paris. (Belgium was also under such arrangements, giving Germany firm military control over its westernmost territories facing Britain.)

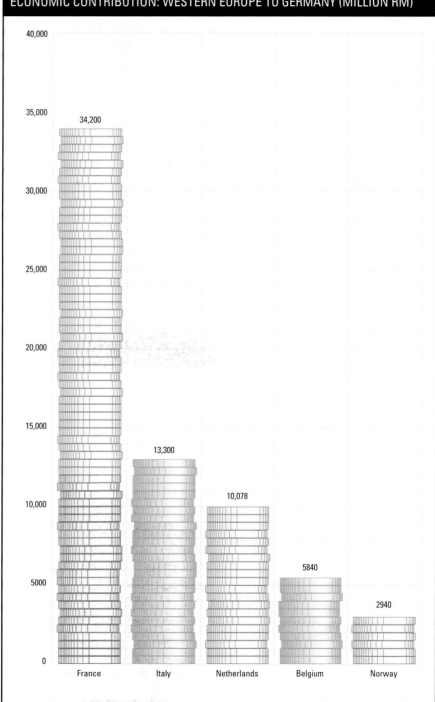

ECONOMIC CONTRIBUTION: WESTERN EUROPE TO GERMANY (MILLION RM)

France 34,200; Italy 13,300; Netherlands 10,078; Belgium 5840; Norway 2940

Resources

German rule over Western Europe could be undeniably harsh. All political opposition was ruthlessly crushed, and the economic resources of once-sovereign nations were exploited or plundered. The *Reichswerke Hermann Göring* – a vast German state-controlled enterprise created to seize the means of steel production and industrial output from private hands – took direct control of huge swathes of European industry.

Other foreign companies were set to work directly for their German overlords, and were forced to sell their goods to the occupiers at derisory prices. They became central to the German war effort – France, for example, produced 2517 aircraft for the *Luftwaffe*. The occupied territories also had to pay 'occupation costs' to the tune of 53 billion RM. Historian Richard Overy notes that 'The whole of German-controlled Europe, including satellite states, contributed 120 billion marks, or approximately 20% of the money spent on the war' (Overy, *Historical Atlas of the Third Reich*, p.89). It was clear that Western Europe was under new rule, and the old order had gone.

Eastern Europe

In Eastern Europe, virtually all pretence of civilized administration was discarded. Poland, the Baltic States and the western Soviet Union experienced the full horror of Nazi racial policies, with all sectors of society suffering. Poland was substantially restructured. Its western parts were absorbed directly into Germany, while its eastern territories would become part of *Reichskommissariat Ostland* (see below).

Its central region, however, was converted into the *Generalgouvernement* (General Government), under the brutal rule of Governor-General Hans Frank.

The *Generalgouvernement*, which included the cities of Warsaw and Cracow, was essentially a slave colony, and it also became a focal point for the Nazi extermination of Eastern Europe's Jews. Conditions within the *Generalgouvernement* were appalling for Jews and non-Jews alike, with brutality, arrest, torture, casual killings, deportations and starvation being common experiences.

Looking further east, the Nazis' rule of former Soviet territory was often equally inhumane. The conquered regions were divided into two principal zones – *Reichskommissariat Ostland*, which consisted of eastern Poland, the Baltic States, parts of East Prussia and western Belorussia, and some western parts of the Ukraine, and *Reichskommissariat Ukraine*, which principally covered the Ukraine and some adjacent parts of Poland and Belorussia. Both of the *Reichskommissariate* were run essentially as Nazi colonies, and they were systematically divided up into more manageable geographical subdivisions, consisting of *Generalbezirke* (General Regions), then *Hauptgebiete* (Main Districts) and *Kreisgebiete* (Districts), and

Opposite: The map here clearly shows how Poland was carved up by the Nazi authorities in the period 1939–42. Also note how, following the invasion of the Soviet Union, Germany administered the eastern territories as *Reichskommissariate* (Reich Commissions).

COUNTRIES/TERRITORIES CONQUERED BY GERMANY, 1939–45

Country	Date invaded	Date surrendered	Estimated total war dead (military and civilian, including Holocaust)
Poland	1 September 1939	27 September 1939	Up to 6 million
Denmark	9 April 1940	9 April 1940	about 5000
Belgium	10 May 1940	28 May 1940	86,100
Netherlands	10 May 1940	15 May 1940	301,000
France	10 May 1940	22 June 1940	567,600
Luxembourg	10 May 1940	10 May 1940	2000
Greece	6 April 1941	By 30 April 1941	300,000+
Yugoslavia	6 April 1941	17 April 1941	1.02 million
Soviet Union	22 June 1941	Not occupied in entirety	about 25 million
Baltic States	From 22 June 1941	By end of August 1941	about 650,000

OCCUPIED POLAND, 1939–42

SWEDEN

BALTIC SEA

Riga

LATVIA

LITHUANIA

Klaipéda
(Memel)

REICHSKOMMISSARIAT OSTLAND

Kaliningrad
(Königsberg)

EAST PRUSSIA

Kaunas
(Kovono)

Vilnius
(Vilno)

Danzig

REICHSGAU
DANZIG-WEST
PRUSSIA

GERMANY

Olsztyn

Grodno

BIALYSTOK

Minsk

Bydgoszcz
(Bromberg)

Zichenau

Bialystok

Inowroclaw
(Hohensalza)

ZICHENAU

Poznan
(Posen)

REICHSGAU
WARTHELAND

Warsaw

WARSAW DISTRICT

REICHSKOMMISSARIAT
UKRAINE

Kalisz

Lódź
(Litzmannstadt)

GENERALGOUVERNEMENT

LITZMANNSTADT

Radom

Lublin

LUBLIN DISTRICT

RADOM
DISTRICT

Zamosc

Dubno

Katowice

KATOWICE

Cracow

CRACÓW DISTRICT

Lvov
(Lemberg)

CZECHOSLOVAKIA

GALICIA

Polish boundary before 1 September 1939	Annexed by Germany
German-Soviet line	To Slovakia November 1939
Under German civil administration	To Poland 1938. To Upper Silesia October 1939
To Upper Silesia	

0   150 km

0   75 mls

finally *Parteien* (Parties), each subdivision having its own level of leadership.

Managing conquests

This neat description belies the complexity of administering a vast expanse of territory adjacent to a fluid war front. The political realities of the occupied regions also created severe friction within Germany. Take *Reichskommissariat* *Ukraine*, for example. Technically, all conquered regions in the east came under the authority of the *Reichsministerium für die besetzten Ostgebiete* (RMfdbO; Reich Ministry for the Occupied Eastern Territories), a state organization headed by Alfred Rosenberg. Yet the *Reichskommissariat Ukraine* was placed under the personal authority of fanatical Nazi Erich Koch, who ran his region brutally, inefficiently and, by having the direct ear of the Führer, largely without consultation with Rosenberg. Rosenberg's efforts to reclaim authority, aided by SS chief Heinrich Himmler, who was also concerned about the weakening reach of the SS, came to nothing. Almost every aspect of Rosenberg's remit, from economic to military matters, was covered by some other party or military organ in a classic example of the overlapping

---

DECREE OF THE FÜHRER CONCERNING THE ADMINISTRATION OF THE NEWLY OCCUPIED EASTERN TERRITORIES, 17 JULY 1941

In order to restore and maintain public order and public life in the newly occupied Eastern territories I decree that:

■ ARTICLE 1
As soon as the military operations in the newly-occupied territories are over, the administration of these territories shall be transferred from the military establishments to the civil-administration establishments. I shall from time to time determine by special decree, the territories which according to this are to be transferred to the civil administration, and the time when this is to take place.

■ ARTICLE 2
The Civil Administration in the newly-occupied Eastern territories, where these territories are not included in the administration of the territories bordering on the Reich or the General government, is subject to the Reich Minister for the Occupied Eastern territories.

■ ARTICLE 3
Military sovereign rights and powers are exercised by the commanders of the Armed Forces in the newly-occupied Eastern territories in accordance with my decree of 25 June 1941.

The powers of the Commissioner for the 4-year plan in the newly occupied Eastern territories, according to my decree of 29 June 1941, and those of the Reichsführer SS and Chief of *the German Police according to my decree of 17 July 1941, are subject to special ruling, and are not affected by the following regulations.*

■ ARTICLE 4
I appoint Reichsleiter Alfred Rosenberg as Reich Minister for the Occupied Eastern Territories. He will hold office in Berlin.

■ ARTICLE 5
The parts of the newly-occupied Eastern territories which are subject to the Reich Minister for the Occupied Eastern Territories are to be divided into Reich Commissariats [or Reich Commissions], which are to be divided into General Regions [Generalbezirke] and these again into District Areas [Kreisgebiete]. Several District Areas can be joined into a Main Region [Hauptbezirk]. The Reich Minister for the Occupied Eastern Territories will issue more detailed instructions on this subject.

■ ARTICLE 6
At the head of each Reich Commissariat will be a Reich Commissar [or Reich Commissioner]; at the head of each General Region a Commissar-General and at the head of every District Area an Area Commissar [Gebietskommissar]. Where a Main Region is formed, there will be a Head-Commissar [Hauptkommissar] in charge.

The Reich Commissars and the Commissar-Generals will

1942, authorities in Hitler's *Reich*. Rosenberg also suffered a similar humiliation over *Reichskommissariat Ostland*, whose rule was given to Hinrich Lohse, the *Oberpräsident* (Governor) and *Gauleiter* of Schleswig-Holstein.

Yet even with Hitler's candidates in place, authority in the east still experienced local variations, especially around the frontline areas, which remained under military rule.

Certain regions were scheduled to be transferred to the civilian rule of the *Reichskommissariat*, but the transfers never took place, leaving power vacuums to be filled by local SS or *Wehrmacht* authorities.

Future order

The development of war on the Eastern Front limited Hitler's further plans for his administration of Slavic lands. At a conference in July 1941, Hitler had mapped out the full extent of his ambitions for the eastern territories. Two further *Reichskommissariate* were proposed – *Reichskommissariat Moskowien* (Reich Commission of Muscovy) and *Reichskommissariat Kaukasus* (Reich Commission of the Caucasus). The former was intended to include most of Russia from the border of *Reichskommissariat Ostland* across to the Ural

---

be appointed by me, as will the heads of the main sections in the bureaux of the Reich Commissars, as well as the Head Commissars and District Commissars will be appointed by the Reich Minister for the Occupied Eastern Territories.

■ ARTICLE 7
In cases where Article 3 is not applicable, the Reich Commissars will be responsible to the Reich Minister for Occupied Eastern Territories, and will receive instructions exclusively from him.

■ ARTICLE 8
It is the responsibility of the Reich Minister for the Occupied Eastern Territories to legislate for the newly occupied territories under his jurisdiction. He can delegate the legislative power to the Reich Commissars.

■ ARTICLE 9
As regards civil affairs, the Reich Commissars are responsible for the whole administration of their territory.
As long as military operations are in progress, it is the duty of the highest competent authorities of the Reich to guarantee railway and postal services in accordance with the instructions of the Chief of Supreme Command of the Armed Forces. Further ruling will remain pending until the time the military operations cease.

■ ARTICLE 10
In order that the measures taken by the Reich Minister for the Occupied Eastern Territories or by the Reich Commissars in their areas may be brought into harmony with the overall aspects of the interests of the Reich, the Reich Minister for the Occupied Eastern Territories will maintain close liaison with the highest Reich authorities. In differences of opinion which cannot be settled by direct negotiations, my decision is to be obtained through the Reich Minister and Chief of the Reich Chancellery.

■ ARTICLE 11
The necessary regulations for carrying out and supplementing this decree will be issued by the Reich Minister for the Occupied Eastern Territories in agreement with the Reich Minister and Chief of the Reich Chancellery.

Führer's Headquarters, 17 July 1941

The Führer
Signed: Adolf Hitler

Chief of Supreme Command of the Armed Forces
Signed: Keitel

Reich Minister and Chief of the Reich Chancellery
Signed: Dr. Lammers

mc
So
att
put
Mc

wa
ter
oth
co

S

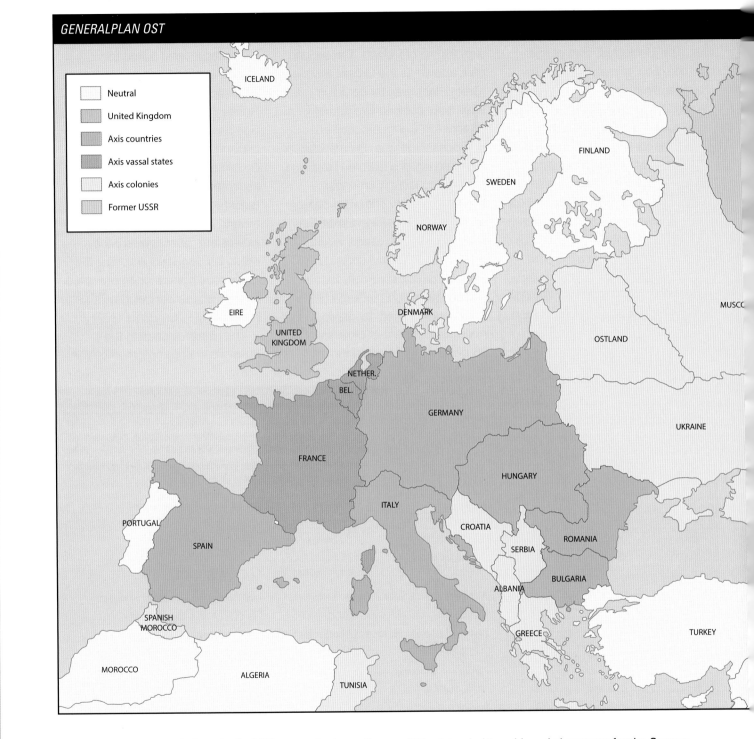

GENERALPLAN OST

Neutral

United Kingdom

Axis countries

Axis vassal states

Axis colonies

Former USSR

Above: How Europe might have looked if Germany had won the war: Hitler intended to achieve *Lebensraum* for the German people with an empire that stretched from the Atlantic coast across to Asiatic Russia, and from Scandinavia to the Middle East. Political arrangements for the states within this empire would range from near independence, albeit under close alignment with German policy, through to total subjugation – the latter particularly applied to the east.

FORMER USSR
(Undemarcated Borders)

CAUKASUS

IRAN

IRAQ

broad diversity of ethnicities, and the variable relations of those ethnicities to the communist regime. Loyalties varied considerably across the regions – at the same time as the Red Army was fighting for every inch of terrain, the Ukraine alone yielded some 20,000 volunteers for the *Waffen-SS*, while in the *Reichskommissariat Ostland* the military volunteers crept well above 30,000.

Yet oftentimes, rather than utilize or foster local support, Hitler and his zealous party officials simply steamrollered over local subtleties and stamped their hardline authority over a region. In the Crimea, for example, Stalin's persecution of the Tartars could have been the ideal lever to generate local support, and also bring out an anti-Soviet commitment from Turkey, which had strong ethnic connections with the Tartars.

Instead, Hitler latched onto a questionable historical theory that the Crimea was historically a place of Germanic peoples who had previously settled Europe, but who had died out in the region in the fifteenth century. Hitler wanted to return the Crimea to its believed Germanic roots, expelling its population through deportation to create 'Gotenland' (Land of the Goths), settled with modern generations of Germans. Hitler even issued a decision, on 3 July 1942, for the deportations to begin, but a more realistic attitude from the local Eleventh Army commander, General Erich von Manstein, resulted in the order being reversed. Thereafter, Manstein attempted to govern the region with more practicality, in spite of the NSDAP's efforts.

Despite Hitler's grand dreams of forging a new racial order across the occupied territories in the east, the reality did not match aspiration. It is true that Poland received large numbers of German settlers – 200,000 by June 1941. It is also true that *Volksdeutsche* – ethnic Germans, deemed of acceptable Germanic ethnicity though born outside Germany – were shifted around in large numbers in the east in general. Yet emigration out east from Germany itself always fell short of expectations – many people did not welcome the idea of swapping a sophisticated lifestyle in Germany for hardship on a confiscated farm in Belorussia or Ukraine. Hitler's vision of around 3.5 million Germans living in the eastern territories by the 1960s never seemed anything other than a pipe dream. Furthermore, the intention to use captive markets in the east as recipients for increased German exports was made ludicrous by Nazi depopulation efforts and the economic subjugation of the local people.

Ultimately, Hitler wanted to remodel Eurasia along his own warped racial lines. Had he succeeded, the long-term consequences are too appalling to imagine, bearing in mind the racial chaos he did in fact create before his defeat in 1945. Hitler's 'masterplan' for his German Empire was rooted in a persistent desire to settle the east, while also dominating the west. There is doubtless a high degree of fantasy in this model, as if such a large part of the world could

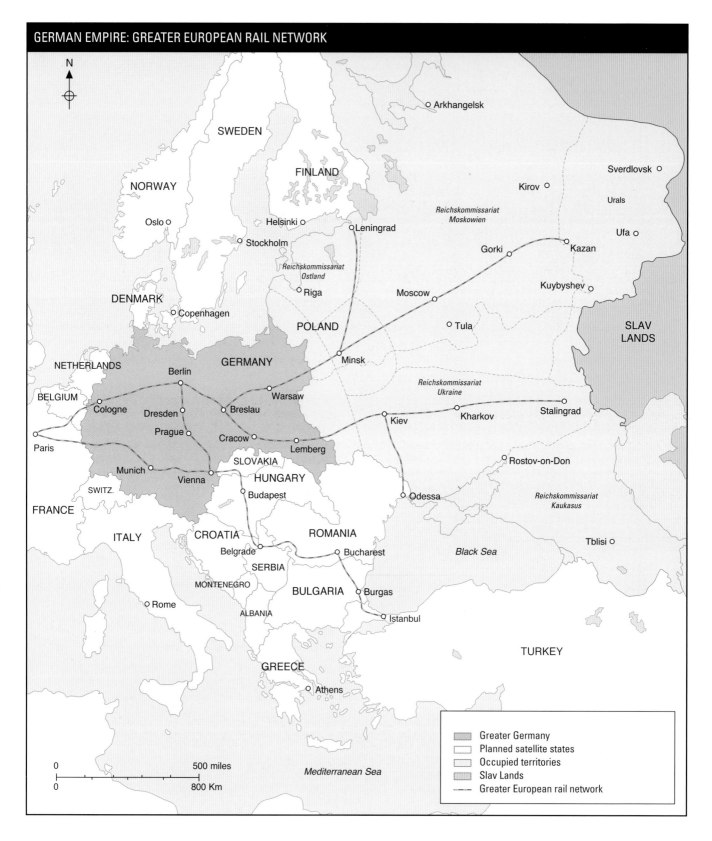

GERMAN EMPIRE: GREATER EUROPEAN RAIL NETWORK

N

SWEDEN

NORWAY

FINLAND

Arkhangelsk

Sverdlovsk

Kirov

Urals

Reichskommissariat
Moskowien

Ufa

Oslo

Helsinki

Leningrad

Stockholm

Gorki

Kazan

Kuybyshev

Reichskommissariat
Ostland

DENMARK

Riga

Moscow

SLAV
LANDS

Copenhagen

POLAND

Tula

NETHERLANDS

GERMANY

Berlin

Minsk

BELGIUM

Cologne

Warsaw

Reichskommissariat
Ukraine

Dresden

Breslau

Kiev

Kharkov

Stalingrad

Prague

Paris

Cracow

Lemberg

Rostov-on-Don

Munich

SLOVAKIA

Vienna

HUNGARY

Odessa

Reichskommissariat
Kaukasus

SWITZ.

Budapest

FRANCE

Tblisi

ITALY

CROATIA

ROMANIA

Black Sea

Belgrade

Bucharest

SERBIA

MONTENEGRO

BULGARIA

Burgas

Rome

ALBANIA

Istanbul

TURKEY

GREECE

Athens

	Greater Germany
	Planned satellite states
	Occupied territories
	Slav Lands
——	Greater European rail network

0   500 miles

Mediterranean Sea

0   800 Km

be remodelled so cleanly along racial lines that were the product of erroneous theory. Yet the idea that he might build this Greater German Reich was persistent, and even endured as the world was starting to collapse on Nazi Germany.

By the later stages of the war, Hitler should have been more concerned with national survival than the dead idea of an international empire. It could be argued that his overwrought sense of territorial destiny was the very thing that caused him to overreach, placing Germany on a certain path to defeat.

Opposite: Hitler envisaged that the new Nazi empire would be linked by an impressive road and rail network to faciliate imperial trade and military movements.

Below: This famous photograph shows Jewish civilians being rounded up by German police units in the Warsaw Ghetto, 1943. Most of the civilians were transported to concentration camps, and almost certain death, as part of the Nazis' wider policy of ethnic cleansing.

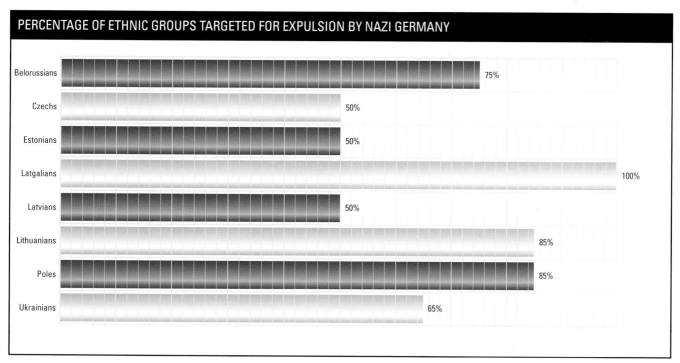

PERCENTAGE OF ETHNIC GROUPS TARGETED FOR EXPULSION BY NAZI GERMANY

Group	Percentage
Belorussians	75%
Czechs	50%
Estonians	50%
Latgalians	100%
Latvians	50%
Lithuanians	85%
Poles	85%
Ukrainians	65%

The Physical Reich

It was Hitler's ambition to make Germany the economic and political hub of the world. He also aspired to re-create the physical nature of the nation, rebuilding it to represent his personal vision of state power.

To this end, during the 1930s Germany underwent one of the most intensive building programmes in its history, expressed through major public works schemes.

Not only did these create hundreds of thousands of jobs, and practically solve Germany's unemployment problems, they also changed the physical face of the nation through a new generation of state buildings, infused with National Socialist ideology and speaking the language of raw power.

Left: The *Königsplatz* in Munich was a visible embodiment of Nazi power. It expressed the Nazi desire to create a legacy along classical lines and was used as a field for the Nazi Party's mass rallies.

Hitler and architecture

Hitler's fondness for architecture went well beyond the bounds of mere artistic interest. He saw buildings as a primary means to express Nazi ideology.

In a 1936 NSDAP sticker album, entitled *Adolf Hitler – Pictures from the Life of the Führer*, there is an essay by Hitler's personal architect, Albert Speer. In it, he acknowledges Hitler's centrality to the new National Socialist architectural movement in Germany, an involvement that goes beyond mere interest:

[Hitler's] great constructions which are beginning to rise in many places today are an essential expression of the thousand-year Movement and are, therefore, a part of the Movement itself. At any rate, the Führer built this Movement. Through its strength he came to power and still today determines its direction down to the smallest detail … As such he commands, just as he commands the purpose and the expression of the Movement, the neatness and the purity of the manner of building, the severity of expression, the nobility of materials and, most importantly, the new inner meaning and the inner character of his buildings.

– Speer, Adolf Hitler

Notwithstanding the sycophantic tone, Speer was correct to identify Hitler's passion for the architectural realization of his National Socialist ideology. Hitler had architectural pretensions from an early age, initially thwarted by his inability to be accepted into art school. Once he was in power from 1933, however, he had the authority to involve himself directly in the architectural redevelopment of the nation. He would work closely with his favoured architects – at first Paul Ludwig Troost until his death in 1934, then the legendary Speer – analyzing and modifying plans throughout the development and building stages, and offering strong opinions on matters of style and visual impression. It is revealing that even as Berlin was crumbling around him in April 1945, Hitler still found time to study fantastical architectural models of how the capital would be rebuilt after the war.

CHAPTERS IN THE 1936 NSDAP STICKER ALBUM PUBLICATION, *ADOLF HITLER – BILDER AUS DEM LEBEN DES FÜHRERS* (ADOLF HITLER – PICTURES FROM THE LIFE OF THE FÜHRER)

Chapter	Title	Translation	Author
	Vorwort	Foreword	Dr Joseph Goebbels
Chapter 1	Der Führer auf Reisen	The Führer Travelling	SS-Brigadeführer Julius Schreck
Chapter 2	Der Führer und das Deutsche Volk	The Führer and the German People	Dr Otto Dietrich
Chapter 3	Der Führer als Redner	The Führer as Orator	Dr Joseph Goebbels
Chapter 4	Der Führer in seinem Privatleben	The Führer in his Private Life	Obergruppenführer Wilhelm Brückner
Chapter 5	Der Führer als Staatsmann	The Führer as Statesman	Dr Joseph Goebbels
Chapter 6	Der Führer und der deutsche Arbeiter	The Führer and the German Worker	Dr Robert Ley
Chapter 7	Der Führer und die Künste	The Führer and the Arts	Dr Joseph Goebbels
Chapter 8	Die Bauten des Führers	The Architecture of the Führer	Albert Speer
Chapter 9	Adolf Hitler und seine Straken	Adolf Hitler and his Highways	Generalinspektor Dr Eng. Fritz Todt
Chapter 10	Unser Hitler: Rundfunk Ansprache an das deutsche Volk zum Geburtstag des Führers	Our Hitler: Radio Broadcast to the German People on the Führer's Birthday	Dr Joseph Goebbels
Chapter 11	Der Führer und die Wehrmacht	The Führer and the Armed Services	Oberleutnant Foertsch
Chapter 12	Der Führer und die Deutsche Jugend	The Führer and the German Youth	Baldur von Schirach
Chapter 13	Der Führer und die nationalsozialistische Bewegung	The Führer and the National Socialist Movement	Philipp Bouhler

Why Hitler was so fascinated with architecture is hinted at by a further passage from Speer's essay. He notes that 'For the Führer architecture is no mere pastime. It is, rather, a most earnest concern of the National Socialist Movement to make its great expression also in stone.' In essence, Hitler strove to rebuild Germany to reflect the greatness of the Nazi state, embodied in neoclassical structures redolent of ancient Greece and Rome, but with a new sense of power and austere authority.

As we shall see, at the same time he also attempted to bring a nostalgic sense of rural living and craftsmanship into German architecture, particularly in domestic housing. From our perspective, what Hitler's architects created was often creepy and overpowering, dominating the people rather than representing them.

Revitalizing the economy

Before analyzing the particular types of architecture created under the Third Reich, and how Hitler saw them representing German identity and destiny, it is important to remind ourselves of how state-funded construction was a key part of Hitler's ostensible 'economic miracle'. The fact remains that German unemployment dropped from six million in 1933 to 302,000 in 1939, in no small measure down to the huge investment in public works projects, among them state buildings, autobahns and hospitals, as well as the digging of irrigation ditches and planting forests. Public spending rose to 33 per cent of Gross National Product (GNP) by

1939 – it had been around 15 per cent a decade earlier.

We must not take the official figures entirely at face value. Jews and women, for example, were not included in the official unemployment figures. The introduction of conscription in 1935 also drove down the figures, with some 1.4 million men in uniform by 1939. Furthermore, general improvements in the world economy made job creation increasingly easy. Nevertheless, it seemed clear to the German people that compared with the bad old days of the late 1920s and early 1930s, Hitler's regime had brought a huge surge in employment and job security.

That is not to say that life for the workers was easy. The abolition of trade unions and the right to strike, plus direct government involvement

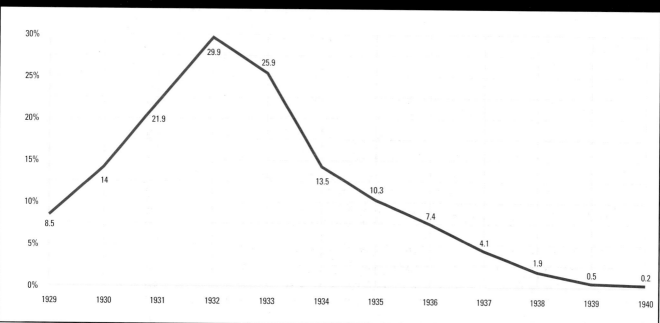

GERMAN UNEMPLOYMENT, 1929–40

in controlling wages and working conditions, meant that the workers were at the mercy of the regime.

In place of the unions came the *Deutsche Arbeitsfront* (DAF; German Labour Front). Created on 10 May 1933, and headed by Dr Robert Ley, this state organization eventually came to manage the affairs of 20 million workers. Ostensibly it was there to promote workers' rights, including improving workplace conditions, stabilizing wages across key industries and providing worker education. Although it did achieve some elements of these goals, at its heart the DAF was committed simply to exploiting the German workforce for maximum profit and productivity. Wages did increase in small annual increments, but these increases were often offset by a leap in working hours – by 1939 many workers in key industries were putting in working weeks of 70-plus hours, with few outlets to redress grievances. Furthermore, wage deductions to compulsory state schemes (including membership of the DAF) also reduced salaries further, the total deductions by 1939 averaging about 18 per cent.

As we can see, Germany's 'economic miracle' was bought at a cost to workers' rights. Germany's foreign currency exchange situation, plus its needs for raw materials,

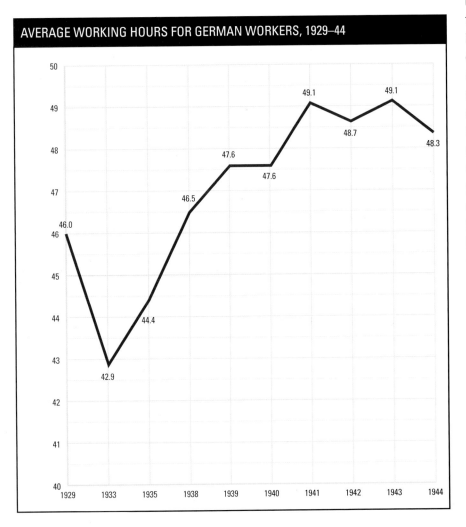

AVERAGE WORKING HOURS FOR GERMAN WORKERS, 1929–44

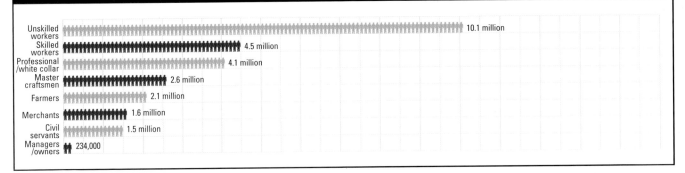

EMPLOYMENT BY OCCUPATIONAL TYPE, 1933

Unskilled workers	10.1 million
Skilled workers	4.5 million
Professional /white collar	4.1 million
Master craftsmen	2.6 million
Farmers	2.1 million
Merchants	1.6 million
Civil servants	1.5 million
Managers /owners	234,000

Above: Adolf Hitler (far right) with Robert Ley, head of the *Deutsche Arbeitsfront* (DAF, or German Labour Front), greet young DAF members at a Nuremberg Rally, 1935.

meant that the economic rise could not be sustained indefinitely. For Hitler, however, such considerations did not affect his plans to create the physical structure of a 'Thousand-Year Reich'.

State architecture

One of the most visible reminders of the new National Socialist regime was its state and party buildings.

During the 1920s and early 1930s, there had been much debate amongst architects, and interested party members, about the appropriate architectural style to manifest National Socialist ideology 'in stone'. One of the most influential voices to emerge from the chatter

was Paul Schultze-Naumburg, an ardent nationalist who struck a chord with Hitler.

Schultze-Naumburg condemned the industrial starkness of modernist architecture, and instead wanted a return to traditional German forms of design, plus the orderly beauty and authoritarianism of classical Roman and Greek edifices. Hence the defining quality of Nazi architecture was to be *Ordnung* (Order) – a building had to project balance, symmetry and authority in a controlled way.

The Nazis latched onto the anti-modernist trend in earnest, seeing modernism as representative of the industrial forces that had alienated the workers from their identity and sense of worth. In its place, at least in terms of public buildings, came a return to neoclassicism, but with an emphasis on power through sheer scale, and ornamentation influenced by the baroque period. The use of traditional skills in stonemasonry and mosaics was also meant to inject the designs with elements of traditional craftsmanship.

THE *REICHSKANZLEI* (REICH CHANCELLERY)

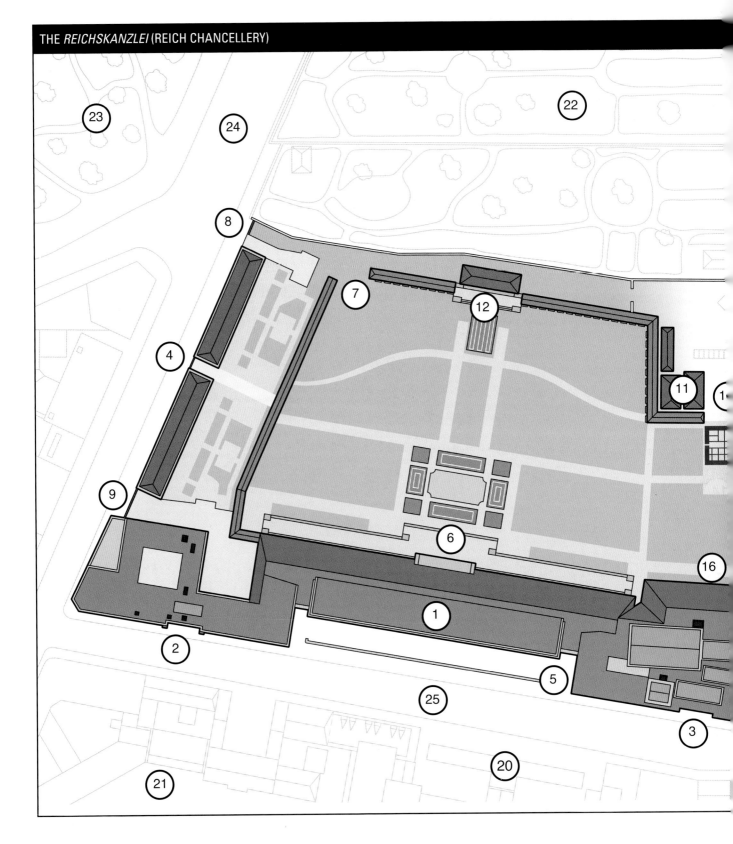

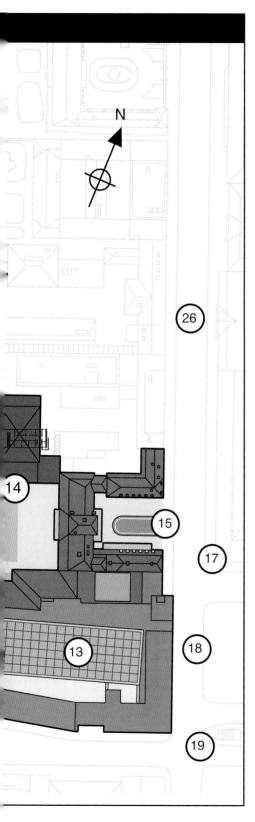

1. Mittelbau mit Marmorgalerie (Mittelbau Marble Gallery)
2. Eingang zur Reichskanzlei (Entrance to the Reich Chancellery)
3. Eingang zur Präsidialkanzlei (Entrance to the Office of the Reich President)
4. Kasernenbauten (Barracks Buildings)
5. Hebebühne zu den Katakomben (Lift to the Catacombs)
6. Gartenportal zu Hitlers Arbeitszimmer (Garden portal to Hitler's Office)
7. Bauzufahrt zum Führerbunker (Entranceway to the Führer Bunker)
8. Zufahrt – Tiefgarage und Führerbunker (Access: Underground Parking and Führer Bunker)
9. Einfahrt – Tiefgarage und Feuerwehr (Entrance – Parking and Fire Brigade)
10. Zufahrt – Führerbunker (Access – Führer Bunker)
11. Haus Kempka (Kempka House)
12. Gewächshaus (Greenhouse)
13. Ehrenhof (Courtyard of Honour)
14. Festsaal mit Wintergarten (Ballroom and Conservatory)
15. Alte Reichskanzlei (Old Reich Chancellery)
16. Speisesaal (Dining Hall)
17. Propagandaministerium (Ministry of Propaganda)
18. Erweiterungsbau zur Reichskanzlei (Reich Chancellery Extension)
19. U-Bahn-Eingang Wilhelmsplatz (Wilhelmsplatz Subway Entrance)
20. Kaufhaus Wertheim (Wertheim Department Store)
21. Leipziger Platz (Leipziger Plaza)
22. Ministergärten (Ministry Garden)
23. Tiergarten (Animal Garden – Zoo)
24. Hermann-Göring-Straße (Herman Göring Street)
25. Voßstraße (Voss Street)
26. Wilhelmstraße (Wilhelm Street)

An early major project undertaken after Hitler took over the chancellorship was the refurbishment and rebuilding of the *Reichskanzlei* (Reich Chancellery), a process that began under Paul Troost in 1933 but was completed by Albert Speer in 1939. Speer utterly transformed the *Reichskanzlei* with a monumental new annexe built along the length of the *Voßstraße* (Voss Street). The work cost the equivalent of $1 billion in today's money, and utilized the services of 4000 workers, but it more than fulfilled Hitler's aspirations of a worthy seat for the Nazi leadership.

Every aspect of the building was designed to overawe the visitor. The entrance was through the imposing gates of the *Ehrenhof* (Courtyard of Honour) on *Wilhelmstraße* (Wilhelm Street). The visitor would thereafter move through a series of mighty rooms and galleries, the most impressive of which was 150m

Left: The *Reichskanzlei* (Reich Chancellery) was Hitler's seat of power in Berlin. It was a vast complex, designed to overawe visitors with its grandeur. The plan of the chancellery here shows the building after its extensive reconstruction by Albert Speer, a redevelopment that cemented Speer's influence within the Third Reich. Hitler was extremely interested in every aspect of its design, as he felt it had to express National Socialist ideology – he once stated that 'Berlin must change its face to adapt to its new mission'. The chancellery was eventually demolished by Soviet occupiers.

DIAGRAMMATIC VIEW OF THE *KÖNIGSPLATZ*, MUNICH, 1940

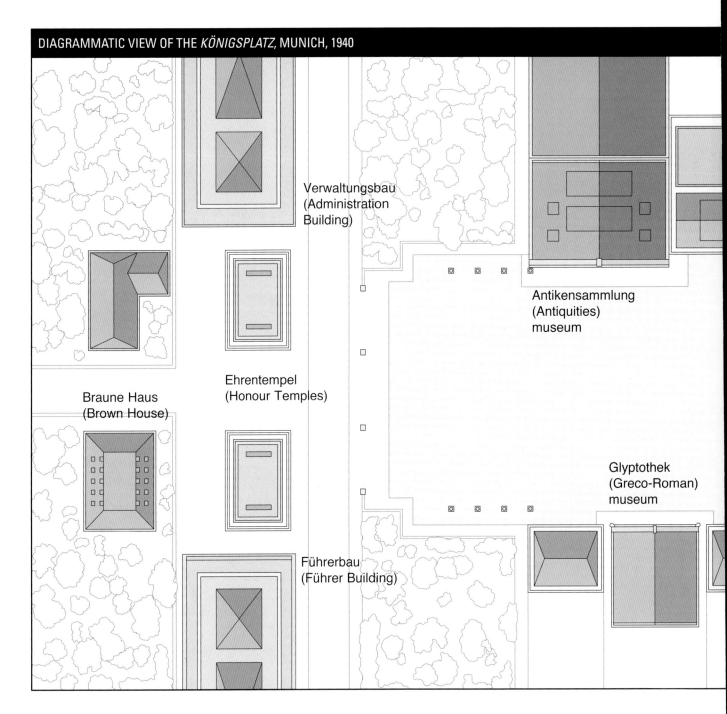

Verwaltungsbau
(Administration
Building)

Antikensammlung
(Antiquities)
museum

Ehrentempel
(Honour Temples)

Braune Haus
(Brown House)

Glyptothek
(Greco-Roman)
museum

Führerbau
(Führer Building)

Above: Munich was the spiritual home of the Nazi movement, so it was not surprising that it came in for substantial architectural redevelopment from 1933. The *Königsplatz* was a former royal square that the Nazis used for ceremonies and parades. The *Ehrentempel* (Honour Temples) held particular importance in the square's symbolism, as they stood in memory of those who had died during the failed 'Beer Hall Putsch' of 1923. They were framed by Nazi government buildings, and at the opposing end of the square stood the temple-like Propyläen monument. The whole effect was that of austere classicism. The *Braune Haus* (Brown House) was the national headquarters of Hitler's Nazi Party.

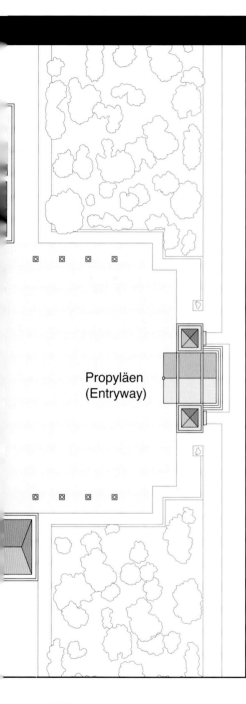

Propyläen
(Entryway)

(480ft) long, created from huge marble pillars and leading to Hitler's own office, itself an overwhelming 400 square metres (4306 square feet).

ALBERT SPEER

Right: Albert Speer (left) applauds at a Nazi conference. To his right is Joseph Goebbels, Reich Minister for Propaganda.

Birth: *19 March 1905*
Death: *1 September 1981*
Parents: *Albert and Luise Speer*
Place of birth: *Mannheim*
Marital status: *Married Margarete Weber, 28 August 1928*
Children: *Six*
Education: *Studied architecture at University of Karlsruhe, Technical University of Munich and Technical University of Berlin*
Early employment: *1927 – assistant to Heinrich Tessenow, Technical University of Berlin; 1931 – property manager for his father's estate*
Political affiliations: *Joined NSDAP in 1931; joined the SS in 1932*
Career landmarks: *1933 – Commissioned by Goebbels to renovate Nazi Party HQ in Berlin; commissioned to design Nuremberg rally at Tempelhof Field, 1 May 1933; appointed Commissioner for the Artistic and Technical Presentation of Party Rallies and Demonstrations*
1934 – made head of the Chief Office for Construction; designs 340,000-seat stadium Zeppelinfeld
1936 – Works on the Olympic Stadium in Berlin
1937 – Designs the German Pavilion for the International Exposition in Paris; appointed General Building Inspector for the Reich Capital
1938 – Rebuilds Reich Chancellery
1942 – Appointed Minister of Armaments following the death of Fritz Todt in an air crash

Dominating buildings

Although the Nazis were ostensibly creating buildings for the German people, the new *Reichskanzlei* tended to produce an alienating, echoing and slightly threatening feel, like some huge mausoleum. Nor was it unique. The *Reichskanzlei* was just one of dozens of looming buildings put up by the regime. Munich – the essential birthplace of the National Socialist movement – received several monumental works. The *Haus der deutschen Kunst* (House of German Art), for example, was a Troost design opened in 1937 to display approved Nazi art, and featured an imposing stone construction fronted by a 21-column colonnade. On Hitler's instructions, Troost also revitalized the city's *Königsplatz* (King's Square), used to hold Nazi Party rallies. Troost redecorated the nearby *Braune Haus* (Brown House), the NSDAP's national headquarters building, but also built two classical *Ehrentempel* (Honour Temples) in the square, solemn monuments to those who had died in the 1923 Beer Hall Putsch.

Other neoclassical edifices in the square included the *Führerbau* (Leader's Building), which was used for Hitler's staff, and a mirroring *Verwaltungsbau* (Administration Building). Both featured great halls, adorned with tapestries and stirring art, and dramatically-lit galleries.

Berlin was naturally a major recipient of public works projects. New municipal buildings included the Tempelhof Airport by Ernst Sagebiel, with an imposing stone frontage that measured 1.2km (0.7 miles). Speer contributed much to the city's landscape, with displays of authority such as the *Propagandaministerium* (Propanganda Ministry) building and the great *Olympiastadion* (Olympic Stadium), constructed specifically to impress the watching world at the 1936 Olympic Games. These and scores of other buildings were embellished with the potent motifs of the Nazi era – the swastika and the eagle – which served as definite reminders of the political status of such structures.

Party rallies

As well as his Berlin designs, Speer is also remembered for his part in arguably the most powerful visual achievements of the Nazi era – the Nuremberg rallies.

The rallies were held near Nuremberg on the *Reichsparteitagsgelände* (Reich Party Rally Grounds), an expanse of ground covering 11 square kilometres (4.2 square miles). It was a thoroughly imperial space, and although many of the buildings were constructed before the Nazis took power, they soon adjusted them to their own visual purposes. The site's central axis was the *Große Straße* (Great Street), which ran two kilometres (1.2 miles) and 40m (132ft) wide through the centre of the grounds, with deployment areas at each end – the *Luitpoldarena* (named after Luitpold, Prince Regent of Bavaria) to the north; the uncompleted *Märzfeld* (March Field) to the south. The latter was to feature 24 granite towers, each 38m (125ft) high; only 11 were completed.

Off the main axis of the grounds was the *Kongresshalle* (Congress Hall), a mighty circular four-tiered Romanesque structure standing 39m (129ft) high and with a diameter of 250m (843ft). Designed primarily by Ludwig and Franz Ruff, with later additions by Speer, the *Kongresshalle* was, like many of the Nazis most ambitious buildings, never entirely finished, but it was completed to a sufficient extent to add further grandeur to an already imposing location.

Hitler worship

One of the most important spaces was the *Zeppelinfeld* (Zeppelin Field), designed by Speer, which featured a large parade ground overlooked by an imposing grandstand, from which Hitler often delivered his addresses. It was in the *Zeppelinfeld* that Speer, Goebbels and other Nazi officials created events of insidious majesty. Night-time gatherings involving more than 200,000 people, all in military garb, were framed by 130 searchlights ringing the circumference of the field, each throwing up a shaft of light miles into the sky. The effect was to create a 'Cathedral of Light'. Combined with Hitler's oratory, vast ranks of swastikas and the mass use of flaming torches, all this caused the rallies to be burned into the minds of those who attended, and of those

NUREMBERG RALLY PROGRAMME, 1938

■ MONDAY, 5 SEPTEMBER – GREETINGS
Press meeting
Reception for Hitler at Nuremberg City Hall

■ TUESDAY, 6 SEPTEMBER
– OPENING OF PARTY CONGRESS
Hitler reviews Hitler Youth flags
*Official opening of the Party Congress – Speeches by
    Rudolf Hess, Julius Streicher, Adolf Wagner*
Imperial Crown Jewels presented to Hitler
*Exhibition 'Kampf in Osten' ('Struggle in the East') opens to
    attendees – Speech by Alfred Rosenberg*
*Presentation of National Prizes for Art and Science –
    Speeches by Alfred Rosenberg, Adolf Hitler*

■ WEDNESDAY, 7 SEPTEMBER
– DEUTSCHE ARBEITSFRONT (DAF) DAY
*DAF parade – Speeches by Konstantin Hierl and
    Adolf Hitler*
DAF parade through Nuremberg
*Party Congress continues – Speeches by Alfred
    Rosenberg, Erich Hilgenfeldt and Adolf Wagner*

■ THURSDAY, 8 SEPTEMBER – DAY OF FELLOWSHIP
Athletic competitions
*Party Congress continues – Speeches by Fritz Todt and
    Dr Otto Dietrich*
Torchlight parade

■ FRIDAY, 9 SEPTEMBER – DAY OF THE LEADERS
*Party Congress continues – Speeches by Konstantin Hierl,
    Walter Darré and Max Amann*
*Presentation by National Socialist Women's Association –
    Speech by Gertrude Scholtz-Klink*
*Review of political leaders on the Zeppelinfeld – Speeches
    by Robert Ley and Adolf Hitler*

■ SATURDAY, 10 SEPTEMBER – HITLER YOUTH DAY
*Review of the Hitler Youth – Speeches by Rudolf Hess and
    Adolf Hitler*
*Committee meeting of DAF – Speeches by Robert Ley and
    Hermann Göring*
Final athletic games
*Party Congress continues – Speeches by Robert Ley,
    Fritz Reinhardt and Joseph Goebbels*

■ SUNDAY, 11 SEPTEMBER – DAY OF THE SA AND SS
*Mass meeting – Speeches by Viktor Lutze and
    Adolf Hitler.*
Parade through Nuremberg
Meeting of political leadership – Speech by Rudolf Hess

■ MONDAY, 12 SEPTEMBER – ARMED FORCES DAY
*Review and mass presentation of the Army – Speech by
    Adolf Hitler*
Closing ceremony – Speech by Adolf Hitler

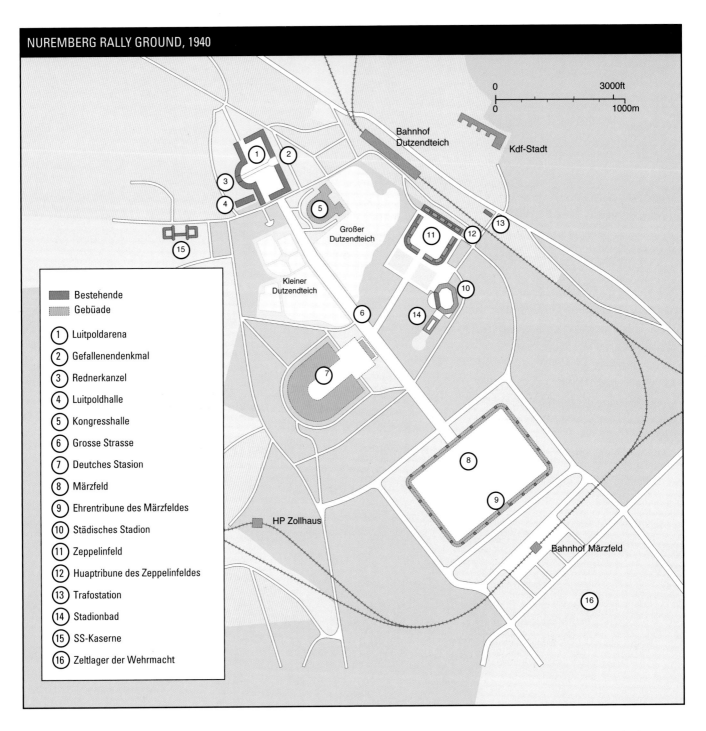

NUREMBERG RALLY GROUND, 1940

Legend:

- Bestehende
- Gebüade

1. Luitpoldarena
2. Gefallenendenkmal
3. Rednerkanzel
4. Luitpoldhalle
5. Kongresshalle
6. Grosse Strasse
7. Deutches Stasion
8. Märzfeld
9. Ehrentribune des Märzfeldes
10. Städisches Stadion
11. Zeppelinfeld
12. Huaptribune des Zeppelinfeldes
13. Trafostation
14. Stadionbad
15. SS-Kaserne
16. Zeltlager der Wehrmacht

Map labels: Bahnhof Dutzendteich, Kdf-Stadt, Großer Dutzendteich, Kleiner Dutzendteich, HP Zollhaus, Bahnhof Märzfeld

Scale: 0 — 3000ft / 0 — 1000m

Above: The Nuremberg rallies, also called the *Parteitage* (Party Days), were spectacular political/ceremonial events in the Nazi calendar. The rally ground was never quite developed to the full extent of Hitler's ambitions, but it was an imposing space nevertheless. The main road that ran down the central axis of the ground measured more than 2km (1.2 miles) in length and was 40m (132ft) wide. Towers, temple-like structures, stadia and public address platforms, plus the theatrical lighting additions of Albert Speer, made the Nuremberg venue a place of great visual power.

who witnessed the spectacle at the cinema. Such stirring visions were carefully and manipulatively crafted, but they illustrated the clear understanding the Nazis had about the relationship between visual effects and the development of what became known as 'Führer worship'.

Imperial plans

Although Hitler oversaw huge public works during his time in power, he envisioned an even greater future for Germany and its architecture. Berlin, in particular, was to have become *Welthauptstadt Germania* (World Capital Germania) – quite literally, the centre of the world.

To demonstrate this status, it would have to be transformed into a place of transcendent grandeur, the perfect vision of a thousand-year empire. The guiding lines of *Welthauptstadt Germania* were to be provided by two huge avenues, forming a crossroads at their meeting point. At the intersection was to be a huge triumphal arch more than 100m (328ft) high, similar in style to the *Arc de Triomphe* in Paris. The north-south avenue – known as the 'Avenue of Victory' – ran through the arch, and would be five kilometres (three miles) in length. At the northern end was to be a huge open forum, the *Großer*

Platz (Great Square), dominated by the vast, domed *Volkshalle* (People's Hall). Sketched out by Hitler himself (although given to Speer to realize), this building was much inspired by the Pantheon of Rome, but was on an even greater scale. The height at the summit of the dome was to be 290m (950ft) from the street, while the dome's diameter would measure 250m (820ft). Inside, three tiers of seating would have enclosed an echoing, lofty space – the building would have acted as a great meeting hall, capable of seating more than 150,000. The southern end of the avenue would feature expansive rail terminals,

STRUCTURE OF THE *REICHSWERKE HERMANN GÖRING*, 1945

◆ **FÜHRERHAUPTQUARTIER** *Führer's Headquarters*

Vierjahresplan *(Four-Year Plan)* **& Rüstungsministerium** *(Defence Ministry)*
 └─■ Reichswerke Hermann Göring
  ├─■ Montan- und Rüstungsgesellschaften *(Mining and Defence Companies)*
  ├─■ Waffen- und Maschinenblock *(Weapons and Machines Section)*
  ├─■ Schiffahtsblock *(Shipping Section)*
  ├─■ Berg- und Hüttenwerksgesellschaften Ost *(Mining and Metallurgical Companies East)*
  ├─■ Sonstige Monopolgesellschaften *(Other Monopolies)*
  ├─■ Spinnstoff- und Fasergesellschaft *(Textile and Fibre Company)*
  ├─■ Chemie-Ost *(Chemistry East)*
  ├─■ Superphosphat Ost *(Superphosphate East)*
  ├─■ Konstinental Öl AG *(Konstinental Oil AG)*
  ├─■ Betriebliche Ostwirtschaft *(Eastern Economy Operations)*
  ├─■ Betriebliche Wirtschaft Serbiens *(Economic Operations Serbia)*
  ├─■ Betriebliche Wirtschaft Rumäniens *(Economic Operations Romania)*
  ├─■ Gesamte Kohlewirtschaft *(Total Coal Production)*
  ├─■ Treuhänder gesamter Erzbergbau *(Trustee Ore Mining)*
  ├─■ Sonstige Treuhandsch. HGW mit SS-Betrieb *(Other Trusts – HGW with SS-Operations)*
  └─■ Militärgouverneue, zivile Parteverwaltg. im Osten *(New Military Governments, Civilian in the East)*

destined to bring thousands of people into the heart of the Reich. Other buildings planned to border the great axes included a House of Nations meeting hall, a 21-storey hotel, numerous cinemas, theatres and opera houses, a swimming pool constructed like a Roman baths and luxurious restaurants.

It should be noted that Hitler was not the only German leader to have grandiose architectural visions for the future. The exceptionally vain Hermann Göring, for example, had his own ideas for how to immortalize himself in stone and iron. Göring centred his expanding *Reichswerke Hermann Göring* on the city of Salzgitter in Lower Saxony.

In 1942 Göring had incorporated the city and outlying districts into a single independent state entity, known as the *Stadtkreis Watenstedt-Salzgitter*. His ultimate vision was eventually to create *Hermann Göring Stadt*, a large area of industrial development that would form the centre of his economic empire. The city would be a self-contained entity, and would include parks and woodlands, areas of workers' housing, commercial districts, major rail and road links, plus the areas designated for mining and heavy industry. As with Hitler's vision for *Welthauptstadt Germania*, however, the realities of war put paid to such ambitions, and much of the plans remained unrealized in 1945.

Völkisch housing

While great municipal and national buildings certainly occupied much of Hitler's attention, there was another side to his plans to redevelop the German landscape.

Hitler had an affection for the *völkisch* movement, a nationalistic philosophy dating back to the nineteenth century that emphasized rural, local traditions over industrial, urban modernity. In many ways it was a purely nostalgic movement, longing to get back to an authenticity of lifestyle that in reality was largely a myth. For the Nazis, furthermore, the rural people

Below: Hermann Göring discusses the latest Nazi four-year plan during a speech, 1936. Behind him, to the right, are Joseph Goebbels and Rudoph Hess.

of Germany came to represent racial and ideological purity, and a connection with the ancient roots of German greatness.

From a practical point of view, the Nazi affection for the rural community made some sense. If Germany was to attain autarky, then its self-sufficiency had to extend to food production, which meant maximizing the yields from German farmland. For farmers and agricultural workers, the Nazis did bring some real benefits. The government stabilized the prices paid for agricultural goods, gave farmers tax relief and low interest rates, and protected German food markets from cheap foreign imports. Wages amongst agricultural workers rose, albeit slowly.

There were plenty of negatives, however. Levels of debt amongst farms was high, and the rural lifestyle remained unforgiving. Escaping from poor conditions on the farm was made much harder by the *Reichserbhofgesetz* (Reich Hereditary Farm Law) of 15 May 1933. In a misguided attempt to preserve the traditions of small-scale farming, the Nazis prohibited the sale of any farm of 7.5–125 hectares (18.5–309 acres) and ordered that farms could be inherited by only a single heir. In effect, the new law simply chained many farmers to their industry, regardless of conditions. The Nazis also interfered with farming practices, and they could take over farms that were not meeting central guidelines about productivity.

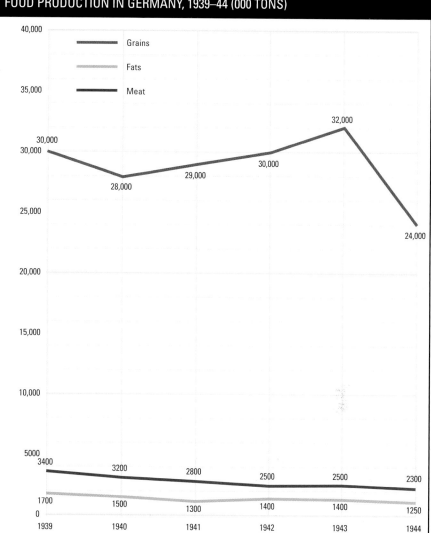

FOOD PRODUCTION IN GERMANY, 1939–44 (000 TONS)

The Nazi affection for rural life extended to housing. There was a limited attempt to encourage development of rural-style housing for German workers, using traditional materials and design techniques. In a similar vein to the 'model villages' built by British industrialists and philanthropists during the nineteenth century, several hundred housing projects for industrial workers were authorized into construction by the Nazis. In the form of detached houses, the *völkisch* architecture tended to consist of relatively simple single- or two-storey homes, regular in shape and in the layout of the windows, and built using local material and craftsmen. Unlike the flat-roofed configuration of many modernist buildings, the Nazi houses tended to have steeply sloped roofs reflecting local design influences, again built of traditional materials such as thatch, slate and wood. Windows were often decorated with painted wooden shutters.

In terms of interiors, the *völkisch* houses refused the modernist tendency for open plan designs, returning to the older layouts in which every room had a distinct space and purpose. Small but picturesque gardens attempted to complete the picture of an idyllic home. Of course, in the inner cities, where space was at a premium, the houses were much more compressed in nature (they were often terraced or semi-detached), but the designers still sought to give them the veneer of traditionalism, even if the options were limited to a gaudily coloured window box.

Architectural intentions

The creation of völkisch housing was not a widespread phenomenon, as the Nazi regime was far more interested in buildings that would awe the population rather than

TYPICAL *VÖLKISCH* HOUSE LAYOUT

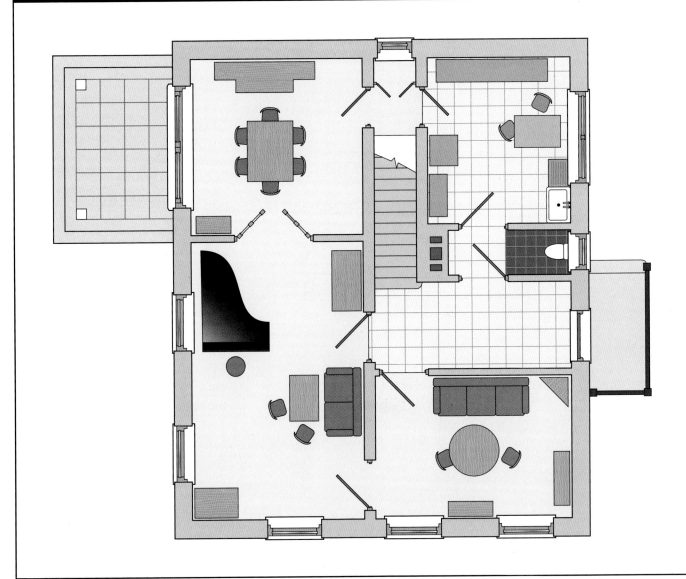

welcome them in. This is one of the inconsistencies of the architectural Third Reich – on the one hand, the Nazis declared themselves a grass-roots, traditionalist movement, while at the same time developing a cold state architecture that unnerved the unfamiliar visitor, and which celebrated the impersonal power of the state over the individual member of that state.

Prora

Before looking at other aspects of the Nazi public works programmes, a different development for the workers is worth special consideration. The *Kraft durch Freude* (Strength through Joy) movement, discussed in more detail in the next chapter, aimed to provide holiday travel and facilities for thousands of the Reich's workers and party members. One expression of this effort was the construction of a sprawling tourist resort on the island of Rügen on the Baltic coastline. Known as Prora, the resort was essentially a holiday camp but – true to Nazi form – on an intimidating scale. (Note that the Nazis planned to create five such resorts at different locations, but Prora was the only one that progressed beyond conception).

Construction began in 1936, and the project consumed thousands of the Reich's workers. Yet in 1939, when war broke out, Prora became nothing more than an expensive drain on resources, and all construction was stopped, leaving gloomy, half-finished buildings that remain to this day.

Instead, the complex was eventually applied to a variety of wartime purposes, including sheltering refugees from bomb-struck Hamburg and for training various auxiliary forces. As with many of Hitler's projects, reality got the better of ambition.

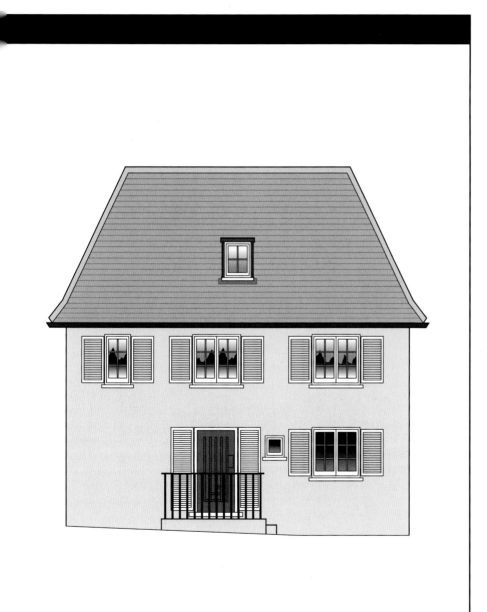

Left: The exterior and interior plan of the *völkisch* house followed patterns of conformity, regularity and tradition. The sloping roof, window decorations and compartmentalized rooms reflected a Nazi rejection of modernism. Applying such a design style to urban rather than rural buildings was problematic.

THE PRORA COMPLEX IN CONCEPTION

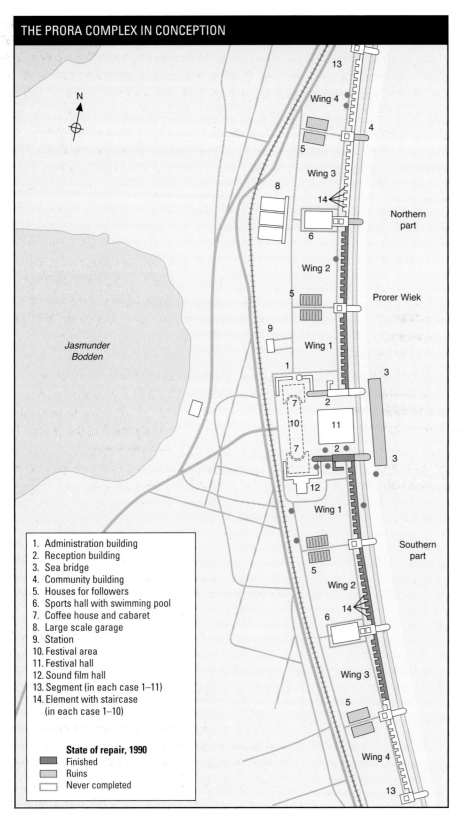

N

13

Wing 4

4

5

Wing 3

8

14

Northern
part

6

Wing 2

5

Prorer Wiek

9

Wing 1

*Jasmunder
Bodden*

1

3

7

2

10

11

7

2

3

12

Wing 1

Southern
part

5

Wing 2

14

6

Wing 3

5

Wing 4

13

1. Administration building
2. Reception building
3. Sea bridge
4. Community building
5. Houses for followers
6. Sports hall with swimming pool
7. Coffee house and cabaret
8. Large scale garage
9. Station
10. Festival area
11. Festival hall
12. Sound film hall
13. Segment (in each case 1–11)
14. Element with staircase
   (in each case 1–10)

State of repair, 1990
Finished
Ruins
Never completed

Factories and workplaces

The places in which the population worked also received some attention from architects keen to make the German population feel spiritually at home. While there was always a limit to how convivial an industrial unit could feel, there was an attempt to make factories and workplaces more traditional in appearance, while also providing a salubrious environment in which to work.

From a design perspective, the new-build German buildings often tried to play down industrial angularity, preferring instead to use as many 'soft' edges as possible and sloping the roofs slightly. As in state buildings and *völkisch* domestic premises, construction materials such as red brick and local stone were used alongside glass and steel in an attempt to give workplaces greater warmth.

Inside the workplace, the *Schönheit der Arbeit* (Beauty of Labour) movement exerted some influence. Part of the *Deutsche Arbeitsfront*, *Schönheit der Arbeit* dedicated itself to giving the

Left: Eight housing blocks, set in two huge complexes, were to hold 20,000 people, with a predicted annual capacity of several million tourists. Each 5 x 2.5m (16 x 8ft), two-bed room overlooked the sea, and shower and toilet facilities were shared. Hitler's plans for the complex were particularly grandiose. He commissioned designs for a vast 20,000-seat festival hall, docking facilities for liners, railway stations, cinemas and restaurants.

humble worker 'the feeling for the worth and importance of his labour'. It therefore encouraged industrialists to provide all manner of workplace facilities, to foster personal development as much as hourly productivity. Some of these measures were eminently practical – such as decent ventilation systems, noise-reduction measures and well-stocked and inexpensive canteens. Others, however, were designed to promote more inner contentment and reflection. Factories were often accompanied by peacefully landscaped grounds, giving the workers somewhere to walk and contemplate when they were not at their machines. There were recreational facilities such as gyms and concert halls. Libraries proliferated – 4000 industrial units had their own libraries by 1938, with books lent out free or for a cost of 10 pfennigs per book.

Working conditions

Of course, as with so much in the Third Reich, there was a gulf between propaganda and reality. Much of German labour, particularly in mining and similar heavy industries, endured tough working conditions. Once the war began in 1939, workers had to endure increasingly punishing hours to meet war production demands, and their workplaces were frequently shattered or damaged by the effects of Allied bombing (see below). Yet there is no denying that the early Nazi regime made some identifiable efforts to enhance the German

workplace, even if these efforts were ultimately another piece in the jigsaw of ideological control.

Autobahns and the automobile

Impressive new state buildings were not the only visible sign of Hitler's Third Reich. He also began the process of reshaping Germany's road transport network through the famous *Reischsautobahn* (State Motorway).

Hitler was a notable believer in the social potential of the automobile. An enthusiast of Henry Ford, the US industrialist who had essentially given America mass car transportation, Hitler saw automobiles as an ideal form of personal transport for the people. In the *Adolf Hitler* album referred to earlier, Fritz Todt – the man who would be appointed the Inspector General for construction of the *Autobahnen* – noted that:

The Führer especially values automobile travel since no other mode of transportation is able to link up the traveller with the people as closely … Even before coming to power … he developed his mature idea of the necessity of creating a network of roads that would be open to motor traffic.
– Todt, *Adolf Hitler*, 1936

Todt gives the impression that Hitler's vision of the autobahns was original to him. That is not the case, and large state and private initiatives were pursued during the 1920s.

Yet it was Hitler who, via his public works projects, galvanized the scheme into life. Todt quotes from a speech given by Hitler on 11 February 1933:

Just as bridle paths were built and railroads laid in accordance with need, so automobile traffic now demands special roadways. Just as we used to measure distances between people in the past by the railroad, in the future we shall be measuring by highways.
– Hitler, 1933

Hitler was proposing that Germany revolutionize its infrastructure through roads, although part of this aspiration was simply to catch up with what much of the developed world was already doing.

The autobahns essentially consisted of two-lane motorways, providing fast road links between Germany's major towns and cities. The most important route would be the Berlin–Nuremberg–Munich–Linz road – the so-called 'Party Road', a Nazi artery connecting the four most politically and symbolically important locations in the Third Reich. (It should be noted that Hitler planned to turn Linz, his birthplace, into something of a cultural and industrial capital. Although significant industrialization did take place, Hitler's plans were never fulfilled.)

The autobahns became the largest of Hitler's public works programmes, using 130,000 workers by 1936. Aesthetic and ideological purposes were as much at the heart of their building as transportation objectives. The autobahns were meant to break down regional barriers, release the pressure of city overcrowding, facilitate military deployments and embody German progress. Special *Landschaftanwalt* (Landscape Councils) were appointed in each autobahn building district to craft the roadside terrain into pleasing contours and features. Bridges were often built using local stone to match the natural surroundings. Indeed, the routes of the autobahns were frequently planned on the basis of scenic quality, taking in alpine views or winding through hilly landscapes, even when less attractive but more direct routes were available.

Despite the sheer volume of muscle and industry being applied to the autobahns, they never quite reached the hoped-for extent. In total, Hitler aimed to lay 14,000km (8700 miles) of autobahn, but by 1940 – when construction of the roads practically stopped – only 3736km (2321 miles) had been put

down, and thousands of kilometres sat unfinished. Moreover, the autobahns did not achieve all the intended effects. Much military traffic, for example, was too heavy for the autobahns' surface, so had to rely on the rail network instead

(which was more practical anyway for heavy armoured vehicles). Problems with fuel supply during the war also limited the amount of traffic on Germany's roads.

A further blow to the autobahns, and the German people in general,

Opposite: The creation of the autobahns used huge amounts of German manpower – at times more than 100,000 men were employed in their building. They formed the world's first high-speed road network, but war brought construction to a virtual stop.

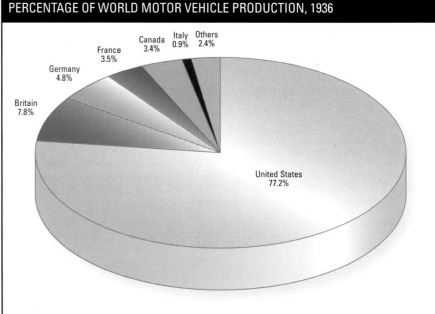

PERCENTAGE OF WORLD MOTOR VEHICLE PRODUCTION, 1936

Canada 3.4%
Italy 0.9%
Others 2.4%
France 3.5%
Germany 4.8%
Britain 7.8%
United States 77.2%

TOTAL LENGTH OF THE AUTOBAHNS, 1935–40

1935								
1936								
1937								
1938								
1939								
1940								

00km   500km   1000km   1500km   2000km   2500km   3000km   3500km   4000km

MAP OF COMPLETED AND PLANNED AUTOBAHNS

Legend:
- Border of the Reich, 1942
- **Autobahns:**
- Completed by 1939
- Planned for 1939
- Planned for 1950
- Party Road
- ⬤ Führerstadt
- ○ Industrial capitals
- ● Other planned Nazi development

SWEDEN

North Sea

DENMARK

Baltic Sea

Reichskommissariat Ostland

○ Copenhagen

● Rugen

● Danzig

East Prussia

● Hamburg

U S S R

○ Amsterdam

Hanover ●   Wolfsburg ●   ⬤⬤ Berlin

● Posen

● Warsaw

NETHERLANDS

Watenstedt-Salzgitter ●

POLAND

○ Brussels

● Cologne

BELGIUM

● Koblenz

● Limburg

● Breslau

Generalgouvernement

GERMANY

● Lux

○ Prague

○ Cracow

● Bayreuth

Nuremberg ⬤

Vitkovice ○

FRANCE

● Strassburg

Linz   Vienna ⬤

SLOVAKIA

Munich ⬤

N

LIECHT

AUSTRIA

HUNGARY

SWITZERLAND

● Klagenfurt

ITALY

ROMANIA

0   100 miles

0   200 Km

CROATIA

BULGARIA

Above: The Volkswagen Type 1 was a highly innovative vehicle. It had a rear-mounted air-cooled engine, which delivered rear-wheel drive and could power the car to a top speed of 100km/h (62mph). It was influenced by the design of a Czech vehicle, the Tatra V750 – the Tatra's designer, Hans Ledwinka, an Austrian, knew Hitler and Ferdinand Porsche personally.

was that the dream of private motoring was also unrealized for many. In the pre-war years, Hitler sought to remedy the lack of a decent home-built German car: in 1933, he commissioned the engineer and vehicle designer Ferdinand Porsche to create a mass-produced vehicle similar in principle and availability to Henry Ford's famous Model T. The key requirements were that it carry four adults and would sell for under 900 RM.

Volkswagen
The result, delivered in final prototype form in 1938, was one of the most famous vehicles of all time – the *Volkswagen*. With its smooth, curvilinear shape and rear-mounted four-cylinder engine, it was a revolution in car design, and has endured to this day in the form of the Volkswagen Beetle. Selling of the *Volkswagen* began even before the car entered production. The KdF promoted a special scheme under which workers could pay 5 RM each week towards the total purchase cost of the vehicle – 990 RM. More than 336,000 Germans joined the scheme, but when war broke out in 1939 all vehicle production was diverted to military purposes, and the investors simply lost their money. (As it happens, part of the original design brief for the *Volkswagen* was that it should be capable of carrying three soldiers and a machine gun, so military repurposing was always a background possibility.)

Destruction

Hitler's dream was for a Third Reich of imperial splendour, a place of lofty, imposing cities, broad avenues, industrial might and national ardour. By May 1945, in contrast, his ambitions had largely reduced urban Germany to a smoking shell, the great buildings of the Nazis reduced to ash and rubble.

Much of this destruction was inflicted by the Allied strategic bombing campaign, delivered in earnest between 1942 and 1945. Although the bombing campaign did not achieve the decisive strategic effects for which the Allies hoped, the devastation wrought upon Greater Germany was appalling. In total, more than 1.5 million tonnes (1.48 million tons) of bombs were dropped onto German towns and cities. These bombs killed 305,000 civilians and wounded 708,000. They also made 7.5 million people homeless, destroying nearly 30 per cent of German domestic housing. A total of about 20 per cent of all buildings in Germany were destroyed, or damaged to some degree, and 20 million people ended up living without basic utilities such as running water and electricity. Roads, bridges and rail networks were also heavily impaired, resulting in severe problems in transporting raw materials around the Reich.

Aside from the material devastation of Germany, the bombing had some wider physical repercussions. Air raid shelters, for example, were built across Germany. While many people took refuge in opportunistic or improvised shelters, such as cellars or tunnels,

RAF & USAAF BOMB TONNAGES DROPPED ON GERMANY, 1939–45 (TONNES)

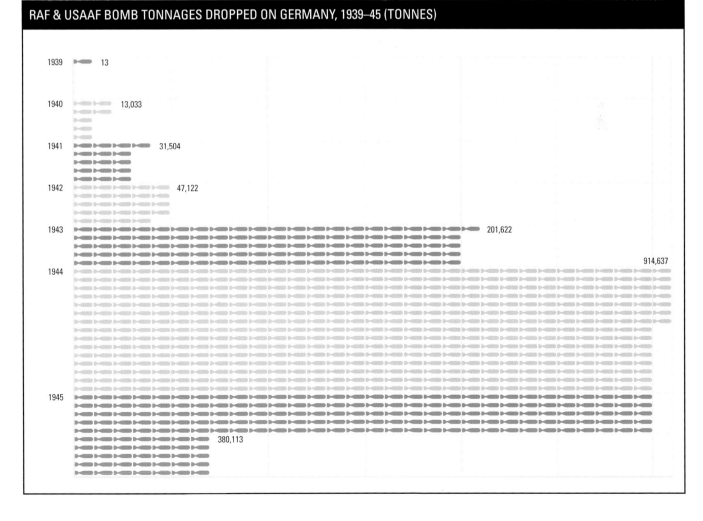

1939   13
1940   13,033
1941   31,504
1942   47,122
1943   201,622
1944   914,637
1945   380,113

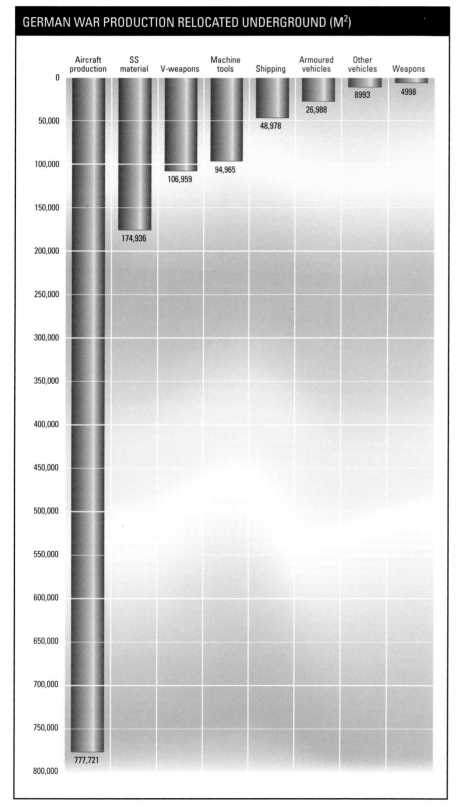

GERMAN WAR PRODUCTION RELOCATED UNDERGROUND (M²)

hundreds of thousands flocked into state-produced shelters. Typically, these consisted of massive *Luftschutzhäuser* (air raid protection buildings) and *Luftschutztürme* (air raid protection towers) – the latter were circular in floorplan, rather than rectangular. These overground shelters looked almost medieval – usually windowless except for small observation slits – and were built from sections of reinforced concrete, metres thick to resist Allied bombs.

Wartime Germany also produced eight *Flaktürme* (flak towers), even larger structures that combined air raid shelters with numerous anti-aircraft guns and communications systems to coordinate air defence. Walls could be up to 3.5m (11ft 5in) thick, and the AA systems on the roof numbered more than 50 guns of various calibres, together capable of throwing up 8000 rounds a minute.

They were designed to shelter up to 10,000 people, although during the apocalyptic last days of the war each could be crammed with up to 30,000 souls. Such was their durability that most remain today – attempts at demolition were often fruitless – and their gloomy interiors hint at the sheer misery and desperation of those who hid within them during the darkest days of the war.

Another effect of the Allied bombing was to drive large portions of German industrial life underground. By building factories beneath ground level, in hardened structures, it was hoped that German production facilities would be able to function at full capacity regardless of the effects of bombing. Yet by the time at which these plans became necessary, conditions in Germany were becoming too chaotic to fulfil them comprehensively. Just under 8.7 million square metres (94 million square feet) of underground industrial facilities were planned, but only 1.2 million square metres (13.3 million square feet) were completed, more than 60 per cent of that figure devoted to aircraft production.

The *Führerbunker*

No building more perfectly represents the failure of Hitler to create a 'Thousand-Year Reich' than his *Führerbunker* (Führer's Shelter), located more than 8m (26ft) beneath the grounds of the old Reich Chancellery (although the entrance was through the new Chancellery annexe). Wrapped in concrete up to 4m (13ft) thick, the *Führerbunker* was Hitler's

Right: Clockwise from top left, the pairs of diagrams here show the three generations of flak tower design. Atop the flak towers were numerous anti-aircraft guns of varying calibres. The fire from these guns, with a combined rate of about 8000rpm, would be coordinated by radar, and it could make for a very hostile environment for Allied bombers. Although the flak towers were very exposed structures, the ferro-concrete walls were up to 3.5m (11ft 5in) thick, meaning that they could withstand direct hits from high-explosive bombs.

near-impregnable refuge from the bombs and chaos on the streets of Berlin above. The *Führerbunker* was, however, no luxury habitation. Austere, frequently cold and damp, and gloomy, it was built on two levels. The upper level (*Vorbunker*) largely held the servants' quarters

and utility rooms plus the dining facilities, while the lower level included Hitler's personal space (three rooms), plus functional rooms such as a map room, bathrooms, telephone exchange and a place for Hitler's dog, Blondi. The lower levels also included bedrooms for

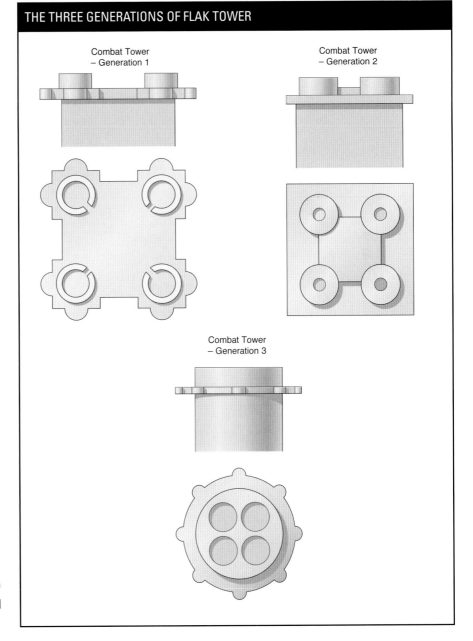

THE THREE GENERATIONS OF FLAK TOWER

Combat Tower – Generation 1

Combat Tower – Generation 2

Combat Tower – Generation 3

THE *FÜHRERBUNKER*

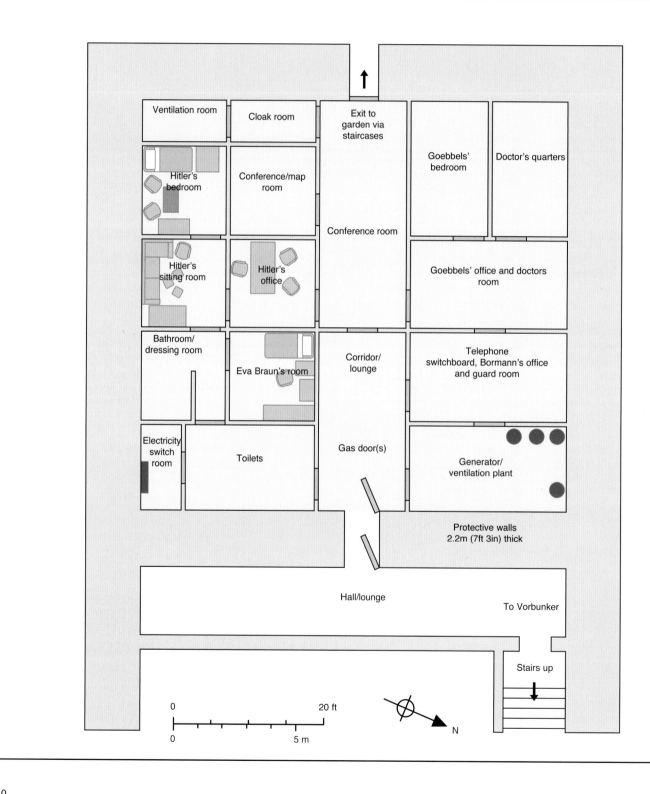

Ventilation room

Cloak room

Exit to garden via staircases

Goebbels' bedroom

Doctor's quarters

Hitler's bedroom

Conference/map room

Conference room

Hitler's sitting room

Hitler's office

Goebbels' office and doctors room

Bathroom/ dressing room

Eva Braun's room

Corridor/ lounge

Telephone switchboard, Bormann's office and guard room

Electricity switch room

Toilets

Gas door(s)

Generator/ ventilation plant

Protective walls 2.2m (7ft 3in) thick

Hall/lounge

To Vorbunker

Stairs up

0   20 ft

0   5 m

N

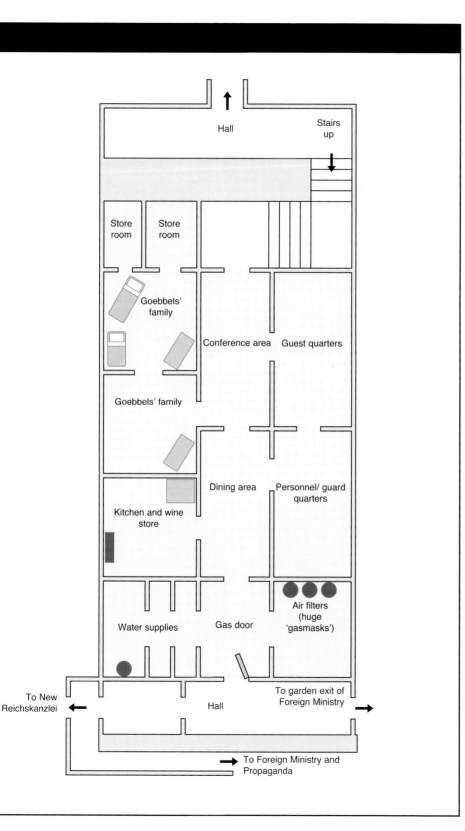

Hall

Stairs
up

Store
room

Store
room

Goebbels'
family

Conference area   Guest quarters

Goebbels' family

Dining area   Personnel/ guard
quarters

Kitchen and wine
store

Air filters
(huge
'gasmasks')

Water supplies   Gas door

To New
Reichskanzlei

Hall

To garden exit of
Foreign Ministry

To Foreign Ministry and
Propaganda

officials such as Joseph Goebbels
and Hitler's personal physician, Dr
Ludwig Stumpfegger.

The last days of Hitler in the
Führerbunker have been well
documented elsewhere. The
descriptions evoke a febrile, anxious,
deluded atmosphere, with the
physically and mentally sick Hitler
continuing to make wild plots for
victory that were always impossible.

Ultimately, with the Soviet Red
Army just streets away from the
bunker complex, the reality dawned
on him, and he shot himself on 30
April 1945. His body was burnt,
along with that of Eva Braun, in
a pit in the shattered Chancellery
gardens. Rather than building a
monument to Germany's greatness,
Hitler had brought the country
to ruin. Unfortunately, Hitler had
dragged much of the world to a
similar fate.

Going down fighting

By the end of 1944, the writing was
on the wall: caught between the
rock of the Western Allies' advance

Left: The infamous *Führerbunker* was
Hitler's subterranean refuge beneath
the Reich Chancellery, and the site of
his death in April 1945. The *Vorbunker*
(right) was an older structure beneath
the rear of the old Chancellery, and it
contained living quarters for Goebbels'
family and various utility and conference
rooms. The *Führerbunker* itself was at a
lower level than the *Vorbunker*, and to
the southwest. Sections of the bunkers
still survive today, although they have
been sealed from access.

and the even-harder place of the Red Army's rampage, the only thing left to do was to go down fighting. If there was little appetite on the Western side for a negotiated peace, there was on the part of the Soviet Union no desire for anything but revenge. Millions had died; many more millions of Soviet citizens had suffered in what had been not just an anti-communist crusade but an anti-Slavic race war.

For ordinary Germans, the outlook was dismal: once the spree of rape and casual killing was over, they had years of subjection, hardship and humiliation ahead. For their Nazi rulers, though, the future promised public humiliation; torture; endless imprisonment or death; slave labour in Siberian ignominy – and that was it. With nothing to hope for by surrender and nothing to lose by standing and fighting to the last, a crazy resolve to resist to the death made perfect sense.

Left: Slow to acknowledge the reality of defeat, Hitler was determined to go down fighting.

The outlook for the Allies could hardly have been more different: from their point of view, the war was all but won. And today we know it was – which gives their victory an aura of inevitability. At the time, they certainly didn't see things that way. Instead, they were haunted by the possibility that, holding triumph in their hands, they might let it go.

Hence the fear that the Nazis were preparing to hole up in an Alpine redoubt, from which they would sally forth to conduct an ongoing guerrilla war. With a complex of fortifications, camps, caves and underground workings to fall back on, they could conduct a campaign of terror in occupied Germany and beyond.

National redoubt

Documents recently released by the British authorities reveal the consternation felt at an apparent Nazi resolve to make a heroic last stand at a secret Alpine stronghold. The Alps was a natural fortress – one aspect that had appealed to Hitler when he had his holiday residence built up here at the Berghof, at Obersalzberg, outside Berchtesgaden. While no one thought the Nazis could directly take

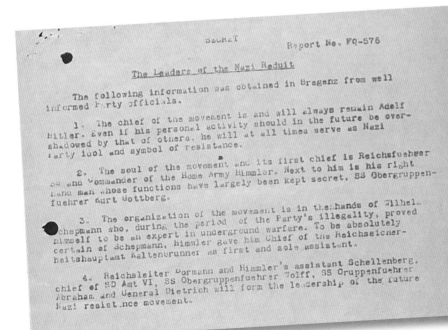

Left: The importance of Adolf Hitler was summarized in this report:
'1. The chief of movement is and will always remain Adolf Hitler. Even if his personal activity in the future be over-shadowed by that of others, he will at all times serve as Nazi Party idol and symbol of resistance.'

TRANSCRIPT OF KEY PARAGRAPHS

Country: Germany/Austria
Subject: Evacuation movement of
  Bavarian localities.
Date of Report: 28 March 1945
Source: Cezanne/French Intelligence
Place of Origin: Switzerland

1. *Thousands of Nazi party officials have recently arrived in the Bavarian localities of Tölz, Fresing and Landshut. They come from the east, west and north of Germany. It is probably, in Source's opinion, that these localities will become important Party centers in case the Party withdraws in Alpine "redoubt".*

2. *At the same time considerable quantities of foods have been transported from Northern Italy through the Brenner pass to Tölz, as well as to Villach through Lienz and Spittal, in Austria.*

3. *Railway repair workshops are being moved from Steinsmanger (Hungary) to Linz-Steyr and Innsbruck (Austria).*

Catalogue Reference:fo/1020/3471

on and defeat the Allies from such a stronghold, they could coordinate fierce resistance for years to come. A briefing of the American Office of Strategic Services (OSS), circulated on 15 March 1945, is clear in its assumption that resolute resistance would be continued from a redoubt.

The philosophy had been hinted at in the defiant speeches of several Nazi leaders, not least the propaganda minister Joseph Goebbels. Far from preparing the way for a rational capitulation, the language of the Nazis was getting more intemperate. 'Rarely in history has a brave people struggling for its life faced such terrible tests …', wrote Goebbels:

We are bearing a heavy fate because we are fighting for a good cause, and are called to bravely endure the battle to achieve greatness.

Was this more than rousing rhetoric, cynically deployed? The Allies were not disposed to take any chances. The 15 March report does seem surprisingly vague and general in its terms. Hitler was the Nazis' 'idol', it informs the reader; he 'is and will always remain' the movement's leader; Himmler, meanwhile, was the movement's 'soul'. A sceptic might say that the writer of the report was in danger of listening too uncritically to the Nazis' mood-music. Rightly or wrongly, though, Allied Intelligence believed that the Nazis continued to believe.

TRANSCRIPT OF KEY PARAGRAPHS

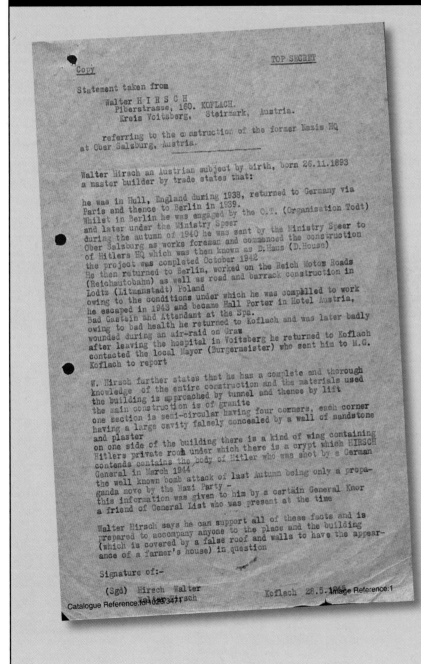

Statement taken from Walther Hirsch, Austria referring to the construction of the former Nazis HQ at Obersalzburg, Germany.

Walter Hirsch an Austrian subject by birth, born 26.11.1893 a master builder by trade states that:

during the autumn of 1940 he was sent by the Ministry Speer to Ober Salzburg as works foreman and commenced the construction of Hitler's HQ which was then known as D.Haus.

The project was completed October 1942

W. Hirsch further states that he has a complete and thorough knowledge of the entire construction and the materials used. The building is approached by tunnel and thence by lift. … on one side of the building there is a kind of wing containing Hitler's private room under which there is a crypt which Hirsch contends contains the body of Hitler who was shot by a German General in March 1944.

Hirsch says he can support all of these facts and is prepared to accompany anyone to the place.

LITERARY RESOURCES UNDER DIRECT SUPERVISION OF THE NSDAP, 1939

Resource	Quantity
Publishing houses	2500
Bookshops	23,000
Authors	3000
National literary prizes	50
Books published annually	20,000

– literature, music, films, theatre, press, fine arts and radio. Although there are plenty of examples of administrative inefficiency in the Third Reich, Goebbels' Propaganda Ministry and the *Reichskulturkammer* seem to have done their job rather competently. From 1933 until the end of the war, therefore, German culture was ruthlessly and rigorously policed.

Literature

The most enduring image of the Nazi attitude towards literature is that of the infamous book burning that took place on 10 May 1933 in *Unter den Linden*, outside the University of Berlin.

Following a torchlit parade, young National Socialists publicly incinerated thousands of books classified as 'un-German', these including works by luminaries such as Thomas Mann, Albert Einstein, Erich Maria Remarque, Lion Feuchtwanger, Marcel Proust, H.G. Wells and Sigmund Freud. This moment, combined with similar acts of barbarism and a tightening state control over writers' output, inspired

dozens of Germany's greatest authors to flee abroad. Those who stayed had to adjust to new straitjackets on their creativity.

Naturally, being a writer in Nazi Germany meant avoiding anything that could be construed as critical of the regime or the *Führer*, or which represented the values to which the Nazis were averse. Thankfully for German writers of the time, the *Reichsschrifttumskammer* (RSK; Reich Literature Chamber) left them in no doubt as to what was suitable subject matter.

Four main genres were defined. *Fronterlebnis* (front experience) referred to essentially military titles that emphasized the heroism of combat, military service and martial comradeship. Works such as Werner Beumelburg's best-selling *Gruppe Bosemüller* did not shy away from the brutalities of combat which, after all, many German citizens had witnessed first-hand. Yet ultimately the fighting experience in such works was about finding purpose, redemption, brotherhood (such novels often had deeply homoerotic undertones) and unity.

Alongside *Fronterlebnis* was a genre that focused on representing the ideals of the National Socialist history or world view, through narratives that involved either lionization of formative *Freikorps* or NSDAP members or tales of fictional individuals who receive the call to greatness, and rise up as leaders within the movement.

The *Heimatroman* (regional novel) and related *Schollenroman*

(novel of the soil), by contrast, were nostalgic fictions centred around the supposed timeless authenticity of the rural world, as opposed to the frenetic chaos of the urban environment. (Again, the Nazis seemed to ignore the fact that most Germans now lived in towns and cities.) Mysticism infused such works, with themes of eternity and nationalism intertwined. Within this genre could be incorporated another, the *Rassenkunde* (ethnology), which addressed Nazi anxieties about race. Such works, ludicrous to modern eyes, could be little more than crude contrasts between the supposed magnificence of the Aryans and the genetically defective races that threatened them. They might also reflect on motherhood and female identity, being keen to emphasize that sex was primarily for nationally essential procreation, not for lascivious pleasure.

Hanging over all the literature was the shadow of the RSK, which could issue a *Schreibverbot* – a veto on publication – if the work did not conform to its standards. There were other tools of coercion, however, before a book could receive the official *Unbedenklichkeitsvermerk* ('safety notice' – a certificate approving its content).

Goebbels' control over the physical processes of the literary world became vast. Not only did his ministry eventually come to control 2500 publishing houses and 23,000 bookshops, it also managed

LOCATION OF MAJOR BOOK BURNINGS, 1933

DENMARK

KIEL
KÖNIGSBERG
ROSTOCK
GREIFSWALD
HAMBURG

HOLLAND

HANOVER
BERLIN
MÜNSTER
BRUNSWICK
GÖTTINGEN
HALLE
LEIPZIG
KÖLN
MARBURG
DRESDEN
BONN
BRESLAU
FRANKFURT
DARMSTADT
WORMS
WÜRZBURG
MANNHEIM
NUREMBERG
KARLSRUHE

CZECHOSLOVAKIA

FRANCE

AUSTRIA

Left: Although the book burnings in 1933 achieved their greatest visibility in Berlin, they occurred in numerous towns and cities across Germany. Those authors whose works were thrown on the bonfires included Erich Maria Remarque, Thomas Mann, Albert Einstein, Marcel Proust, Jack London, Lion Feuchtwanger, Helen Keller and Sigmund Freud. The burnings were officially promoted by the Nazi Party. During the burnings Joseph Goebbels made the pronouncement that 'These flames not only illuminate the end of the old era, they also light up the new.' Note, however, that the burnings were downplayed in the German media, the Nazis being sensitive to accusations of barbarism.

the systems of literary prizes and sponsorship, and even paper allocations. To work outside the system, therefore, was not an option.

What must be acknowledged, however, is that the Nazi Party did appear to drive up reading as an activity. The number of NSDAP-controlled libraries rose from 6000 in 1933 to 25,000 ten years later. Not only that, but 45,000 libraries were established for soldiers near frontline positions. The Nazis seem to have fully realized that controlling the literature that people read was critical if they were to buy the public mind.

Art

The visual arts suffered profoundly under the Nazis. As with many other art forms, the Nazis channelled Hitler's anti-intellectualism and anti-modernism into a campaign of unusual prejudice against some of the greatest artists in history.

The Weimar period, for all its failings, had been highly fertile for German visual arts. Movements such as expressionism, surrealism, cubism, Dadaism and post-impressionism opened up entirely new approaches to art, Germany producing many of the leading members of these fraternities, including Otto Dix, Max Ernst and George Grosz. Hostility to the avant-garde did not arrive with the Nazis – groups such as the 'Combat Leagues of German Culture' launched attacks on the movements on political grounds during the 1920s – but it was Hitler's regime that translated antipathy into decisive social action.

A defining moment in the attack on modernist art came in 1937. To make clear to the public

SELECTIVE LIST OF WRITERS BANNED UNDER THE THIRD REICH

A
Alfred Adler
Hermann Adler
Max Adler
Raoul Auernheimer

B
Otto Bauer
Vicki Baum
Johannes R. Becher
Richard Beer-Hofmann
Walter Benjamin
Walter A. Berendsohn
Ernst Bloch
Felix Braun
Bertolt Brecht
Willi Bredel
Hermann Broch
Ferdinand Bruckner

D
Alfred Döblin
John Dos Passos

E
Albert Ehrenstein
Albert Einstein
Carl Einstein
Friedrich Engels

F
Lion Feuchtwanger
Marieluise Fleisser
Leonhard Frank
Anna Freud
Sigmund Freud
Egon Friedell
Otto Flake
Hans Fallada

G
André Gide
Claire Goll
Oskar Maria Graf
George Grosz

H
Jaroslav Hasek
Walter Hasenclever
Raoul Hausmann
Magnus Hirschfeld
Jakob van Hoddis
Ödön von Horvath
Karl Hubbuch

I
Vera Inber

J
Hans Henny Jahnn
Georg Jellinek

K
Erich Kästner
Franz Kafka
Georg Kaiser
Mascha Kaleko
Hermann Kantorowicz
Karl Kautsky
Hans Kelsen
Alfred Kerr
Irmgard Keun
Klabund
Annette Kolb
Paul Kornfeld
Siegfried Kracauer
Karl Kraus
Adam Kuckhoff

L
Else Lasker-Schüler
Vladimir Lenin
Jack London
Ernst Lothar
Emil Ludwig
Rosa Luxemburg

M
André Malraux
Heinrich Mann
Klaus Mann
Thomas Mann
Hans Marchwitza
Ludwig Marcuse
Karl Marx
Walter Mehring
Gustav Meyrink
Erich Mühsam
Robert Musil

N
Alfred Neumann
Robert Neumann

O
Carl von Ossietzky

P
Adelheid Popp
Hertha Pauli

R
Fritz Reck-Malleczewen
Gustav Regler
Wilhelm Reich
Erich Maria Remarque
Karl Renner
Joachim Ringelnatz
Joseph Roth

S
Nelly Sachs
Felix Salten
Rahel Sanzara
Arthur Schnitzler
Alvin Schwartz
Anna Seghers
Walter Serner
Ignazio Silone
Rudolf Steiner
Carl Sternheim

T
Ernst Toller
Friedrich Torberg
B. Traven
Leon Trotsky
Kurt Tucholsky

W
Jakob Wassermann
Armin T. Wegner
Franz Werfel
Eugen Gottlob Winkler
Friedrich Wolf

Z
Carl Zuckmayer
Arnold Zweig
Stefan Zweig

ART LOOTED BY THE NAZIS DURING WORLD WAR II

These figures are derived from evidence presented during the Nuremberg Trials; they are probably not complete but give some indication of the scale of Nazi looting:

- *5281 paintings, pastels, water colours, drawings*
- *684 miniatures, glass and enamel paintings, illuminated books and manuscripts*
- *583 sculptures, terracottas, medallions, plaques*
- *2477 articles of furniture of art historical value*
- *583 textiles (tapestries, rugs, embroideries, Coptic textiles)*
- *5825 objects of decorative art (porcelains, bronzes, faience, majolica, ceramics, jewellery, coins, art objects with precious stones)*
- *1286 East Asiatic artworks (bronzes, sculptures, porcelains, paintings, folding screens, weapons)*
- *259 artworks of antiquity (sculptures, bronzes, vases, jewellery, bowls, engraved gems, terracottas)*
- *21,903 WORKS OF ART (TOTAL)*

what was 'degenerate' and what was approved, the Nazis put on several exhibitions illustrating the difference. To accumulate their material, Nazi art inspectors from the *Reichskammer der bildenden Künste* (Reich Chamber of Fine Arts) went through Germany's art galleries, museums and collections to conduct a purge of 'subversive' or 'decadent' artworks, or those with a Jewish influence. Up to 16,000 individual artworks were taken, including works by great foreign artists such as Henri Matisse, Vincent van Gogh and Pablo Picasso.

Some of the artworks taken between 1933 and 1939 had an abrupt end – 4000 pieces, for example, were burnt in the courtyard of the Berlin fire brigade headquarters. Others, however, found their way into the *Entartete Kunst* exhibition in Munich, which opened on 19 July 1937.

The exhibition was designed to shock the public with the indulgence, profanity, moral seediness and sheer cost of modernist art. The artworks were arranged in a chaotic, irreverent fashion, and slogans were daubed on the wall to make sure that the audience did not miss the point. Slogans included 'Madness becomes method', 'An insult to German womanhood' and 'Deliberate sabotage of national defence'.

While the publicly expressed opinions of the art were vitriolic, the exhibition suspiciously attracted two

ARTISTS FEATURED IN THE *ENTARTETE KUNST* EXHIBITION IN MUNICH, 1937

■ **A**

Jankel Adler

■ **B**

Ernst Barlach

Rudolf Bauer

Philipp Bauknecht

Otto Baum

Willi Baumeister

Herbert Bayer

Max Beckmann

Rudolf Belling

Paul Bindel

Theo Brün

Max Burchartz

Fritz Burger-Mühlfeld

■ **C**

Paul Camenisch

Heinrich Campendonk

Karl Caspar

Maria Caspar-Filser

Pol Cassel

Marc Chagall

Lovis Corinth

■ **D**

Heinrich Maria
    Davringhausen

Walter Dexel

Johannes Diesner

Otto Dix

Pranas Domsaitis

Hans Christoph Drexel

Johannes Driesch

■ **E**

Heinrich Eberhard

Max Ernst

■ **F**

Hans Feibusch

Lyonel Feininger

Conrad Felixmüller

Otto Freundlich

Xaver Fuhr

■ **G**

Ludwig Gies

Werner Gilles

Otto Gleichmann

Rudolph Grossmann

George Grosz

Hans Grundig

■ **H**

Rudolf Haizmann

Raoul Hausmann

Guido Hebert

Erich Heckel

Wilhelm Heckrott

Jacoba van Heemskerck

Hans Siebert von Heister

Oswald Herzog

Werner Heuser

Heinrich Hoerle

Karl Hofer

Eugen Hoffmann

■ **I**

Johannes Itten

■ **J**

Alexej von Jawlensky

Eric Johanson

■ **K**

Hans Jürgen Kallmann

Wassily Kandinsky

Hanns Katz

Ernst Ludwig Kirchner

Paul Klee

Cesar Klein

Paul Kleinschmidt

Oskar Kokoschka

■ **L**

Otto Lange

Wilhelm Lehmbruck

El Lissitzky

Oskar Lüthy

■ **M**

Franz Marc

Gerhard Marcks

Ewald Mataré

Ludwig Meidner

Jean Metzinger

Constantin von Mitschke-
    Collande

Laszlo Moholy-Nagy

Margarethe (Marg) Moll

Oskar Moll

Johannes Molzahn

Piet Mondrian

Georg Muche

Otto Mueller

■ **N**

Erich Nagel

Heinrich Nauen

Ernst Wilhelm Nay

Karel Niestrath

Emil Nolde

■ **P**

Otto Pankok

Max Pechstein

Max Peiffer-Watenphul

Hans Purrmann

■ **R**

Max Rauh

Hans Richter

Emy Röder

Christian Rohlfs

■ **S**

Edwin Scharff

Oskar Schlemmer

Rudolf Schlichter

Karl Schmidt-Rottluff

Werner Scholz

Lothar Schreyer

Otto Schubert

Kurt Schwitters

Lasar Segall

Friedrich Skade

Friedrich (Fritz) Stuckenberg

■ **T**

Paul Thalheimer

Johannes Tietz

Arnold Topp

■ **V**

Friedrich Vordemberge-
    Gildewart

Karl Völker

Christoph Voll

■ **W**

William Wauer

Gert Heinrich Wollheim

million visitors, many times more than went to similar exhibitions of approved art.

Approved art

So what constituted approved art under Nazi ideology? Nazi art generally ranged between the epic and sentimental. The figures created by painters and sculptors tended to be muscular and powerful in a classical fashion, and exuded heroism and national devotion. Their backdrops could range from idyllic pastoral scenes through to stirring battle depictions. *Kameraden* by Will Tschech, for example, showed two soldiers stoically carrying a wounded comrade across a moodily smoky battlefield, all three looking to the horizon with defiance and gravitas. Other artworks simply reproduced classical nudes with tasteful drapery.

In essence, however, all art had to connote physical health, beauty, strength and a powerful spirit. To balance out the *Entartete Kunst* exhibition, therefore, Munich also hosted a far less popular *Große Deutsche Kunstausstellung* (Great German Art Exhibition), which in many ways was a banal object lesson in *Führer* worship and conformity rather than a show of artistic innovation.

Nevertheless, there must have been an appetite for the work, as such exhibitions were held every year in Munich, with annual attendance figures rising to 720,000 by 1942.

Furthermore, we must not get the impression that the Nazis were

anti-art. In fact, the regime was a passionate sponsor of approved art forms, and ran thousands of art exhibitions in the Reich, gave patronage to many artists and ran more than 170 art competitions each year. Yet as in the case of writers, artists in the Third Reich were also closely policed. Those who transgressed what was acceptable would simply be unable to practise as artists, at least as artists who could publicly display their works.

Official looting

One final, important point about the Nazi attitude to art was that during the war years the regime, and particularly *Reichsmarschall* Hermann Göring, were dedicated looters of foreign art. The *Einsatzstab Rosenberg* (Rosenberg Task Force), headed by Alfred Rosenberg, was commissioned by Hitler and Göring to requisition valued pieces of art and Jewish cultural artefacts and take them back to Germany (many actually ended up in Göring's personal collection). According to Rosenberg's own figures, just under 22,000 cultural artefacts were acquired between October 1940 and July 1944, including works by most of the great masters. Thankfully, most of these artworks were repatriated after the war.

Music and radio

Hitler realized early on in his rise to power that radio would become a critical tool in influencing public

ideas. He even stated that without radios (alongside cars and talking movies), there would be 'no victory for National Socialism'.

The wireless gave Hitler the means to take his ideology straight into people's homes and workplaces, both by broadcasting his speeches (he made more than 50 broadcasts in his first year in office) or the speeches of other Nazi orators, and by controlling the listener's entertainment hours. Through broadcast music, furthermore, the radio would provide a form of escapism, something that became increasingly important during the war years.

A top priority for Hitler, therefore, was to distribute radios widely. This was accomplished with impressive rapidity. From 1933 the price of radios was pushed down to manageable levels for everyone, including the labouring classes, through sets such as the *Volksempfänger 3.31* (People's Receiver) for 76 RM or the *Deutsche Kleinempfänger* (German Mini-Receiver) for 35 RM. Such affordability alone meant that 70 per cent of German households owned a radio by 1942, up from 22.5 per cent in 1933.

Furthermore, the Nazis pushed radios into every nook and crevice of the Third Reich. Factories, offices, restaurants, cafés and other public meeting areas were obliged to have radio sets for communal listening for important public announcements and events. Party 'radio wardens' would also patrol streets and housing blocks, encouraging people to listen to appropriate programming and reporting those who strayed onto foreign radio networks. Grunberger notes that 'Although the war interrupted a comprehensive scheme for the construction of 6,000 loudspeaker pillars, there can be no doubt that the Third Reich achieved a denser radio coverage than any country in the world' (Grunberger, *A Social History of the Third Reich*, p.402).

Note, however, that ownership and distribution of radios does not necessarily translate into good National Socialist listeners. Many Germans became bored with repetitious propaganda and uniform styles of music, and hence indulged themselves in more foreign channels. As Hitler had imperial pretensions, the Reich also concerned itself with pushing Nazi radio broadcasts into other countries. Beginning in 1933, short-wave broadcasts were transmitted across Europe, reaching as far as Denmark. Such broadcasts were a useful preparatory tool for German interventions in Czechoslovakia and Austria during the 1930s. More ambitiously, a massive 100,000kW transmitter, based near Berlin, was eventually able to take the Nazi message to the Americas and East Asia, the programmes going out in a total of 12 languages.

The content of radio broadcasts was, naturally, highly policed by Goebbels' ministry. During the 1930s there was a hefty propaganda quota on the radio, including

---

MOST IMPORTANT FIGURES LISTED ON THE *GOTTBEGNADETEN* (GOD-GIFTED ARTIST) LIST

The Gottbegnadeten-Liste *was assembled in September 1944 by Goebbels' Propaganda Ministry. Running to 36 pages, it listed more than 1000 leading figures from the arts classified as indispensable to the culture of the Third Reich.*

- **SCULPTORS:**
  Arno Breker (1900–1991)
  Fritz Klimsch (1870–1960)
  Georg Kolbe (1877–1947)
  Josef Thorak (1889–1952)

- **PAINTERS/ARTISTS:**
  Hermann Gradl (1883–1964)
  Arthur Kampf (1864–1950)
  Willy Kriegel (1901–1966)
  Werner Peiner (1897–1984)

- **ARCHITECTS:**
  Leonhard Gall (1884–1952)*
  Hermann Giesler (1898–1987)*
  Wilhelm Kreis (1873–1955)
  Paul Schultze-Naumburg (1869–1949)

  * Named as a Reichskultursenator (Reich Culture Senator)

- **WRITERS:**
  Gerhart Hauptmann (1862–1946)
  Hans Carossa (1878–1956)
  Hanns Johst (1890–1979)*
  Erwin Guido Kolbenheyer (1878–1962)
  Agnes Miegel (1879–1964)
  Ina Seidel (1885–1974)

- **COMPOSERS:**
  Richard Strauss (1864–1949)
  Hans Pfitzner (1869–1949)
  Wilhelm Furtwängler (1886–1954)*
  Carl Orff (1895–1982)
  Werner Egk (1901–1983)

- **ACTORS:**
  Otto Falckenberg (1873–1947)
  Friedrich Kayßler (1874–1945)
  Hermine Körner (1878–1960)

---

speeches, programmes explaining National Socialist ideology and various exhortations to service. Yet Goebbels increasingly focused the radio's efforts more on the escapism provided by variety shows and music. Indeed by 1937 some 69 per cent of radio air time consisted of music, up 11 per cent from just five years earlier. During the war years, the radio was even more devoted to defusing the angst of a weary population.

Music itself was the subject of much Nazi scrutiny. In terms of orchestral music, anything experimental or atonal was out, for the same reasons that avant-garde art was vilified, but other more traditional composers also found their way onto the black list. The works of Mendelssohn, for example, were cut on account of his being Jewish, and some operas by Mozart were viewed with disapproval because the libretti had been written by a Jew, Lorenzo Da Ponte. The cumulative prejudices led to a rapid exodus of musical talent (composers, conductors and musicians) from Germany during the 1930s, the emigrants including Paul Hindemith, Arnold Schoenberg and Elisabeth Schumann.

The type of orchestral music preferred by the Nazi regime was rousing and powerful, reflective of national and human greatness. Favoured composers included Richard Strauss, Richard Wagner and Carl Orff. Strauss was himself appointed as the head of the

Reichsmusikkammer (Reich Music Chamber), although his relationship with both Goebbels and the Nazi regime was problematic, and his lack of empathy with Nazi racial theory eventually led to his dismissal from the post. His music, however, continued to be played.

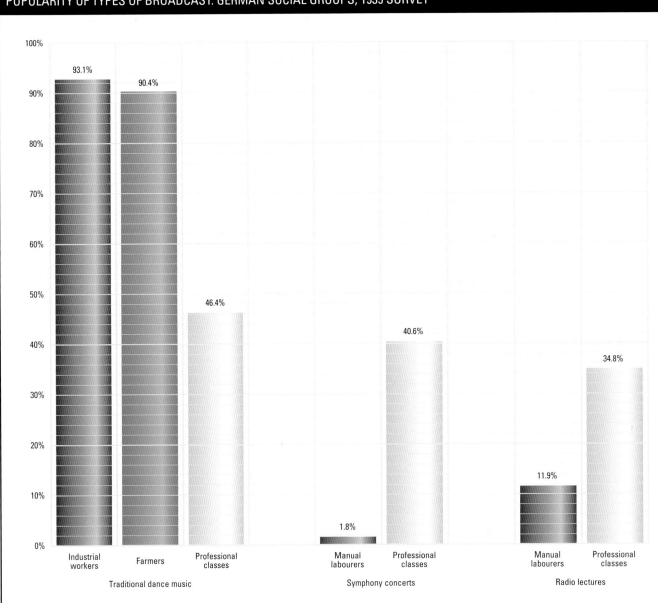

POPULARITY OF TYPES OF BROADCAST: GERMAN SOCIAL GROUPS, 1939 SURVEY

Hitler's regime was energetic in taking music to the widest possible audience, with numerous annual music festivals and cheap access to concerts via the Strength through Joy organization and other groups. Helped by economic improvements during the 1930s, Germany witnessed a huge upsurge in concert attendance, and also a modest growth in practical music-making. Military and NSDAP bands needed plenty of musicians, and choirs were formed in numerous workplaces and communities – in 1938, Goebbels declared that Germany had 25,000 male voice choirs.

Youth music was a far more problematic proposition for the Nazis. Hitler was particularly averse to jazz, associating it with black identity (to which his racial ideas made him hostile) and with lascivious dance steps. The trouble was, it was infectious musically, and the regime attempted to

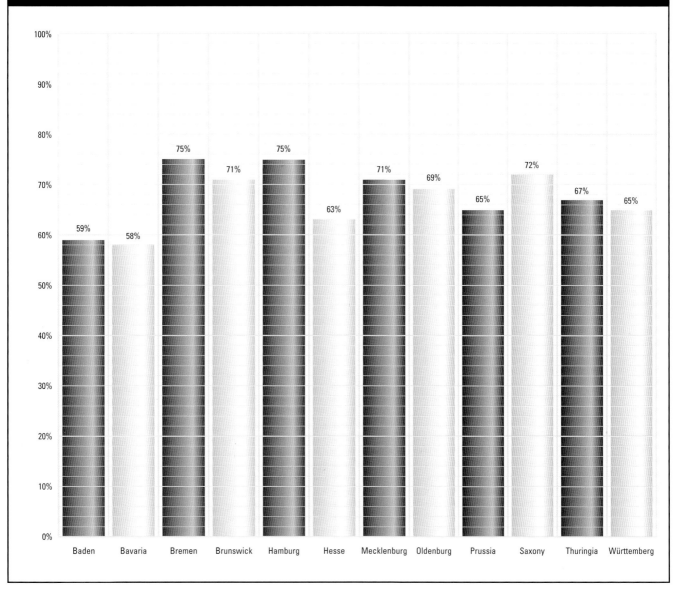

PERCENTAGE OF RADIO LISTENERS BY REGION OF GERMANY, 1941

foster 'German jazz', an anaemic replacement that inspired little enthusiasm from the audience. The Nazis, suspicious of rhythmic bodily movements in general, attempted to find an acceptable form of dance, and settled on folk dancing as both energetic and linked to rural traditionalism. Nevertheless, underground musical youth clubs developed throughout Germany, their members covertly listening to the Western tunes they craved.

Theatre and cinema

It is one of the curiosities of the Third Reich that while the Nazis purged the arts of much that was good, consumption of the approved arts generally rose between 1933 and 1944, after which the impending defeat brought a precipitous collapse in entertainment.

That was certainly the case for the theatre and the cinema. Regarding the former, theatre-going audiences doubled between 1932 and 1942. Part of the reason was that the improved economy simply brought more disposable income, and various Nazi cultural schemes encouraged the populace to spend their money on cultural pursuits.

The Strength through Joy organization reduced the cost of theatre tickets dramatically for its members. Similarly, membership of the 'Cultural Association' cost a total of 1 RM, for which the member could see 10 plays per season, paying half-price for every ticket. In a typically Nazi limitation of the fun, however, the member had no choice

COMPARISON OF CINEMA VISITS: GERMANY, UK AND USA, 1938 – PERCENTAGE OF POPULATION ATTENDING THE CINEMA ON A WEEKLY BASIS

UK 41.2%
USA 34.2%
Germany 8.6%

over the show, venue or time. Other organizations that subsidized theatre tickets included the Hitler Youth and the Reich Labour Service.

The content of the theatre shows in the Third Reich reflected the ideological priorities already outlined. Light comedies were a popular form of escapism, albeit one often injected with some underlying theme relating to Nazi eugenics or militarism. Playwrights of such works had to be especially careful that they did not unwittingly mock the authorities or ideology, or they could find their careers quickly cut short.

Also attracting large audiences were the *Thingspiele*, festival-like alfresco performances that were 'open-air medleys of Nazi "agit-prop", military tattoo, pagan oratorio and circus performance' (Grunberger, p.363).

The theatres for such performances, known as *Thingspielstätten*, were built in an amphitheatre style in natural settings that had, for the rurally inspired Nazis, a mystical resonance, and they often incorporated landscape features such as cliffs, streams and hills directly into their design. A *Thingspiel* performance was meant

to connect the audience with its ancient Germanic roots, and the productions tended to feature huge casts, epic themes, highly physical performances and powerful oratory.

Dramatic content

In conventional theatres, audiences were treated to a predictable feast of drama – plays involving war heroes, 'blood and soil' themes, racial warnings and exhortations to sacrifice. If these were a little too rich, or bland, for some tastes, the Nazis also revived many classic plays, although only those that were seen as posing little threat to public sensibilities. German greats such as Schiller and Goethe were given prominence, but certain works of Shakespeare were also granted the seal of approval. The translations of Shakespeare's work would often be carefully modified to reflect Nazi racial preoccupations, particularly in works with a 'Jewish' content, such as *The Merchant of Venice*.

One area of theatrical entertainment treated with much more caution was cabaret, which was associated with a pre-Nazi licentiousness and subversive character. Cabarets still played, but they were straitjacketed by conformity to appropriate content. Combined with the restrictions on music described above, the cabarets consequently became a shadow of their former selves.

In a similar vein to theatre-going, visits to the cinema also rose significantly under the auspices of the Third Reich.

In 1933 there were approximately 250 million visits to the cinema; by 1942 that figure was at 1000 million. Naturally, Hitler and Goebbels embraced the propaganda potential of this mass medium with gusto. The controlling influence of the Propaganda Ministry over cinema was near total. The *Reichsfilmkammer* (Reich Film Chamber) had a direct say over the films made in Germany, at first exercised through a controlling influence (as a majority shareholder) over Germany's four major film studios, and then through nationalization of the industry in 1942. Jewish and liberal actors, directors, producers and scriptwriters were quickly removed from work, despite their impressive track record during the Weimar period.

The 'factual' elements of cinema programmes – newsreels and documentaries – were filled with images of marching masses, mighty parades, German victories and Hitler doing his rounds of the Reich. By far the most famous of these productions was the singular act of *Führer* worship entitled *Triumph des Willens* (Triumph of the Will; 1936),

by the esteemed female director Leni Riefenstahl. Three hours long, the film was a carefully crafted and highly theatrical portrayal of Hitler at the 1934 Nuremberg Rally. Riefenstahl also went on to make *Olympia*, a Herculean representation of the 1936 Berlin Olympics.

Yet factual programmes were eclipsed in popularity by the

on average 100 dramatic films produced every year under the Third Reich. They occupied the familiar range of genres – musicals, historical dramas, romances, action films, etc – and offered sentimental escapism from the hardships of work and war.

Rural themes were common, the actors demonstrating country virtues

MAJOR FILMS SHOWING IN GERMAN CINEMAS, 1933

Title	Director	Genre
Carmen	Lotte Reiniger	Animation
Der Choral von Leuthen	Carl Froelich, Arzén von Cserépy	War/History
Der Deutsche Reichstag zu Nürnberg	–	Documentary
Don Quichotte	Georg Wilhelm Pabst	Drama
F.P.1	Karl Hartl	Drama/Aviation
I.F.1 ne répond plus	Karl Hartl	Drama/Aviation
Flüchtlinge	Gustav Ucicky	Historical
Gretel zieht das große Los	Carl Boese	Comedy
Hans Westmar. Einer von vielen. Ein deutsches Schicksal aus dem Jahre 1929	Franz Wenzler	Nazi propaganda
Hitlerjunge Quex	Hans Steinhoff	Nazi propaganda
Hitlers Aufruf an das deutsche Volk	–	Hitler address
Ich und die Kaiserin	Friedrich Hollaender	Musical comedy
Lachende Erben	Max Ophüls	Romantic comedy
Liebelei	Max Ophüls	Romantic drama
Meisterdetektiv	Franz Seitz	Comedy
Morgenrot	Vernon Sewell, Gustav Ucicky	War
Der Page vom Dalmasse-Hotel	Victor Janson	Comedy
S.A.-Mann Brand	Franz Seitz	Propaganda
S.O.S. Eisberg	Arnold Fanck	Survival drama
S.O.S. Iceberg	Tay Garnett	Survival drama
Der Sieg des Glaubens	Leni Riefenstahl	Documentary
The Testament of Dr. Mabuse	Fritz Lang	Crime drama
Der Tunnel	Curtis Bernhardt	Drama
Viktor und Viktoria	Reinhold Schünzel	Musical comedy
Was Frauen träumen	Géza von Bolváry	Romantic comedy
Zwei gute Kameraden	Max Obal	Comedy

rather than urban vices. Ideological content was rarely far below the surface, or was right on top. Anti-Jewish films such as *Der ewige Jude* (The Eternal Jew) and *Jud Süß* (Jew Süss) could be particularly vile. In the latter, produced by Terra Filmkunst, the eponymous Jew (the character's name was Oppenheimer) was portrayed as a nauseating caricature, predatory, sly and also sexually manipulative. Appalling to modern eyes, the film nevertheless won its director, Veit Harlan, the 1943 Universum Film Archiv award. (After the war, Harlan was put on trial for war crimes.)

Another type of film favoured by the Nazis was historical drama, as long as it clearly rewrote history in Germany's favour. A popular film of this genre was *Ohm Krüger* (Uncle Kruger), released in 1941. With the title role played by the famous German actor Emil Jannings, *Ohm Krüger* told the story of Stephanus Johannes Paulus Kruger, state president of the South African Republic, or Transvaal Republic, and a key resistance leader against

PLAYS PERFORMED IN THE *BERLINER STAATSTHEATER* (BERLIN STATE THEATRE), 1933–39 SEASONS

■ 1933–34 SEASON

Hanns Johst Schlageter

Hans Christoph Kaergel Andreas Hollmann

Björnson When the New Wine Ripens

William Shakespeare Julius Caesar

Griese Person Made of Earth

Hermann Bahr The Concert

Friedrich Schiller The Bride of Messina

Emil Rosenow Kater Lampe

Hanns Johst The Prophets

Boetticher The King

Heinrichs When the Cock Crows

Benito Mussolini The Hundred Days

Graff The Return Home of Matthuius Bruch

Johann Wolfgang von Goethe Faust I

Blunck The Land in Dämmerung

William Shakespeare Comedy of Errors

C. Hauptmann Music

Schwarz Rebel in England

Otto Erler Struensee

Pedro Calderón de la Barca Life Is a Dream

■ 1934–35 SEASON

Johann Wolfgang von Goethe Faust I

Johann Wolfgang von Goethe Faust II

William Shakespeare Comedy of Errors

Friedrich Schiller The Bride of Messina

Hermann Bahr The Concert

Schwarz Rebel in England

Pedro Calderón de la Barca Life is a Dream

Lessing Meier Heimbrecht

Heinrich von Kleist Die Hermannschlacht

Eugene Scribe A Glass of Water

Hans Rehberg The Grand Kurfürst

William Shakespeare King Lear

Bernard Shaw Pygmalion

Kolbenheyer Heroic Passion

Schwarz Prince of Prussia

Wischmann Voice in the Storm

■ 1935–36 SEASON

Johann Wolfgang von Goethe Egmont

Eugene Scribe A Glass of Water

Hanns Johst Thomas Paine

William Shakespeare King Lear

Christian Friedrich Hebbel Gyges and his Ring

William Shakespeare Hamlet

Niebalgall Datterich

Johann Wolfgang von Goethe Faust I

Bernard Shaw Pygmalion

Hans Rehberg Friedrich Wilhelm I

Pierre de Beaumarchais Happy Days / The Marriage of Figaro

Aeschylus Orestia

Johann Wolfgang von Goethe Faust II

the British during the Boer conflicts of the late nineteenth century.

With production costs of 5.5 million RM, the film was essentially a turgid work of anti-British propaganda, but it attracted an audience of 250,000 people in its first four days of release and was later awarded the *Film der Nation* (Film of the Nation) by the Propaganda Ministry. The film was re-released several times throughout the war, but was eventually banned in January 1945 – it was felt that scenes of British soldiers destroying Boer homes would be too painful for bombed-out German citizens. By this stage of the war, no amount of escapist cinema was enough to mask reality.

Newspapers and magazines

Newspapers can be a nation's most political media, and Hitler faced a significant challenge aligning the country's journalists with his party's ideology. On Hitler's takeover in 1933, Germany was truly a land of newspapers, with a huge range of local, regional and national dailies – 4700 different publications in

■ 1936–37 SEASON

Aeschylus Orestia

William Shakespeare Hamlet

Johann Wolfgang von Goethe Faust II

Pierre de Beaumarchais Happy Days

Knut Hamsun At the Gates of the Reich

Johann Wolfgang von Goethe Faust I

Eugene Scribe A Glass of Water

Paul Apel Hans Sonnenstössers Hellride

Johann Wolfgang von Goethe Egmont

Friedrich Schiller Mary Stuart

Christian Grabbe Don Juan and Faust

Christian Friedrich Hebbel Gyges and his Ring

Gerhart Hauptmann And Pippa Dances

William Shakespeare Richard III

Heinrich von Kleist Amphitryon

Molière The Imaginary Invalid

William Shakespeare Twelfth Night

■ 1937–38 SEASON

William Shakespeare Twelfth Night

Friedrich Schiller Wallenstein I and II

William Shakespeare Hamlet

William Shakespeare Richard III

Molière The Imaginary Invalid

Johann Wolfgang von Goethe Egmont

Richard Billinger The Giant

Gerhart Hauptmann Michael Kramer

Heinrich von Kleist Das Kätchen von Heilbronn

Friedrich Schiller Mary Stuart

E.W. Möller The Overthrow of the Ministers

Bernard Shaw Mrs. Warren's Profession

Hans Rehberg The Seven Years War

Henrik Ibsen Peer Gynt

Otto Erler Struensee

■ 1938–39 SEASON

Henrik Ibsen Peer Gynt

Hans Rehberg The Seven Years War

Bernard Shaw Mrs. Warren's Profession

Wolfgang Götz Gneisenau

Christian Friedrich Hebbel Gyges and his Ring

William Shakespeare Richard III

Gerhart Hauptmann Michael Kramer

Bernard Shaw Pygmalion

Friedrich Schiller Wallenstein

William Shakespeare Twelfth Night

William Shakespeare Hamlet

Bernhard Shaw The Doctor's Dilemma

Johann Wolfgang von Goethe Egmont

Christian Friedrich Hebbel Maria Magdalene

Friedrich Schiller The Maid of Orleans

Richard Billinger On High Seas

Hans Rehberg Queen Isabella

William Shakespeare Richard II

Heinrich von Kleist The Broken Jug

Karl von Holtei 33 Minutes in Grüneberg

GERMAN NEWSPAPER TITLES, 1918–35

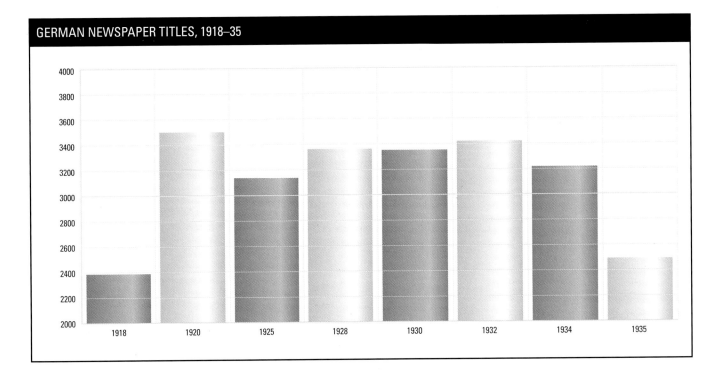

MAJOR NAZI NEWSPAPERS, 1935, WITH CIRCULATION FIGURES

Title	Translation	Location	Circulation
Der Angriff	The Attack	Berlin	95,000
Der Mitteldeutsche	The Midlands	Magdeburg	103,100
Der Stürmer	The Stormer	Nuremberg	450,000
Nationalzeitung	National Times	Essen	140,600
Rheinische Landeszeitung	Rhine Gazette	Düsseldorf	166,200
Völkischer Beobachter	People's Times	Munich/Berlin	400,700
Westdeutscher Beobachter	West German Observer	Cologne-Aachen	187,300
Westfälische Landeszeitung	Westphalian Times	Dortmund	171,800

total – serving diverse communities and interests. The press division of the Propaganda Ministry therefore had two major goals: 1) suppress dissident newspapers and journalists; 2) promote the National Socialist press. In both areas, Goebbels was largely successful.

The answer to newspapers that challenged ideology was in many cases simply to shut them down. Some figures clarify the point. Between 1934 and 1944 the number of German daily newspapers declined by nearly 80 per cent (30 per cent were shut down within the first year of Hitler's rule).

Journals and periodicals went through a similar decline, dropping by 50 per cent between 1934 and 1938. One law used to cull large numbers of papers was the Reich Press Law of 4 October 1933, which focused on purging all journalists and publishers who were Jews or who had liberal leanings. This in itself extirpated some of Germany's oldest or most respected papers, such as the *Vossische Zeitung* and the *Berliner Tageblatt*. Often the assets of the companies would be snapped up by Nazi-approved publishing houses, such as Eher Verlag under Max Amann. Amann was Hitler's former army sergeant, but under Hitler he not only built a vast publishing empire but was also appointed head of the *Reichspressekammer* (Reich Press Chamber) and *Reichsleiter für die Press* (Reich Leader for the Press). By 1944 the Nazis would control 82 per cent of the German press.

Those newspapers and magazines that survived the axe and the new ones that sprang up were naturally mouthpieces for Nazi German propaganda. All press bodies and associations received *Sprachregelungen* (language rulings) via daily briefings from the *Deutsches Nachrichtenbüro* (German News Bureau), to which the content, expression and focus of the day's paper was to conform. Journalistic individuality and research was not encouraged. (*Frankfurter Zeitung*, for example, was finally killed off in 1943 by a critical article on Hitler's personal architect, Paul Troost.)

Although the Nazis eventually promoted hundreds of newspapers, the flagship NSDAP publication was the *Völkischer Beobachter* (*Völkisch* Observer), first published in 1920.

From its early low circulation it came to sell over one million copies daily by 1941, not least because its official status and viewpoint made it essential reading for party members, educators and anyone seriously involved in the public life of the Reich.

Nazi newspapers

Underneath the *Völkischer Beobachter* was a whole host of national and local papers, many with a distinctly paramilitary feel, such as *Der Angriff* (The Attack), *SA-Mann* (SA Man) and the sickening *Der Stürmer* (The Attacker). The latter, owned and run by Nazi faithful Julius Streicher, was little more than a semi-pornographic news-sheet that pushed a vicious anti-semitism and a lingering focus on inter-racial sexual crimes. Goebbels

personally loathed the publication (he hated anything that lacked professionalism), but it generally had Hitler's approval, and with a weekly readership of about 480,000 by 1935, it could not be suppressed for many years. Only in the last year of the war was Goebbels able to use the excuse of paper shortages to shut it down.

In 1940, as a counterbalance to *Der Stürmer*, Goebbels brought out *Das Reich*, a newspaper featuring ostensibly learned articles, news reports and opinions plus an editorial from Goebbels himself (although he did not keep this commitment up for long). Marketed hard, it reached a peak circulation of 1.4 million.

Signal

One other interesting publishing enterprise was *Signal*, a fortnightly magazine produced by the *Wehrmacht* under Propaganda Ministry guidance. Rather than being intended for a home audience – which constituted only a small part of its circulation – *Signal* was intended for sale to the peoples of conquered countries and to neutral states. Filled with political propaganda and lavishly illustrated with photographs and artworks, the magazine achieved a circulation of 2.5 million by 1943 and ran until March 1945. It was produced in a total of 20 foreign editions, including French (the French market took 800,000 copies a fortnight at its peak), Spanish, Russian, Serbian, Turkish and Arabic. It even went into

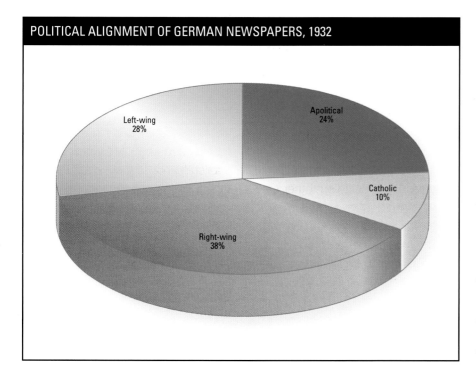

POLITICAL ALIGNMENT OF GERMAN NEWSPAPERS, 1932

Apolitical 24%

Left-wing 28%

Catholic 10%

Right-wing 38%

NUMBERS OF PEOPLE IN GERMANY LEAVING ORGANIZED FAITH, 1932–44			
Date	Catholic	Protestant	Total
1932	52,000	225,000	277,000
1933	34,000	57,000	91,000
1934	27,000	29,000	56,000
1935	34,000	53,000	87,000
1936	46,000	98,000	144,000
1937	104,000	338,000	442,000
1938	97,000	343,000	440,000
1939	95,000	395,000	490,000
1940	52,000	160,000	212,000
1941	52,000	195,000	247,000
1942	37,000	105,000	142,000
1943	12,000	35,000	47,000
1944	6000	17,000	23,000

English, and was distributed to the United States (prior to the attack on Pearl Harbor), the Republic of Ireland and also, following their occupation in 1940, the Channel Islands.

Signal attempted to present the Germans as benefactors to those whose countries they occupied. For this reason, racial vitriol was kept subdued in the magazine. Of course, as the war turned against the Germans from 1943, the rationale of the magazine became harder to sustain. As with all Germany's cultural enterprises, the gap between reality and ideology could be maintained for only so long.

Faith and religion

Hitler's private opinion of Christianity was low – he saw it as weak and Jewish-influenced, whereas he wanted a militaristic and anti-Semitic people. Yet he could not entirely alienate millions of believers. There is no doubt that Hitler was essentially opposed to the practice of Christianity. Yet Germany's long traditions of Catholicism, and its place as the historical centre of the Protestant Reformation, meant that it was a presence he could not openly attack (that attention was the preserve of the Jewish faith, of course). His chosen course, therefore, was a mixture of skewed theology, de facto persecution and begrudging tolerance.

Toleration and theology

It is easy to see why Hitler was antagonistic towards Christianity. Here was a faith that not only had Jewish roots and scriptures (the Old Testament) but also promoted ideas of conciliation, love of enemies, kindness, mercy and forgiveness – all of which notions were anathema to Nazi ideologies of war, violence, hard hearts and racial enmity.

At first, however, the Nazis seemed to buy into a much modified version of Christianity, emphasizing racial and heroic notes at the expense of its gentler doctrines, aided by support from many of the churches, who believed Hitler had rescued German faith from the clamp of Bolshevism. The Nazi Party Programme even expressed support for the practice of 'positive Christianity'.

The Catholic Church, disturbed by a potential loss of authority and the erosion of its influence in Germany, signed a concordat with the Nazis in 1933. This act, as much an attempt to calm international opinion as to protect domestic Catholicism, ostensibly protected the practice of the Catholic faith in Gemany, including the integrity of Catholic schools and youth groups.

At the same time as Hitler was promoting tolerance, he was also attempting to reshape core Christian theology to match his own world view, aided by Nazi theologians such as Professor Ernst Bergmann. Among his books, several of which ended up on the Catholic list of banned titles, Bergmann published *Die 25 Thesen der Deutschreligion* ('The Twenty-five Points of the German Religion'), a work of breathtakingly imaginative theology that amongst its premises claimed that Christ was not Jewish but Nordic, Adolf Hitler was the new messiah and that the Old Testament was no longer considered part of scripture. Bergmann also argued that 'Either we have a German God or none at all.'

The construction of a new German neo-pagan religion based on Nordic deities rather than the Christian god, termed the *Deutsche Glaubensbewegung* (German Faith Movement) and headed by 'Reich Bishop' Ludwig Müller, rankled with Germany's regular Christians, who saw the Nazi religious charade for what it was.

Once German Christians felt direct evidence of Nazi moral failings with the onset of war in 1939, and the persecution of the Jews, there was a backlash amongst elements of the church.

Resistance and persecution

It has to be acknowledged that resistance to Nazism from German Christians was minor. In fact, as the figures on the opposite page show, the numbers of people leaving organized faith during the Nazi era were high, especially during the pre-war years when many Germans did indeed find a new faith in the *Führer*. The principal resistance came in the form of the *Bekenntniskirche* (Confessional Church), headed by Pastor Martin Niemöller. The *Bekenntniskirche*'s declared intention was to keep the Protestant faith pure, and distant from the influence of the *Deutsche Glaubensbewegung*. Some 7000 Protestant pastors signed a declaration saying that Christianity and Nazism were not compatible. This extraordinary act of bravery was to cost them dear.

During the 1930s and the war years, Hitler's policy of tolerance towards the orthodox churches gradually shifted to targeted persecution. The Confessional Church members were destined for concentration camps and/or execution. Niemöller, for example, spent seven years in such camps before his release.

Other Protestant resisters were involved in more active subversion of the Nazi state. The theologian Dietrich Bonhoeffer was another member of the *Bekenntniskirche* who became involved in anti-Nazi

espionage and plots against Hitler. He was eventually arrested in April 1943, and after two years in *Gestapo* prisons and concentration camps was finally executed on 9 April 1945.

Nor was religious resistance only confined to the Protestants. During the 1930s and early 1940s, the Catholic Archbishop of Münster, Clemens Galen, railed against Nazi racial laws and euthanasia programmes. His prominence in the Catholic Church prevented his immediate extirpation, but following the July Bomb Plot in 1944 he finally disappeared into Dachau concentration camp, where he was brutalized but survived the war.

Hundreds of other members of the clergy served peace instead of war during the Nazi era, expressing their beliefs with acts ranging from proclaiming their faith to rescuing Jews from certain death. The fact remains, however, that in the main,

religious believers were a compliant body for the Nazis, or at least one that hid its true voice.

Mythology and symbolism

The Nazi Party had an especially keen eye for symbolism, realizing that powerful imagery was integral to cohesive political and social movements. It consequently created one of the most memorable systems of iconography in history.

Although, as we have seen, Hitler had little time for orthodox religion, his political views did contain spiritual overtones. Hitler's beliefs centred around ideas of messianic destiny; of the power of *Blut und Boden* (Blood and Soil); and on the concept of racial purity. Nazi rituals were akin to high church ceremonies.

Some pro-Nazi thinkers and even Party members began to explore Nordic paganism as a form of Germanic replacement for

NORSE MYTHOLOGY, KEY FIGURES AND PLACES IN NAZI NEO-PAGANISM

Figure	Meaning
Wotan/Odin	Norse warrior king, celebrated for being a military archetype.
Thor	Norse god of thunder and son of Wotan/Odin. Also celebrated for his martial qualities.
Race of giants	A race of Norse giants, enemies of the gods, whom some Nazis saw as archetypes of the enemies with which they struggled, particularly at the end of the war.
Magni and Modi	These sons of Thor were both warrior gods, and together they represented the ideal of total war, expressing ferocity in battle and a complete lack of weakness that appealed to the Nazi mentality.
Jarnsaxa	A giantess who became a god through marriage to Thor. Could represent the status of women in the Third Reich – important but inferior.
Valhalla and Asgard	Asgard was the home of the Norse gods, and Valhalla the 'heaven' within Asgard – the place for fallen warriors. Both places had martial connotations, and so were more stirring to the Nazis when compared with Christian notions of heaven.

the Christian faith. Yet while some scholars have attempted to forge substantial links between Nazism and pagan or even occult practices, the link should not be taken too far. Hitler actually frowned on overt occultism, and some mystics such as Friedrich Bernhard Marby were even dispatched to concentration camps for more extreme attempts to revive old German religions.

Yet while the Nazis may have opposed outright pagan religiosity, they were intensely interested in the symbolism and legends of antiquity. The Aryan mythology often revolved around ideas of a lost ancestral centre, or historical patterns of racial destiny, mixed with pseudo-religious imagery. The *Thule Gesellschaft* (Thule Society), for example, was a nationalistic and anti-Semitic organization formed in the early post-World War I years. It was named after a mythical Nordic country and used mystical symbols in its iconography, including the swastika. Its quest to define the spiritual and geographical homeland of the Aryan race attracted several thousand members, including Nazi Party authorities such as Rudolf Hess and Alfred Rosenberg.

Ritual images

Looking at Nazism for signs that it was an organized religion or cult are misguided. What was certain, however, was that the Nazis had a deeply spiritual relationship to their symbolism. The SS, for example, relied heavily on runic symbols in its insignia, with uniform collars and

hats bearing symbols for death, victory, fidelity and so on.

By far the most definable emblem of Nazi ideology, however, was the *Hakenkreuz* ('Hook Cross', or swastika). Although the swastika has come to be identified with the Nazi era, it is actually a symbol of great antiquity. It is first seen in decorative arts in Persia back in the fourth millennium BC, and was subsequently used as a religious symbol in ancient Greece, India and Japan. The Nazis adopted the swastika as their official

emblem – often combined with the German eagle – because of its connections with the Aryan Indians and the perceived associations of racial purity (on account of the Indian caste system). Whatever the philosophy, the swastika was wielded with powerful national pride by the Nazis, and was treated as virtually a sacred motif of nationhood. Ultimately, Nazi symbolism was largely about style over substance, but both Goebbels and Hitler realized that the former was often what motivated people.

SWASTIKA FLAG VARIATIONS

Image	Flag	Example
	45° black swastika, set on a white disc	NSDAP flag
	45° black swastika, set in a white lozenge	Hitler Youth flag
	45° black swastika, set in a white outline	Tail marking on Luftwaffe aircraft
	45° black swastika, outlined by white and black lines, set on a white disc	German War Ensign (used by the Kriegsmarine)
	Upright black swastika, outlined by white and black lines, set on a white disc	Adolf Hitler's personal standard
	45° swastikas in gold, silver, black, or white; often set on or being held by an eagle	Numerous military badges and flags
	Upright swastika with curved arms, described in white outline on black background, forming a circle	Emblem of Waffen-SS Nordland Division

NAZI SYMBOLISM

Image	Symbol	Origins	Nazi meaning and application
	Hakenkreuz (Swastika)	Uncertain – prevalent across Indo-European cultures from the Bronze Age	National flags and offical emblem of NSDAP
	Sonnenrad ('Sunwheel' Swastika)	Old Norse symbol for the sun	Divisional sign for Waffen-SS divisions Wiking and Nordland
	Eagle	Roman Empire	Represented Nazi Party (when looking to right) and Nazi Germany (when looking to left)
	Totenkopf (Death's Head)	Ancient; eighteenth-century European military symbol	Used by SS as official badge
	Sig rune	Ancient/medieval Germanic alphabets	Symbolized victory. Two side by side became the official emblem of the SS
	Opfer rune	Ancient/medieval Germanic alphabets	Symbolized self-sacrifice. Used in SA Sports Badge for War Wounded
	Odal rune	Ancient/medieval Germanic alphabets	Symbolized family and racial cohesion. Used by the SS Race and Settlement Department
	Ger rune	Ancient/medieval Germanic alphabets	Symbolized faith. Alternative divisional sign for Waffen-SS Division Nordland
	Heilszeichen	Ancient/medieval Germanic alphabets	Symbolized success. Used on SS Death's Head ring
	Wolfsangle (Wolf's Hook)	Medieval German	Symbolized liberty. Early motif of NSDAP and used by Waffen-SS Division Das Reich
	Toten rune	Ancient/medieval Germanic alphabets	Symbolized death, hence used on official SS documents alongside date of death
	Tyr rune	Ancient/medieval Germanic alphabets	Symbolized leadership in battle. Used on SS grave markers
	Eif rune	Ancient/medieval pagan Germanic alphabets	Symbolized enthusiasm, passion. Worn by SS adjutants in the 1930s
	Hagall rune	Ancient/medieval Germanic alphabets	Symbolized fidelity (to Nazi cause). Featured on SS Death's Head ring

Racial War

*Throughout this book, Hitler's racial hatred
has been the sinister heartbeat of so much of Nazi policy.
As we have seen in the ideas of* Lebensraum, *the views
expressed in* Mein Kampf *and the Nazis' policies on the arts,
racial theory was a driving force in Hitler's strategic
decision-making.*

*His hatred towards Jews and Slavs in particular
would lead to arguably the greatest crime against humanity
in history – the systematic murder of six million Jews in
a camp system designed expressly for that purpose.
For this reason alone, it was necessary that the
Third Reich be destroyed.*

Left: Prisoners line up in the concentration camp at Sachsenhausen, Germany, December 1938.

Persecution in the 1930s

Chapter 1 outlined the essence of Hitler's extreme anti-Semitism, a viewpoint that would eventually lead to mass murder. It should be remembered that Hitler was not working in an vacuum when it came to hatred of the Jewish people.

Anti-Semitism had a long, shameful history of persecution and alienation stretching back to Roman times, and even in the twentieth century it persisted in varying degrees throughout Europe and the United States. Hitler simply tapped into a vein of prejudice already there, but magnified it greatly using a mish-mash of spurious biological theory, nationalism and political ideology.

While anti-Semitism was common in Germany, as elsewhere, that reality should not mask the fact that by the 1920s the Jewish people were fully integrated into German society at every level, largely without problem. A total of about 240,000 Jews lived in Germany, and they played a key role in the financial, administrative and commercial life of the nation. Furthermore, by the 1920s one in four German Jews were marrying non-Jews, signifying that a large portion of the population had no issue with Jewish people or society.

Such 'interbreeding' infuriated Hitler, who associated it with weakening the supposedly noble Aryan bloodline. In all his writings and speeches, Hitler sought to dehumanize the Jews on every level, almost literally presenting them as alien creatures clinging to the German state like parasites. He argued that Jews, unlike 'true' German citizens, had no affiliation to a particular country but instead wandered the world latching onto nations from which they could feed economically. Such perspectives would have remained the ravings of a madman had not Hitler steered his way to power in 1933.

In talking of Hitler's 'masterplan' for a racial war against the Jews in particular, as expressed in the Holocaust, we need to be clear about our terminology. Holocaust historians broadly fall into two camps: 'Intentionalists', who see the Holocaust as Hitler's direct long-term goal, and 'Functionalists', who argue that the Holocaust was an emerging policy that responded to circumstances and opportunities, rather than being based on an overall plan.

The debates between these two camps are complex, and space does not allow us to unpack them here, nor to give a full history of the Holocaust. What we can say, however, was that the ultimate sanction and direction of the Holocaust had to originate in Hitler, in whom all power was concentrated in the Third Reich.

Anti-Jewish policy, 1933–39

What became the Holocaust was a long process, taking place over a period of 12 years. When Hitler came to power in 1933, direct, murderous action against the Jews would not have been tolerated by many Germans, nor by the international community. Instead, Hitler's initial policy towards German Jews was to drive them out of the nation's society, and out of Germany itself, through steadily tightening restrictions and persecution.

Hitler's first year in power set the scene. He quickly banned Jews from practising law, then through his 'Law for the Restoration of the Professional Civil Service' expelled them from working in the German government at any level. On 1 April he also attempted a boycott of Jewish shops, aided by intimidation from members of the SA, who quickly found that they could harass, assault and humiliate Jewish people virtually with legal impunity. And 1933 was just the beginning. Between 1933 and 1939, Jews were banned from practising as journalists, dentists, doctors, veterinarians, university lecturers, teachers, soldiers and artists. They were steadily muscled out of commercial activity through confiscation of their businesses and livelihoods; a law of April 1938 meant that all Jewish assets over 5000 RM had to be registered with the government, and these assets put at the government's disposal.

At the level of citizenship, the Nazis enacted the 'Law for the Protection of German Blood and German Honour' and the 'Reich Citizenship Law' in 1935. Together these laws not only stopped marriage between Jews and non-Jews, but they also stripped Jews of rights of citizenship, reducing them to 'subjects' of the state and therefore placing them at the government's mercy. In an ominous sign, all Jews had to insert the name 'Sarah' or 'Israel' as an identifying middle name from August 1938, and two months later their passports were marked with a 'J'.

Although there was some resistance to Jewish persecution, particularly from church groups, many in German society eventually accepted, complied with or embraced the new anti-Semitism. The effects were clearly seen on the night of 9/10 November 1938,

ESTIMATES OF REMAINING JEWISH POPULATIONS: DATA PRESENTED AT THE WANNSEE CONFERENCE, 1942

Old Reich	131,800
Austria	43,700
Eastern Territories	420,000
General Government	2,284,000
Bialystok	400,000
Bohemia/Moravia	74,200
Estonia	0
Latvia	3500
Lithuania	34,000
Belgium	43,000
Denmark	5600
France occupied	165,000
France unoccupied	700,000
Greece	69,600
Netherlands	160,800
Norway	1300
Bulgaria	48,000
England	330,000
Finland	2300
Ireland	4000
Italy	58,000
Albania	200
Croatia	40,000
Portugal	3000
Romania	342,000
Sweden	8000
Switzerland	18,000
Serbia	10,000
Slovakia	88,000
Spain	6000
Turkey	55,500
Hungary	742,800
USSR	1,558,832
Belorussia	446,484
Ukraine	2,994,684

when SA and SS squads embarked on a government-sanctioned bout of violence against Jewish communities throughout Germany, supposedly in response to the shooting of a German embassy official in Paris by a young Jewish man. In what became known as *Kristallnacht* ('Night of the Broken Glass'), 91 Jews were murdered and 7500 Jewish businesses and 200 synagogues destroyed. Up to 30,000 Jewish men were also arrested and taken off into the burgeoning concentration camp system.

Emigration

Hitler's ultimate goal to be achieved by such actions was still not necessarily extermination. One Nazi

---

KRISTALLNACHT ORDER, 9 NOVEMBER 1938

To – all headquarters and stations of the State Police.

All districts and sub-districts of the SD

Urgent! For immediate attention of Chief or his deputy!

Re: Measures against Jews tonight

Following the attempt on the life of Secretary of the Legation vom Rath in Paris, protests against the Jews are expected in all parts of the Reich during the coming night, 9/10 November 1938. The instructions below are to be used for handling these events:

1. The chiefs of the State Police, or their deputies, must immediately upon receipt of this telegram contact, by telephone, the political leaders in their respective areas – Gauleiter or Kreisleiter – who have jurisdiction in their districts, and arrange a joint meeting with the inspector or commander of the Ordnungspolizei to discuss the arrangements for the demonstrations. At these discussions the political leaders will be informed that the German police has received instructions, detailed below, from the Reichsführer-SS and the Chief of the German Police, with whom the political leadership is asked to coordinate its own measures:

a) Only those measures should be taken that do not endanger German lives or property (i.e., synagogues are to be burned down only if the fire presents no danger to nearby buildings).

b) Places of business and apartments belonging to Jews may be destroyed but not looted. The police are instructed to implement this order and to arrest looters.

c) In commercial streets particular care is to be taken that non-Jewish businesses are completely undamaged.

d) Foreign citizens – even if they are Jews – are not to be molested.

2. Assuming that the guidelines detailed under para. 1 are observed, the demonstrations are not to be prevented by the police, which are only to supervise the following of the guidelines.

3. On receipt of this telegram, police will seize all archives to be found in all synagogues and offices of the Jewish communities so as to prevent their destruction during the demonstrations. This refers only to material of historical value, not to contemporary tax records, etc. The archives are to be handed over to the local officers of the SD.

4. Control of the measures of the Security Police regarding the demonstrations against the Jews is vested in the authority of the State Police, unless inspectors of the Security Police have given their own instructions. Officials of the Criminal Police, members of the SD, of the Reserves and the SS in general may be utilized to apply the measures taken by the Security Police.

5. As soon as the events of the night allow the release of the officials required, as many Jews in all districts – especially the rich – as can be accommodated in existing prisons are to be arrested. For the time being only healthy male Jews, who are not too old, are to be detained. After the detentions have been carried out the appropriate concentration camps are to be contacted immediately for the prompt accommodation of the Jews in the camps. Special care is to be taken that the Jews arrested in accordance with these instructions are not ill-treated....

Signed Heydrich,
SS Gruppenführer

MAJOR ANTI-SEMITIC LAWS IN GERMANY, 1933–38

Date	Law	Terms
7 April 1933	Law for the Restoration of the Professional Civil Service	Bans Jews from the German civil service
7 April 1933	Law Regarding Admission to the Bar	Peoples of non-Aryan descent denied access to the Bar
25 April 1933	Law Against the Crowding of German Schools and Institutions of Higher Learning	The numbers of 'non-Aryan' Germans within an educational establishment have to be lower than those of 'pure' German pupils
15 September 1935	Law for the Protection of German Blood and German Honour	Marriage or 'extramarital intercourse' between Jews and non-Jews is forbidden. Jews are forbidden to fly the Reich and national flag and to display Reich colours
15 September 1935	Reich Citizenship Law	Strips Jews of their German citizenship and rights
14 November 1935	First Supplementary Decree to the Reich Citizenship Law	Clarifies the conditions of the Reich Citizenship Law
17 August 1938	Second Decree for the Implementation of the Law Regarding Changes of Family Names	Jews whose names do not conform to the Guidelines on the Use of Given Names are forced to adopt an additional given name – 'Israel' in the case of males and 'Sarah' in the case of females

policy was to 'encourage' Jews to emigrate, and tens of thousands did so, including 100,000 to the United States and 150,000 to Palestine. (Britain took 45,000.) Notably, the Nazi hierarchy even toyed with the idea of creating a Jewish colony on the island of Madagascar, to which all Germany's Jews would be expelled – the idea was naturally untenable, but the fact that it was even considered shows a worrying desire to innovate. Hitler had attempted to remove Jews from positions of social and cultural influence and to denude them of their human rights – and had succeeded. As yet, however, his Jewish policies were purely directed at the unfortunate citizens of Germany itself and those regions annexed or occupied during the pre-war period. From 1939, the situation would change entirely.

The problem of conquest

In Hitler's twisted world, the German conquests of 1939–42 heightened the issue of the 'Jewish Question', which essentially amounted to 'What to do with the Jews?'

The conquest of Poland, Western Europe and large portions of the Soviet Union brought literally millions of Jews under Nazi control (Poland alone had 3.3 million Jews in 1939). Nor were the Jewish people the only ones deemed racially problematic. Hitler had an almost equal enmity towards the Slavs, whom he described as *Untermenschen* (sub-humans). If the Germans were to enjoy the full fruits of *Lebensraum*, then as far as Hitler was concerned something had to be done with these populations.

In Poland, the initial policy was containment in ghettos, compact areas of towns and cities whose conditions were so dreadful that possibly 500,000 Jewish men, women and children died in them before 1942, when the extermination camps roared into life in earnest. Furthermore, SS *Einsatzgruppen* (Task Forces) – special murder units

formed from SS and security police personnel – began field massacres of any groups of Poles, including Jews, deemed threatening to the Nazi regime.

Invasion of Soviet Union

The activities of the *Einsatzgruppen* were to intensify horrifically during Operation *Barbarossa*, the invasion of the Soviet Union, from June 1941. Four huge *Einsatzgruppen* were formed to trail in the wake of the advancing conventional forces, and these units were literally commanded to murder tens of thousands of Jews and 'political' opponents, clearing entire regions of age-old communities.

During 1941 and 1942, 1.4 million Jews were executed with utmost barbarity, most simply forced at gunpoint to remote locations and shot at close range. In one action alone, near Kiev in the Ukraine in September 1941, 33,771 people were killed in the ravine of Babi Yar in just two days. Here was the

MAP OF OPERATIONAL AREAS OF EASTERN EINSATZGRUPPEN, 1941–44*

Einsatzgruppe A – Baltic Republics
Einsatzgruppe B – Belorussia
Einsatzgruppe C – Northern and central Ukraine
Einsatzgruppe D – Bessarabia, southern Ukraine, Crimea, Caucasus

* Shows 1939 borders

Above: The operational areas of the *Einsatzgruppen* from June 1941 extended from the Baltic States in the north down to the southern Ukraine and beyond. At first the *Einsatzgruppen* simply moved behind the German forces advancing under Operation *Barbarossa*, but then established fixed operational regions, organized under a police and security service command structure. The *Einsatzgruppen* murdered in these regions with impunity until the Soviet advances of 1943 and 1944 pushed them back. Although the Holocaust has been identified largely with the death camps, it began in earnest with the activities of the *Einsatzgruppen*.

true beginning of the Holocaust, although as yet the official use of extermination camps had not begun.

The war in the east was, on Hitler's orders, to be conducted very differently from that in the west. In the west, the conflict was primarily about conquest; in the east, it

SELECTED POLISH VILLAGES SUBJECTED TO NAZI 'PACIFICATION' OPERATIONS

Village name	Killed	Village name	Killed
Borów	232 (103 children)	Szczecyn	368 (71 children)
Cyców	111	Wanaty	109
Jamy	147	Zamosc	470
Kaszyce	117	Szczebrzeszyn	208
Kitów	174	Labunie	210
Krasowo-Czestki	257 (83 children)	Krasnogród	285
Krusze	148	Mokre	304
Kulno	100	Nielisz	301
Lipniak-Majorat	more than 370	Nowa Osada	195
Lazek	187	Radecznica	212
Michniów	203 (48 children)	Skierbieszow	335
Milejów	150	Stary Zamosc	287
Mrozy	more than 100	Suchowola	324
Olszanka	103	Sulów	252
Rajsk	more than 143	Tereszpol	344
Rózaniec	about 200	Wysokie	203
Skloby	265	Zwierzyniec	412
Smoligów	about 200	Kitowa	165
Sochy	183	Królewiec/Szalas	more than 100 each
Sumin	118		

was as much about expulsion and extermination. Through his speeches and instructions to commanders, Hitler made it clear that the war in the east was to be waged without mercy or compassion.

In a speech to *Wehrmacht* officers in March 1941, Hitler emphasized that 'The war against Russia will be such that it cannot be conducted in a knightly fashion. This struggle is one of ideologies and racial differences and will have to be conducted with unprecedented, unmerciful and unrelenting harshness.' What this meant in real terms was a conflict that would result in the deaths of an estimated 25 million Soviet citizens, including at least 1.1 million Jews. It is terrifying to consider, but the death toll could have been even worse if one of the Nazis' other plans had been fulfilled.

Hunger plan

A central problem for the Nazis was how the food production system of the Soviet Union would support the invading German forces, and eventually also feed the millions of intended German settlers, as well as the indigenous population. (Hitler stated in a speech that 'my long-term policy aims at having eventually a hundred million Germans settled

in these territories'.) In early 1941, before the invasion of the Soviet Union was launched, the German agronomist Herbert Backe came up with a plan.

It involved systematically diverting food supplies in the conquered territories away from the civilian populations of major cities and into German hands. The useful corollary of this plan was that an estimated 30 million Slavs would literally starve to death. Hence the plan would solve Germany's food problems and destroy vast numbers of people into the bargain, clearing the way for German settlement. The full implications of the *Hungerplan* (Hunger Plan), as it came to be known, were spelled out in a report prepared by the Economic Staff East, Agricultural Group on 23 May 1941:

It follows from all that has been said that the German administration in these territories may well attempt to mitigate the consequences of the famine which undoubtedly will take place, and to accelerate the return to primitive agricultural conditions. An attempt might be made to intensify cultivation in these areas by expanding the acreage under potatoes or other important food crops giving a high yield. However, these measures will not avert famine. Many tens of millions of people in this area will become redundant and will either die or have to emigrate to Siberia. Any attempt to save the population there from death by starvation by importing surpluses from the black soil zone would be at the expense of supplies to Europe. It would reduce Germany's and Europe's power to resist the blockade. This must be clearly and absolutely understood.

Highest approval

The concepts of the *Hungerplan* were approved at the highest levels of the Nazi administration, despite the appalling implications. Rosenberg, the minister for the Eastern Territories, stated that mass starvation would be 'a harsh necessity that stands outside any sentiment', while Goebbels explained publicly 'that Russia has nothing to expect from us and we will let it starve to death'.

Göring, Himmler and many other senior Nazis also expressed their knowledge of and agreement with the *Hungerplan*, but even some senior *Wehrmacht* commanders acknowledged that the plan was a necessity.

The *Hungerplan* was thankfully never implemented in its fullest expression, partly through German

---

EXTRACT FROM THE JÄGER REPORT

The following are just two pages from a six-sheet document listing the killings of Jews in Lithuania by *Einsatzkommando 3*, written by the commander of the liquidation squad. The final total of executions listed on sheet six was 137,346.

Date	Place	Details	Total
2.10.41	Zagare	633 Jews, 1,107 Jewesses, 496 Jewish children (as these Jews were being led away a mutiny rose, which was however immediately put down; 150 Jews were shot immediately; 7 partisans wounded)	2,236
4.10.41	Kauen-F.IX	315 Jews, 712 Jewesses, 818 Jewish children (reprisal after German police officer shot in ghetto)	1,845
29.10.41	Kauen-F.IX	2,007 Jews, 2,920 Jewesses, 4,273 Jewish children (mopping up ghetto of superfluous Jews)	9,200
3.11.41	Lazdijai	485 Jews, 511 Jewesses, 539 Jewish children	1,535
15.11.41	Wilkowiski	36 Jews, 48 Jewesses, 31 Jewish children	115
25.11.41	Kauen-F.IX	1,159 Jews, 1,600 Jewesses, 175 Jewish children (resettlers from Berlin, Munich and Frankfurt am main)	2,934
29.11.41	Kauen-F.IX	693 Jews, 1,155 Jewesses, 152 Jewish children (resettlers from from Vienna and Breslau)	2,000
29.11.41	Kauen-F.IX	17 Jews, 1 Jewess, for contravention of ghetto law, 1 Reichs German who converted to the Jewish faith and attended rabbinical school, then 15 terrorists from the Kalinin group	34
EK 3 detachment in Dunanberg in the period 13.7-21.8.41:		9,012 Jews, Jewesses and Jewish children, 573 active Comm.	9,585
EK 3 detachment in Wilna: 12.8-1.9.41 City of Wilna		425 Jews, 19 Jewesses, 8 Comm. (m.), 9 Comm. (f.)	461
2.9.41 City of Wilna		864 Jews, 2,019 Jewesses, 817 Jewish children (sonderaktion because German soldiers shot at by Jews)	3,700
		Total carried forward	99,084

Date	Place	Details	Total
12.9.41	City of Wilna	993 Jews, 1,670 Jewesses, 771 Jewish children	3,334
17.9.41	City of Wilna	337 Jews, 687 Jewesses, 247 Jewish children and 4 Lith. Comm.	1,271
20.9.41	Nemencing	128 Jews, 176 Jewesses, 99 Jewish children	403
22.9.41	Novo-Wilejka	468 Jews, 495 Jewesses, 196 Jewish children	1,159
24.9.41	Riesa	512 Jews, 744 Jewesses, 511 Jewish children	1,767
25.9.41	Jahiunai	215 Jews, 229 Jewesses, 131 Jewish children	575
27.9.41	Eysisky	989 Jews, 1,636 Jewesses, 821 Jewish children	3,446
30.9.41	Trakai	366 Jews, 483 Jewesses, 597 Jewish children	1,446
4.10.41	City of Wilna	432 Jews, 1,115 Jewesses, 436 Jewish children	1,983
6.10.41	Semiliski	213 Jews, 359 Jewesses, 390 Jewish children	962
9.10.41	Svenciany	1,169 Jews, 1,840 Jewesses, 717 Jewish children	3,726
16.10.41	City of Wilna	382 Jews, 507 Jewesses, 257 Jewish children	1,146
21.10.41	City of Wilna	718 Jews, 1,063 Jewesses, 586 Jewish children	2,367
25.10.41	City of Wilna	1,776 Jewesses, 812 Jewish children	2,578
27.10.41	City of Wilna	946 Jews, 184 Jewesses, 73 Jewish children	1,203
30.10.41	City of Wilna	382 Jews, 789 Jewesses, 362 Jewish children	1,553
6.11.41	City of Wilna	340 Jews, 749 Jewesses, 252 Jewish children	1,341
19.11.41	City of Wilna	76 Jews, 77 Jewesses, 18 Jewish children	171
19.11.41	City of Wilna	6 POW's, 8 Poles	14
20.11.41	City of Wilna	3 POW's	3
25.11.41	City of Wilna	9 Jews, 46 Jewesses, 8 Jewish children, 1 Pole for possesion of arms and other military equipment	64

CASE STUDY – THE BABI YAR MASSACRE

The actions of Einsatzgruppe C *at Babi Yar from 29 September 1941 are a typically horrifying example of how* Einsatzgruppen *operations were conducted, and how they generated such dizzying death tolls.*

On 19 September 1941, Kiev, the capital of the Ukraine, fell to the Germans as part of Operation Barbarossa, and Einsatzgruppe C *quickly moved into the streets to vent its wrath on the city's large Jewish community. The Jewish population of Kiev was huge, but any vestige of mercy was lost through the German casualties taken by booby traps left by the retreating Soviet forces.*

Einsatzgruppe C's commander, SS-Brigadeführer Otto Rasch, consulted with the local HSSPF, SS-Obergruppenführer Friedrich Jeckeln, to decide on a course of action. The selected option was the liquidation of all Kiev's Jews, the chosen execution site being the large ravine of Babi Yar just outside the city. The operation would be assisted by various security service and Waffen-SS *personnel, plus units of local auxiliary police, formed into two special Kommandos, who appeared more than willing to help out with the operations.*

First the Germans had to assemble the Jews. Leaflets were distributed that read out the following message:

All Jews of the city of Kiev and its environs must appear on Monday, September 29, 1941, by 8:00 am on the corner of Melnikov and Dokterivsky streets (near the cemetery). You are to take your documents, money, valuables, warm clothes, linen etc. Whoever of the Jews does not fulfill this order and is found in another place, shall be shot. Any citizen who enters the apartments that have been left and takes ownership of items will be shot.

On 29 September 1941, the first, huge columns of Jews were led out to the ravine at Babi Yar. As they approached the ravine, they were stopped and ordered to remove all their clothes and hand over their valuables. They were then channelled between tight ranks of SS soldiers to the edge of the ravine, where they were formed up into large groups and machine-gunned or shot individually and cast into the ravine. *Some 33,771 people were killed in this way in a period of only two days, according to the official SS reports.*

The Babi Yar ravine was the site of Einsatzgruppen *murder operations for a long period after the initial actions against Kiev's Jews. Gypsies, Soviet POWs and psychiatric patients also joined the ranks of the dead in the bottom of the ravine, which ultimately may have held up to 100,000 corpses.*

By mid-1943, the war was turning against the Germans, and it was desperately realized that Babi Yar constituted profound evidence against the SS. At that point the SS decided to remove that evidence, and during a grim six-week operation local concentration camp inmates were forced to exhume and burn the rotting bodies.

Paul Blobel, the commander of Sonderkommando 4a, *a sub-unit of* Einsatzgruppe C, *later testified to the Nuremberg trial judges about the body removal operations, which he witnessed in August 1943:*

During my visit in August I myself observed the burning of bodies in a mass grave near Kiev. This grave was about 55m [180ft] long, 3m [10ft] wide and 2.5m [8ft] deep. After the top had been removed the bodies were covered with inflammable material and ignited. It took about two days until the grave burned down to the bottom. I myself observed that the fire had glowed down to the bottom. After that the grave was filled in and the traces were now practically obliterated.

In this way the SS managed to remove many of the traces of its hideous work. Enough survivors and scraps of evidence remained, however, to bring the crime to light. Furthermore, although massacres such as that perpetrated at Babi Yar resulted in an enormous death toll, Himmler came to regard such killings as grossly inefficient, and looked for other methods of execution. This led to the development of the infamous death camps.

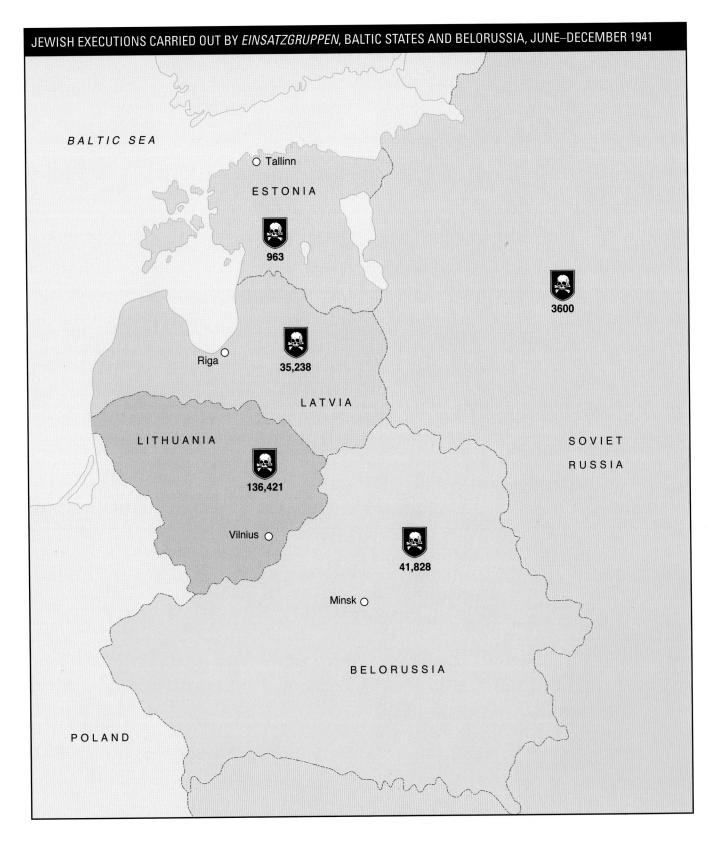

JEWISH EXECUTIONS CARRIED OUT BY *EINSATZGRUPPEN*, BALTIC STATES AND BELORUSSIA, JUNE–DECEMBER 1941

BALTIC SEA

○ Tallinn

ESTONIA

963

3600

○ Riga

35,238

LATVIA

LITHUANIA

136,421

Vilnius ○

41,828

Minsk ○

SOVIET

RUSSIA

BELORUSSIA

POLAND

administrative inefficiences and partly through the way that the war in the east actually developed. There is no doubt, however, that the Nazis' policy of denying food to targeted populations resulted in the starvation and deaths of millions of people. Jews were herded into confined ghettos where they were often denied subsistence levels of nutrition (even non-Jewish Polish citizens often received only about 700 calories a day).

In the Soviet Union, *Wehrmacht* and *Waffen-SS* units would often simply take over a rural house and eject the occupants into the wilderness, to starve or freeze. Had Germany not been defeated, the death toll from the Nazi occupation of foreign lands could have been vast, and would have dramatically altered the ethnic composition of the east. Even in the west, a German food embargo on the Netherlands in late 1944, aggravated by a harsh winter, resulted in the deaths of 18,000 people.

SS racial culture

The SS was, as we have seen repeatedly, an organization with tortured racial logic. Himmler, in his desire to define the racial purity of true Germans, involved his SS in curious and often horrible experiments in massaging history and in racial engineering.

An SS pocket diary and information book entitled *Der Soldatenfreund* ('The Soldier's Friend'), published in 1943, gave the following explanation of the *SS-Hauptamt*, emphasizing its role in preserving SS racial quality:

It is the task of the SS Main Office to create a strictly organized elite order. Therefore it is charged with the selection of suitable men for the SS and with the recording of the SS members and their families, furthermore with the ideological and political guidance, schooling, and education of the entire SS and police as well as the care of the organizations committed within the frame of the SS and police.

A further task is the physical education and the physical training of the SS before and after military duty. Of special importance is the selection, the establishment, and the leadership of the SS in the Germanic countries, and the prevailing of the Germanic idea in all spheres of life.

As this passage makes clear, in one way or another, physical 'quality' and racial health were at the core of SS culture and thinking. Although, as we have seen, clear racial purity was not borne out in practice, particularly within the *Waffen-SS*, there was a definite sense that the SS was on a racial mission. We have already seen several ways in which this was expressed, including the ultimate horror that was the Holocaust and more benign programmes such as *Lebensborn*. Yet the SS desire to create a pure Aryan society developed in other, often bizarre ways. Some were mere exercises in academic curiosity, while others were cruel attempts at genetic engineering.

On 30 September 1947, the US Military Tribunal at Nuremberg sat to consider the 'RuSHA Case', the

CIVILIAN LOSSES IN THE SOVIET UNION IN WORLD WAR II, BY CAUSE

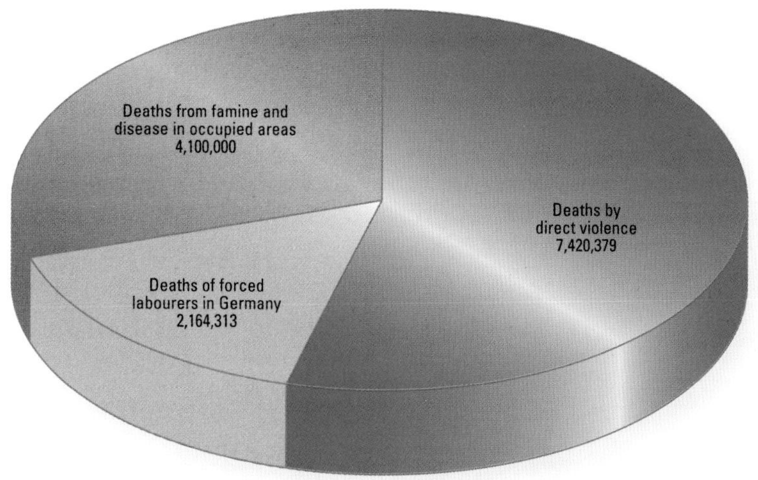
Deaths from famine and disease in occupied areas 4,100,000
Deaths by direct violence 7,420,379
Deaths of forced labourers in Germany 2,164,313

RuSHA CASE – DEFENDANTS, 1947–48

- ULRICH GREIFELT

SS-Obergruppenführer; *General of Police; Chief of the Staff Main Office (Stabshauptamt) of the* Reichskommissar für die Festigung des Deutschen Volkstums *(Reich Commissioner for the Strengthening of the German Nation; RKFDV); Chief of* Amtsgruppe B *of the Staff Main Office.*

- RUDOLF CREUTZ

SS-Oberführer; *Deputy to Greifelt; Chief of* Amtsgruppe A *of the Staff Main Office of the RKFDV.*

- KONRAD MEYER-HETLING

SS-Oberführer; *Chief of* Amtsgruppe C *of the Staff Main Office of the RKFDV.*

- OTTO SCHWARZENBERGER

SS-Oberführer; *Chief of* Amt V *in* Amtsgruppe B *of the Staff Main Office of the RKFDV.*

- HERBERT HÜBNER

SS-Standartenführer; *Chief of Branch Office Poznan of the Staff Main Office of the RKFDV; representative of the* SS-Rasse- and Siedlungshauptamt *(SS Race and Settlement Main Office; RuSHA) for the Warthegau.*

- WERNER LORENZ

SS-Obergruppenführer; *General of the* Waffen-SS *and Police; Chief of the* Hauptamt Volksdeutsche Mittelstelle *(Ethnic German Main Assistance Office; VOMI) of the SS.*

- HEINZ BRÜCKNER

SS-Sturmbannführer; *Chief of* Amt VI *of VOMI.*

- OTTO HOFMANN

SS-Obergruppenführer; *Chief of RuSHA, 9 July 1940–20 April 1943; Higher SS and Police Leader (HSSPF) for southwestern Germany.*

- RICHARD HILDEBRANDT

SS-Obergruppenführer; *General of Police; Chief of RuSHA, 20 April 1943–May 1945.*

- FRITZ SCHWALM

SS-Obersturmbannführer; *Chief of Staff of RuSHA and principal RuSHA representative at the* Einwandererzentrale Lodz *(Immigration Centre, Lodz; EWZ)*

- MAX SOLLMANN

SS-Standartenführer; *Chief of* Lebensborn, e.V. *('Fount of Life' Society) of the SS; Chief of Main Department A of* Lebensborn.

- GREGOR EBNER

SS-Oberführer; *Chief of the Main Health Department of* Lebensborn.

- GÜNTHER TESCH

SS-Sturmbannführer; *Chief of the Main Legal Department of* Lebensborn.

- INGE VIERMETZ

Deputy Chief of Main Department A of Lebensborn.

---

trial of 14 members of the *SS-Rasse- und Siedlungshauptamt* (SS Race and Settlement Main Office; RuSHA). The indictments contained a broad sweep of crimes against humanity in the occupied countries, and contained some chillingly unusual charges read out by the prosecution, including:

a. *Kidnapping the children of foreign nationals in order to select for Germanization those who were considered of 'racial value';*

b. *Encouraging and compelling abortions on Eastern workers for the purposes of preserving their working capacity as slave labor and of weakening Eastern nations;*

c. *Taking away, for the purpose of extermination or Germanization, infants born to Eastern workers in Germany;*

d. *Executing, imprisoning in concentration camps, or Germanizing Eastern workers and prisoners of war who had had sexual intercourse with Germans, and imprisoning the Germans involved;*

e. *Preventing marriages and hampering reproduction of enemy nationals.*

As is evident from these charges, the RuSHA Case covered a lot of ground, too much to cover in detail here. Yet one aspect is particularly worthy of exploration – the kidnap of children as part of an extension of the *Lebensborn* programme. In a speech at Bad Schachen in October

1943, Himmler acknowledged that the occupation had brought Germany into contact with a huge range of peoples and cultures, a fact that threw up some new possibilities for racial engineering:

Obviously in such a mixture of peoples there will always be some racially good types. Therefore I think that it is our duty to take their children with us, to remove them from their environment, if necessary by robbing or stealing them. Either we win over any good blood that we can use for ourselves and give it a place in our people or we destroy this blood.

RuSHA CASE VERDICTS	
Name	*Sentence*
Ulrich Greifelt	Life Imprisonment
Rudolf Creutz	15 Years Imprisonment
Konrad Meyer-Hetling	Acquitted & Released
Otto Schwarzenberger	Acquitted & Released
Herbert Hübner	15 Years Imprisonment
Werner Lorenz	15 Years Imprisonment
Heinz Brückner	15 Years Imprisonment
Otto Hofmann	25 Years Imprisonment
Richard Hildebrandt	25 Years Imprisonment
Fritz Schwalm	10 Years Imprisonment
Max Sollmann	Acquitted & Released
Gregor Ebner	Acquitted on two charges, convicted on the third but released for time served
Günther Tesch	Acquitted & Released
Inge Viermetz	Acquitted & Released

In terms of the options that Himmler presents in the last sentence, he obviously invested heavily in the latter. Yet his attempt to find 'good blood that we can use for ourselves' had terrible repercussions for thousands of children and their families from the Eastern occupied territories.

Following the occupation of Poland, the Baltic states and the Soviet Union, Himmler's RuSHA agents spread out through the territories, on the lookout for children who physically matched the Aryan ideal – blonde hair, blue eyes, strong physique. In an attempt to 'Germanize' these young people, they were literally kidnapped from their parents (the parents were themselves often destined for concentration camps). Orphans – of which there were plenty owing to the massive death toll amongst Eastern

European civilians – were another major source.

The numbers of children taken are hard to ascertain, as the records have either been destroyed, lost or not compiled in the first place. It is thought that up to 100,000 children from Poland alone were extracted, and tens of thousands from the Soviet territories. The total figure may be in the region of 250,000. Additional numbers were also taken from other parts of the occupied territories. Although the Germans utterly destroyed the village of Lidice in Czechoslovakia in 1942 (the reprisal action for the assassination of Reinhard Heydrich), for example, and killed most of its population, some 91 children were still selected for Germanization, and were sent back to infant camps in Germany.

Once in the hands of the Germans, the infants were to be

raised in SS homes or nurseries under strict educational guidelines. (While the majority of children went en masse into special SS-run centres, decent numbers were adopted directly by SS families. Those raised from babies would never know their origins.)

The word 'strict' was operative – in SS eyes the growing children had to have the contamination of their original parentage and upbringing worked out of them. Beatings were commonly administered to those children who, doubtless emotionally scarred by their fractured childhoods, displayed behavioural problems. In fact, an extremely high percentage of the children taken by the SS were ultimately sent on to extermination camps like so much troublesome garbage to be disposed of. At the end of the war, only 25,000 children were identified and sent back to their families. In a horrible twist to the story, many of the children had, indeed, had their characters reshaped by their SS education, and no longer fitted back into the societies from which they came.

The Final Solution

On 20 January 1942, the future of occupied Europe's already beleaguered Jews took an appalling turn. On that day, a small group of key Nazi officials attended a conference at a lakeside villa in the Berlin suburb of Wannsee; the conference was chaired by *SS-Obergruppenführer* Reinhard Heydrich, head of the *Reichssicherheitshauptamt* (RSHA; Reich Main Security Office). The previous July, Hermann Göring had issued a carefully crafted

Below: The ghetto system was integral to the Final Solution. When Einsatzgruppen moved into an urban area with a high concentration of Jews, a certain area of the city was sealed off by German forces and the Jewish people were relocated into a ghetto. Once in the ghetto, the Jews could be controlled more easily in terms of deporting them to the concentration and extermination camps, or liquidating them in batches in Einsatzgruppen operations. The horrible conditions inside the ghettos also added a daily attrition.

GHETTOS IN OCCUPIED EUROPE, 1939–45*

KEY
■ Ghetto established 1939–May 1941
■ Ghetto established June 1941–1943
■ Ghetto established 1944

* Shows 1939 borders

order to the RSHA to 'carry out all preparations with regard to organizational, factual and financial viewpoints for a total solution to the Jewish question in those territories in Europe under German influence'. The conference at Wannsee would define the new Nazi policy.

Minutes from the meeting at Wannsee were taken by SS officer Adolf Eichmann. These minutes essentially laid out a blueprint for mass murder. The core passage of the 'Wannsee Protocol' laid out a chilling future for the Jewish people:

Under proper guidance, in the course of the 'Final Solution', the Jews are to be allocated for appropriate labour in the East. Able-bodied Jews, separated according to sex, will be taken in large work columns to these areas for work on road, in the course of which a large portion will be eliminated by natural causes. The possible final remnant will, since it will undoubtedly consist of the most resistant portion, have to be treated accordingly, because it is the product of natural selection and would, if released, act as the seed of the new Jewish revival (see the

experience of history). In the course of the practical implementation of the 'Final Solution', Europe will be combed through from west to east.

Seen through the prism of subsequent history, and of events already in progress, the Wannsee Conference outlined two ghastly futures for the Jewish peoples of occupied territories – forced labour, which would in itself be a means of mass murder, and literal extermination.

Authority behind the Holocaust

Given that Hitler's signature is not directly on the Wannsee Protocol, to what extent can we say that the Holocaust was an integral part of his plan for Europe, and not the invention of the SS or other members of the Nazi bureaucracy? First, Hitler's racial views were an explicit driving force behind much of Nazi policy, and the language of extermination and expulsion was present in his writing and oratory back in the 1920s. In itself we must not overwork this point; such language was not uncommon in anti-Semitic writings of the nineteenth and early twentieth centuries, and should not necessarily be interpreted as an evolved plan.

Yet the fact remains that Hitler was the undoubted centre of authority in the Third Reich, and it is inconceivable that the Final Solution could have been designed or implemented without his fiat and approval. Numerous Nazi officials

WANNSEE CONFERENCE, 20 JANUARY 1942: PARTICIPANTS LISTED IN OFFICIAL MINUTES OF MEETING	
Participant	**Position/Department**
SS-Obergruppenführer Reinhard Heydrich	Chief of the RSHA and Reichsprotektor of Bohemia-Moravia
Dr Josef Bühler	Administration of the General Government
Dr Roland Freisler	Reich Ministry of Justice
SS-Gruppenführer Otto Hofmann	Race and Resettlement Main Office
SA-Oberführer Dr Gerhard Klopfer	NSDAP Chancellery
Ministerialdirektor Friedrich Wilhelm Kritzinger	Reich Chancellery
SS-Sturmbannführer Dr Rudolf Lange	Deputy Commander of the SS in Latvia
Reichsamtleiter Dr Georg Leibbrandt	Reich Ministry for the Occupied Eastern Territories
Dr Martin Luther	Foreign Office
Gauleiter Dr Alfred Meyer	Reich Ministry for the Occupied Eastern Territories
SS-Gruppenführer Heinrich Müller	Chief of Amt IV (Gestapo), Reich Main Security Office (RSHA)
Erich Neumann	Director, Office of the Four-Year Plan
SS-Oberführer Dr Karl Eberhard Schöngarth	SD, assigned to the General Government
Dr Wilhelm Stuckart	Reich Ministry for the Interior
SS-Obersturmbannführer Adolf Eichmann	Head of Referat IV B4 of the Gestapo, recording secretary

at the highest levels – including Göring, Himmler and Heydrich – plus legions of SS soldiers, security and police personnel, Nazi administrators, *Wehrmacht* soldiers and commanders were either direct participants in the Holocaust or witnesses to it; some commanders even made official complaints about the executions of Jews by *Einsatzgruppen* teams in the Soviet Union. The idea that such activity could have taken place without Hitler's assent has no credibility.

Camp system

Another important consideration is that by the time of the Wannsee Conference, the Holocaust was in fact already materializing, and not only in the horrifying activities of the *Einsatzgruppen*. The Nazi concentration camp system, for example, had reached huge proportions, with dozens of camps spread throughout Germany and the occupied territories.

Right: The Auschwitz II-Birkenau facility was essentially a factory of death, designed to 'process' thousands of people, from their arrival by train – note the close position of the railway platform to the gas chambers – to the disposal of their bodies in the crematoria near to the gas chambers. About 1.1 million Jews died inside the camp between 1941 and early 1945, some 90 per cent of them Jews from Eastern Europe. The first gassings there took place on 3 September 1941, and the first mass transports of Jews arrived in February 1942.

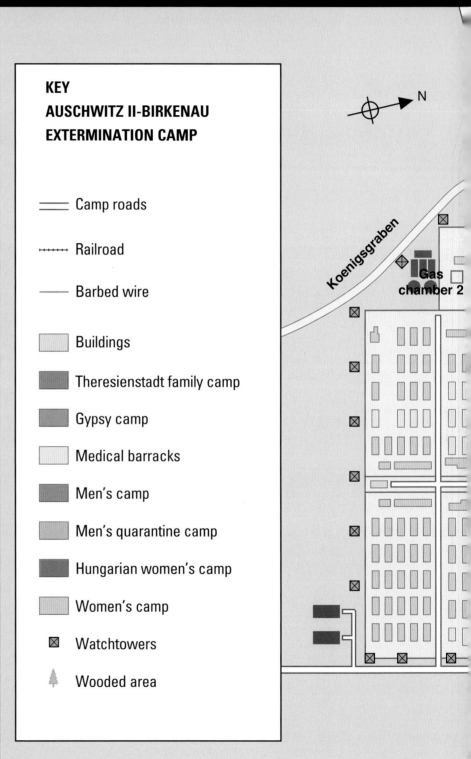

MAP OF AUSCHWITZ II-BIRKENAU

**KEY
AUSCHWITZ II-BIRKENAU
EXTERMINATION CAMP**

Camp roads

Railroad

Barbed wire

Buildings

Theresienstadt family camp

Gypsy camp

Medical barracks

Men's camp

Men's quarantine camp

Hungarian women's camp

Women's camp

Watchtowers

Wooded area

Koenigsgraben

Gas chamber 2

N

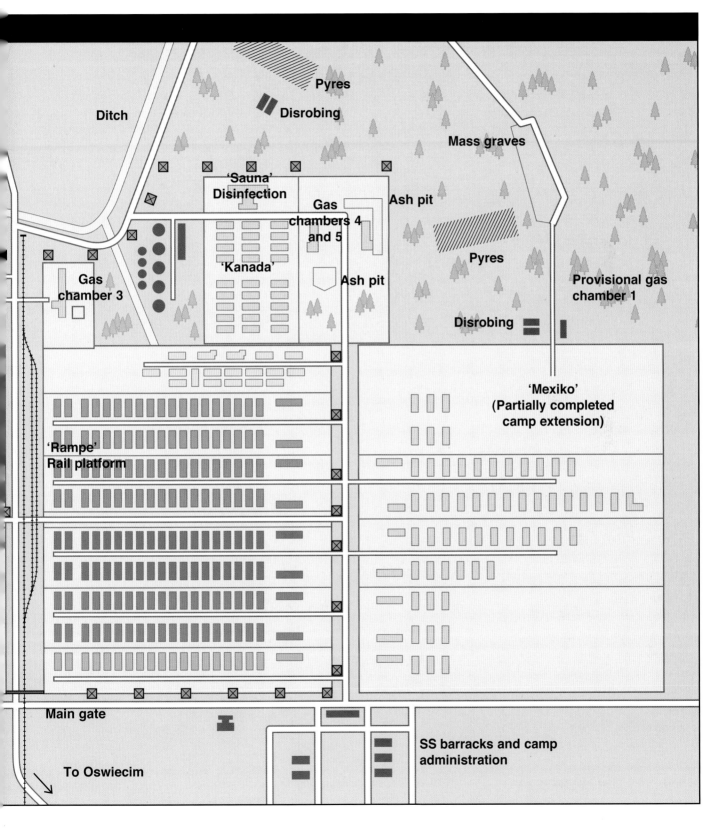

Pyres

Ditch

Disrobing

Mass graves

'Sauna'
Disinfection

Gas
chambers 4
and 5

Ash pit

'Kanada'

Ash pit

Pyres

Gas
chamber 3

Disrobing

Provisional gas
chamber 1

'Mexiko'
(Partially completed
camp extension)

'Rampe'
Rail platform

Main gate

SS barracks and camp
administration

To Oswiecim

The first camps were established at Dachau (the earliest, opened in March 1933), Oranienburg, Lichtenburg and Esterwegen shortly after the Nazis took power, initially intended for political prisoners. The number of people who fell under this category, however, grew ever wider – there were 50,000 inmates by 1939, and some 3.5 million Germans alone would have passed into the camp system by the end of the war, although many would not appear on the other side. By 1939 the numbers of Jews held in the camps were swelling by the month, incarcerated for little reason other than their faith or ethnic background, prisoners at the mercy of a regime stripping itself of mercy.

Nazi eugenics

Jewish people were not the only unfortunate objects of Hitler's racial derangement. Other hated groups included gypsies and homosexuals – both would also experience the Holocaust first-hand.

Hitler was also unsettled by the presence of the physically and mentally disabled. In *Mein Kampf*, he explains – using a cowardly language of pity – how such individuals needed to be genetically managed by the state:

Those who are physically and mentally unhealthy and unfit must not perpetuate their own suffering in the bodies of their children. From the educational point of view there is here a huge task for the People's State to accomplish. But in a future era this work will appear greater and more significant than the victorious wars of our present bourgeois epoch. Through educational means the State must teach individuals that illness is not a disgrace but an unfortunate accident which has to be pitied, yet that it is a crime and a disgrace to make this affliction all the worse by passing on disease and defects to innocent creatures out of mere egotism....

If for a period of only 600 years those individuals would be sterilized who are physically degenerate or mentally diseased, humanity would not only be delivered from an immense misfortune but also restored to a state of general health such as we at present can hardly imagine. If the fecundity of the healthy portion of the nation should be made a practical matter in a conscientious and methodical way, we should have at least the beginnings of a race from which all those germs would be eliminated which are to-day the cause of our moral and physical decadence.

– Hitler, *Mein Kampf*

In such views were the beginnings of the Nazi eugenics programme, the sickening attempt – based upon fantastical and racially motivated biological theory – that 'racial hygiene' could be achieved through a form of selective breeding.

The passage from *Mein Kampf* contains troubling hints at what was to come, directly suggesting sterilization and implicitly suggesting murder. In July 1933, the Nazis passed the 'Law for the Prevention of Offspring with Hereditary Illnesses', which resulted in the forced sterilization of perhaps 360,000 people. Those who fell foul of the law came under a broad range of categories, not only the mentally and physically disabled (which included sufferers from conditions such as epilepsy and schizophrenia) but even alcoholics or those with basic behavioural problems. In October 1935, the 'Law to Safeguard the Hereditary Health of the German People' further extended the remit of Hitler's doctors, legalizing abortion in cases where either the pregnant woman or the father were carrying hereditary diseases.

Underlying these laws was the implicit threat that sterilization and abortion could mutate into 'euthanasia' (a term used to mask the reality of murder). Hitler already had some spurious intellectual foundations for such a policy. Eugenics theory had burgeoned since the late 1800s, beginning in Britain and the United States but soon being co-opted by some German nationalists. A book entitled *The Permission to Destroy Life Unworthy of Life*, published by German university professors Alfred Hoche and Karl Binding in 1920, explicitly advocated killing those deemed genetically deficient.

Hitler and eugenics

Hitler more than embraced such ideas. According to post-1945 war crimes testimony, Hitler began discussing the outlines of a euthanasia programme with his officials as early as 1935. In the spring and summer of 1939 he began to translate these discussions into action. Through consultation with Philipp Bouhler and Karl Brandt, his chancellery director and physician respectively, Hitler planned out a programme by which certain doctors and medical staff would be given the authority to kill those mentally and physically disabled people who fell outside of Nazi racial guidelines.

At first, the killings were directed against disabled children. On the recommendations of Nazi medical staff, such children were selected for euthanasia and taken from their parents or guardians, usually by fooling them into thinking that the child was going to a special treatment centre.

In fact, the child would be killed by lethal injection, his or her demise typically listed on the records as caused by 'pneumonia'. In such a way, some 5000 children would meet their deaths. Making the action even more horrific, all medical staff who dealt with infants were obliged from August 1939 to report signs of physical and mental problems in children under three years old directly to the authorities.

Aktion T4

In September 1939, the euthanasia programme underwent a significant expansion. In a directive dated 1 September 1939, but signed by Hitler himself in October, the killing of vulnerable people was scaled up and extended to institutionalized adults. This new phase would be directed by Karl Brandt and Philipp Bouhler and was known as *Aktion T4* (Action T4). (The 'T4' referred to the project headquarters address – Tiergartenstraße 4 in Berlin.)

NAZI JUSTIFICATIONS FOR A EUTHANASIA PROGRAMME

The following excerpt is taken from Karl Bareth and Alfred Vogel, Erblehre und Rassenkunde für die Grund- und Hauptschule *(Heredity and Racial Science for Elementary and Secondary Schools), 2nd edition (Bühl-Baden: Verlag Konkordia, 1937). It was intended to explain to children why mentally or physically disabled people were a burden on the state.*

Hereditary illness places the state under a great burden: The cost to the state per day is:

- *For a normal pupil: 1/3 Reich Mark*
- *For a backward pupil: 11/2 Reich Marks*
- *For a mentally ill pupil: 24/5 Reich Marks*
- *For a blind or deaf pupil: 4 Reich Marks*

In 1932, one German city listed the following expenses:

- *A person on a small pension: 433 Reichmarks*
- *An unemployed person on welfare: 500 Reichmarks*
- *Costs for someone mentally ill: 1944 Reichmarks*

The total extra costs for caring for those hereditary illnesses in 1930 were about 1 billion Reich Marks, and 350 million Reich Marks went to handling such cases during the 1933/34 Winter Relief Program.

To protect the healthy population from the dangers of hereditary illness and weakness, the National Socialist State enacted the Law for the Prevention of Offspring with Hereditary Illnesses on 14 July 1933. Under this law, the genetically inferior are sterilized for the following diseases:

1. *Backward mentality*
2. *Schizophrenia*
3. *Manic depression*
4. *Epilepsy*
5. *St. Vitus' Dance*
6. *Blindness*
7. *Deafness*
8. *Major physical deformity*
9. *Severe alcoholism*

The intended scale of the killing would require new methods, and experiments were conducted using specially constructed gas chambers to kill numbers of people at a time. Six such gassing installations were created in Germany and Austria at Brandenburg, Grafeneck, Bernburg, Sonnenstein, Hartheim and Hadamar. Carbon monoxide gas was used, pumped into the room from running engines.

The scale of euthanasia

Aktion T4 ran from October 1939 until August 1941. During that time, tens of thousands of people were taken from government institutions and murdered, their families simply informed of the death when they received an urn full of ashes (the ashes were taken from a communal pile of cremated victims) and a death certificate.

Yet the programme was on such a scale, and affected so many people, it could not stay secret for long. Public awareness brought an outcry from the Church and other groups, and Hitler was eventually forced to call the programme to a halt. Yet it still continued in secret, particularly directed against children, and was also extended into occupied territories in the east, where it became a convenient tool for ridding the Reich of its 'political' enemies.

It is estimated that the Nazi euthanasia programme took the lives of 200,000 people. What is significant is that the events clearly show how Hitler willingly directed his racial views into an extermination policy. *Aktion T4* also provided the Nazis with practical experience that they would unleash on a far larger scale on the Jews themselves.

The *Lebensborn* programme

There existed, however, a very different side to the Nazi eugenics movement, known as the *Lebensborn* (Fount of Life) programme, established in December 1935. While much of Nazi racial policy was focused on removing 'undesirable' racial stock, *Lebensborn* was essentially a breeding and family support project, in which the best of SS manhood would procreate with Aryan women, thereby ensuring 'pure' bloodlines. The purposes of *Lebensborn* were spelt out by Himmler in a directive of 13 September 1936:

1. *Aid for racially and biologically-hereditarily valuable families.*
2. *The accommodation of racially and biologically hereditarily valuable mothers in appropriate homes, etc.*
3. *Care of the children of such families.*
4. *Care of the mothers.*

The women selected for the programme were not necessarily married – perpetuation not propriety was the goal of the programme – and in 1940 some 70 per cent of the mothers were unmarried. The pregnant women were cared for by the SS for the duration of their pregnancy. Once the children were born, they were taken into special SS nurseries, where they would be brought up as supposedly perfect representatives of German nationhood.

The *Lebensborn* programme was not Hitler's only policy designed to increase birth rates amongst the German people. In 1933, for example, the government introduced a marriage loan system, in which an average interest-free loan of 600 RM was paid to newlyweds, with a deduction of 25 per cent of the amount to be repaid for every child produced by the family. There were also several other financial incentives for having children, including systems of tax breaks. Medals and other awards were given to German mothers with large families.

Limitations

Yet Hitler's plan to encourage reproduction, and so ensure the future numbers of Aryan Germans, was mostly a failure. During the war years, German men went off in their millions to serve in the *Wehrmacht*, leaving one million single women and 5.4 million childless women by the end of 1939 alone. Furthermore, by the later war years women had been channelled heavily into working for key industries, leaving less time and inclination to build large families.

Perhaps because the limitations of German population were realized, the *Lebensborn* programme spread out from the confines of Germany and into the occupied countries of Western Europe and Poland. Apart from the 10 *Lebensborn* homes established in Germany, there were also nine in Norway, two in Austria and one each in Belgium, the Netherlands, France, Luxembourg and Denmark.

Holocaust

The Wannsee Conference formalized the industrial slaughter of occupied Europe's Jews. Even as Adolf Eichmann was writing down the minutes, the 'Final Solution' was already being enacted.

Within the *Einsatzgruppen*, concerns over the traumatic effects, and the apparent 'inefficiences', of close-quarters shootings led to the introduction of gas vans onto the Eastern Front in September 1941. Each van (a large lorry) featured a hermetically sealed cargo box, with the engine exhaust fumes directed into the box interior. Dozens of Jews at a time would be forced into the cargo box and the doors closed, then the van would drive from the place of collection to the location of body disposal – the people inside would be gassed to death over a 15-minute period by the carbon monoxide fumes. In the camps, the *Aktion T4* experience was utilized in gassing experiments at Auschwitz in Poland, also in September 1941, and mass killings by gas were conducted at Chelmno camp in December.

Yet it was between 1942 and 1945 that the full terror of the 'Final Solution' was unleashed. In addition to numerous pure labour camps, in which Jews and other

targeted groups (such as Soviet POWs) were starved, tortured and worked to death in their hundreds of thousands, six major extermination camps were established in occupied Poland: Auschwitz-Birkenau (Auschwitz II), Belzec, Chelmno, Majdanek, Sobibor and Treblinka.

These were literally factories of death. Jews would be transported

by rail from across the occupied Reich according to carefully planned timetables. Days or even weeks on a train without food or water killed many, but on arrival, those who were still alive would – in pure extermination camps such as Chelmno – be immediately dispossessed of their belongings, stripped naked and sent to the gas

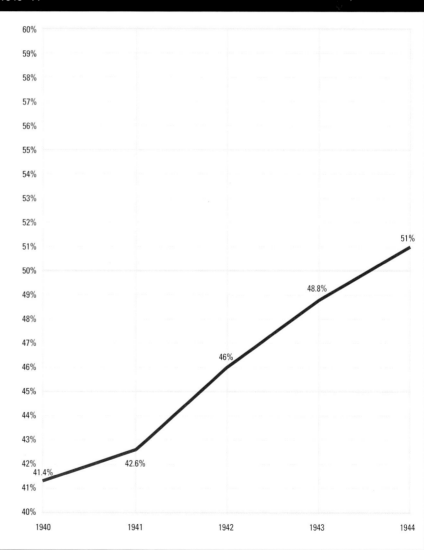

PERCENTAGE OF GERMAN FEMALES AS PART OF TOTAL WORKFORCE, 1940–44

LOCATIONS OF MAJOR CONCENTRATION AND EXTERMINATION CAMPS, 1939–45*

KEY
■ Extermination camps
■ Concentration camps

ESTONIA
Klooga
Vaivara

LATVIA
Kaiserwald

LITHUANIA
Kaunas
Vilnius

Maly Trostenets

Stutthof

Neuengamme   Ravensbrück
Papenburg   Sachsenhausen   Plaszów   Treblinka   POLAND
                                                WARSAW
Belsen   BERLIN   Chelmno   Sobibór
AMSTERDAM   Arbeitsdorf   Lvov   Belzec
                                            Majdanek
Breendonk   Dora-Mittelbau   Schileben   Lvov
BRUSSELS   Auschwitz-Birkenau
             Buchenwald   PRAGUE
Drancy   Ohrdruf   Lety   Hodonín
PARIS   GERMANY   Flossenbürg   Novaky
Natzweiler   VIENNA   Sered
          Dachau   Mauthausen   Kistarcsa
Landsberg   Nartheim   BUDAPEST

                                    HUNGARY   ROMANIA

          Bolzano
FRANCE   Jasenovac
                                        Sajmiste
          Asti   Schabatz
                                            Nisch
Le Vernet   ITALY   Banjica

* Shows 1939 borders

chambers and murdered. In mixed labour/extermination camps such as Auschwitz, SS 'doctors' would decide who would go to be worked to death, and who would go straight to the gas chambers – the latter group typically included children, women with dependent children and the old and sick. The process reached literally industrial levels of efficiency, and at its maximum capacity the camp system was killing thousands of Jews a day, every single day.

A detailed account of the Holocaust is impossible here, and has been recounted in many other sources. By the time the camps were shut down, either by panicking German guards in late 1944 or 1945, or by Allied liberation, six

ESTIMATED PERCENTAGE OF JEWISH POPULATION KILLED, BY COUNTRY

Country	Percentage
Austria	35%
Belgium	45%
Bohemia-Moravia	60%
Bulgaria	0%
Denmark	0.8%
Estonia	44%
Finland	0.3%
France	22%
Germany	93%
Greece	87%
Hungary	74%
Italy	17%
Latvia	84%
Lithuania	85%
Luxembourg	55%
Netherlands	71%
Norway	45%
Poland	91%
Romania	84%
Slovakia	80%
USSR	36%
Yugoslavia	81%

Left: The German concentration camps were located mainly in Germany and Poland, although there were camps as far west as France and Belgium, and as far south as Italy and the Balkans. The pure extermination camps were located exclusively in Poland, where they could more effectively dispose of the Jews of Poland and Eastern Europe and were hidden from the eyes of the regular German population. Most of the other concentration camps were labour camps, although mass executions did take place there, and the labour and living conditions were so severe that they killed hundreds of thousands of people without the need for bullets or gas.

million Jews had been murdered. In addition, some 3.5 million of the 5.7 million Soviet POWs had also been starved or worked to death, or executed. In the annals of history, murder has scarcely ever reached such intensity.

Total annihilation

Taking all the evidence together, Hitler's ultimate goal appears to have been the entire eradication of occupied Europe's Jews, in fulfilment of his racial theory. Some countries virtually experienced this end state – Poland, for example, lost 3 million of its 3.3 million Jews to the Holocaust, and the 650,000-strong Jewish population of Hungary was reduced to 200,000 in a few frenzied months of killing in 1944. We cannot tell if Hitler would have

achieved his ultimate goal had he not been defeated in the war. Even based on the numbers the Nazis did murder, some historians believe that today's world Jewish population is about half of what it would have been if the Holocaust had not been perpetrated. Given the sheer volume of people the extermination camps could 'process' each day by 1943 and 1944, it appears likely that Europe could have been virtually emptied of Jewish people by the late 1940s or the 1950s.

On the route to destruction, the Jews were employed as free labour, in what became a huge commercial enterprise for Himmler's SS and many major German industrial concerns. Industries and plants supported by slave labour came to include brickworks, stoneworks, quarries and mines, porcelain and pottery factories, armaments production, food production, textiles and leatherworking. The profits from these enterprises are uncertain, and would have been higher if there had not been such high mortality amongst the workers, but they are certain to have been in the hundreds of millions of Reichsmarks.

The deeply unpleasant persistence of Holocaust denial amongst small groups of neo-Nazis today flies in the face of an overwhelming body of documentary, photographic and personal evidence. As we have seen, there is plentiful evidence to show that the full depth of the Nazi regime, including Hitler at the top, was implicated in this terrible crime.

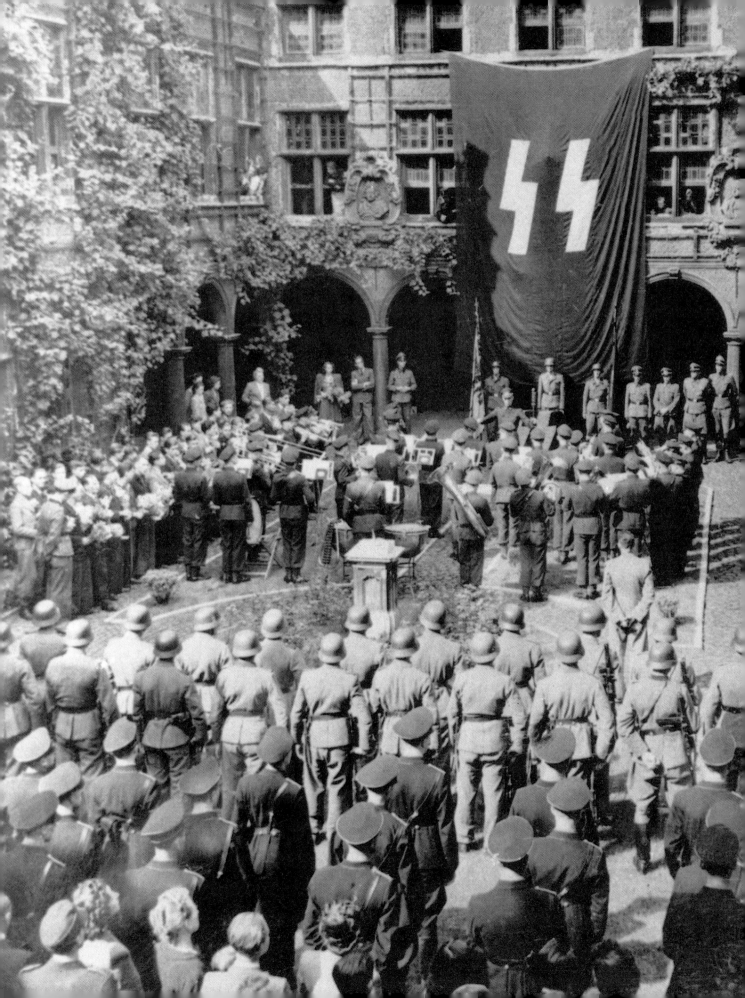

Servants of the Reich

Hitler's plans for Europe, and the world,
were not feasible without a vast army of willing
(or at least compliant) helpers.

Outside the conventional armed forces,
the Nazis therefore established powerful organizations
to manage the affairs of the Third Reich, and watch over the
citizens of Germany and the occupied territories.

As the war went on, furthermore,
foreign workers, soldiers, police and auxiliaries
would become increasingly central to keeping
the war effort running.

Left: New SS recruits parade in Brussels, summer 1944. As the SS expanded its numbers, foreign volunteers were used to fill the ranks. More than 40,000 Belgians joined the SS, mainly to fight on the Eastern Front.

The SA

The Nazi Party had a paramilitary undercurrent from its earliest days. Politics during the Weimar era was a rough-and-ready business, and each political organization needed muscular support if it was to survive in a frequently violent environment.

For Hitler's NSDAP, that muscle initially came in the form of politically committed *Freikorps*, but in 1921 these elements were formalized as the *Sturmabteilung* (SA; Storm Detachment). Like the later SS, the SA was essentially a thuggish paramilitary formation with a military-type structure, including its own versions of regiments, battalions, companies and sections. From 1930 Hitler resided at the head of the SA, but the chief of staff below him had practical command, an authority that the organization would later pay for in blood. The group had its own distinctive, and eventually infamous, brown uniform that earned the SA the nickname 'Brownshirts'.

By 1931 the SA numbered 100,000 members, but it was about to be transformed under a new chief of staff, Ernst Röhm. A large, scarred and ebullient character, Röhm had been involved with the SA and the NSDAP since their earliest days, and had been a participant in the failed Beer Hall Putsch of 1923, after which he was imprisoned. He was soon released, and with a ban on the SA in place in Bavaria he maintained the group under an alternative name, the *Frontbann* (Front Unit). Yet Röhm steadily began to pull in a different direction to Hitler. He wanted an anarchic, violent, revolutionary organization, whereas Hitler had committed himself after 1923 to the legal and presentable takeover of power. Röhm felt increasingly at odds with the NSDAP leadership, and left Germany in 1928 to serve as a military advisor to the Bolivian Army.

The SA grew increasingly belligerent in nature, and Röhm was summoned back as chief of staff in 1931 to bring some order. Röhm now transformed the power of the SA. Membership certainly grew significantly – by August 1934 it numbered 2.9 million, up from around 400,000 members just two years previously. In fact, the SA was growing a little too powerful for Hitler's comfort. The organization saw itself as an alternative power to the *Reichswehr*, a tendency that troubled German military leaders, whom Hitler wanted to keep on his side.

Moreover, once Hitler came to power in 1933, the SA leadership began to fear that they would now be sidelined, particularly with the growth of the SS (see below), and that the 'revolution' would be allowed to dissipate. In June 1933, Röhm even stated that 'The SA and SS will not tolerate the German revolution going to sleep or betrayed at the halfway stage by non-combatants.' Violent attacks by the SA continued, not just on Jewish people or communist supporters, but even on *Reichswehr* personnel. When Röhm began to mutter about the possibility of merging the SA with the *Reichswehr* to create a new 'People's Army', and bring about a 'second revolution', it was a step too far for Hitler.

PERSONS HOLDING THE RANK OF *OBERSTER SA-FÜHRER* (*CHEF DES STABES* FROM 1930)	
Name	Period
Emil Maurice	1920–21
Hans Ulrich Klintzsche	1921–23
Hermann Göring	1923
No OSAF	1923–25
Franz Pfeffer von Salomon	1926–30
Adolf Hitler	1930–31
Ernst Röhm	1931–34
Viktor Lutze	1934–43
Wilhelm Scheppmann	1943–45

SA MEMBERSHIP, 1930–39

December 1930	about 100,000
January 1932	about 400,000
August 1934	2.9 million
April 1939	1.2 million

In June 1934, on Hitler's direct orders, the SS were unleashed in a coordinated 48-hour operation to exterminate the SA leadership. During those two days, 600 key members of the SA were arrested and executed, including Röhm himself, shot dead in Dachau concentration camp. The 'Blood Purge' did not destroy the SA, but it crushed its revolutionary aspirations. Membership declined, not least because the establishment and growth of the *Wehrmacht* pulled men away into regular military service, while the SS under Himmler grew to be the dominant political army of the NSDAP. During the war years, SA personnel were used on security and training duties, but from 1934 they were never in a position again to challenge Hitler's authority. The case of the SA illustrates how Hitler's political priorities changed over time. The bullish and violent tendencies of the SA worked well during the scrappy early days of Hitler's political career, but they did not fit in with his rise to statesman.

The SS

Of all the organizations within Hitler's Third Reich, the SS remains one of the most historically notorious. Its crimes against humanity were legion and ranged from running the *Einsatzgruppen* death squads in the Soviet Union through to administering and delivering the Holocaust.

Like the SA that it eventually subjugated, the SS laid its foundations during the early days

REINHARD HEYDRICH

Left: Reinhard Heydrich, head of the Reich Security Main Office, was, along with Heinrich Himmler and Adolf Eichmann, one of the chief architects of the Holocaust. His assassination in the summer of 1942 led to horrifying reprisals, including the obliteration of the entire village of Lidice in Czechoslovakia, in which SS soldiers killed 172 men and boys and sent the women and children to their deaths in the concentration camps.

Birth:	7 March 1904
Death:	4 June 1942 (following assassination attempt on 27 May 1942)
Place of birth:	Halle, near Leipzig
Father:	Richard Bruno Heydrich
Mother:	Elisabeth Anna Maria Amalia Heydrich (née Kranz)
Education:	Reform-Realgymnasium; also joined the Maracker Freikorps in 1914
Military service:	Joined German Navy in 1922, forced to resign his commission in 1931 for 'conduct unbecoming an officer and a gentleman'
Nazi Party positions:	Member of the NSDAP (1931)
	Member of the SS (1931)
	Head of the SD (1932)
	Heinrich Himmler's deputy (1933)
	Head of Reich Central Office for Jewish Emigration 1939)
	Head of the Reich Security Main Office (RHSA) (1939)
	Deputy Reich Protector of Bohemia and Moravia (1941)

of the NSDAP. Its root was the *Stabswache* (Headquarters Guard), formed in 1923 as a bodyguard unit for the Nazi leadership. This in turn was replaced by the *Stoßtruppe Adolf Hitler* (Shock Troop Adolf Hitler), which included men who would become powerful figures in the later growth of the Nazi Party, including Rudolf Hess, Josef 'Sepp' Dietrich and Ulrich Graf. This small unit (it probably numbered less than 20 men) was disbanded after the failure of the Beer Hall Putsch, but once Hitler returned to the political scene in 1925 he sought to create a more permanent formation. This came in the form of the SS, a bodyguard force loyal directly to Hitler himself, rather than the Nazi Party per se. Sensing a potential conflict between the SA and the SS, Hitler deliberately kept the SS small to placate the SA leadership – by 1929 its membership numbered around 1000. This bred low morale amongst the SS personnel, as did the fact that the SS men had to receive orders from local SA commanders. Nevertheless, Hitler emphasized the importance of the SS character, each man having to display a total loyalty to National Socialist ideals and a rigorous self-discipline.

The transformation of the SS from small political force to Hitler's second army began in effect in 1929, when it came under the leadership of Nazi bureaucrat Heinrich Himmler. With Hitler's approval, Himmler expanded the membership levels and influence of the SS, attracting new members through an emphasis on the organization's elite status, helped by a striking black uniform and the chilling death's head badge. Hitler's ascent to the chancellorship in 1933 also gave a huge boost to SS membership, taking it to a strength of 204,000 by the end of that year. Once the SA was subdued by the 'Blood Purge', the SS remained as the central paramilitary body of Hitler's regime. Yet this was just the beginning of its reign.

Allgemeine-SS

To understand the power the SS attained, it is best to examine it in its two main constituent parts: the *Allgemeine-SS* (General SS), which was essentially its administrative component; and what became the *Waffen-SS* (Armed SS), the combat wing. Both sides of the SS were integral to fulfilling Hitler's visions, and almost to the very last weeks of the war they offered their *Führer* unwavering loyalty.

The *Allgemeine-SS* consisted of full- or part-time members, and dealt with administrative, economic, legal, racial, intelligence, security and personnel issues. It was at the height of its powers during the 1930s, after which the *Waffen-SS* naturally took a more central role because of its direct involvement in the wartime fighting. Nevertheless, the authority of the *Allgemeine-SS* remained considerable, and this sprawling organization came to control interests ranging from the police and security services through

to the concentration camp system. In terms of overall structure, the *Allgemeine-SS* came to be arranged into *SS-Oberabschnitte* (Senior Districts), territorial commands that roughly corresponded to the *Wehrkreis* (Military District) administrative system used by the German armed forces. At the organization's peak extent in 1944, there were 17 *Oberaschnitte* in Germany and six in the occupied territories. These districts were in turn divided into *Abschnitte* (Administrative Districts), then into *Standarten* (Regiments) that could number anywhere from 400 to 2000 men. The further subdivisions of the SS regiment were the *Sturmbanne* (Storm Units), *Stürme* (Companies), *Züge* or *Truppe* (Platoons or Troops), then finally the smaller elements, the *Scharen* (Sections) and *Rotten* (Files).

Such was the core hierachical organization of the *Allgemeine-SS*, and presiding over both the *Allgemeine-SS* and the *Waffen-SS* until the last acts of the war was Heinrich Himmler, the *Reichsführer-SS* (RFSS), served by an extensive personal staff organization that provided administrative services for Himmler but also conducted key policy research. (During the war years, the staff organization also aided Himmler in his military leadership roles, and came to include combat elements.) Beneath Himmler was a broad range of SS main command offices, each with responsibility for a particular aspect of SS life. These came to include

STRENGTH OF THE *ALLGEMEINE-SS*, 1938

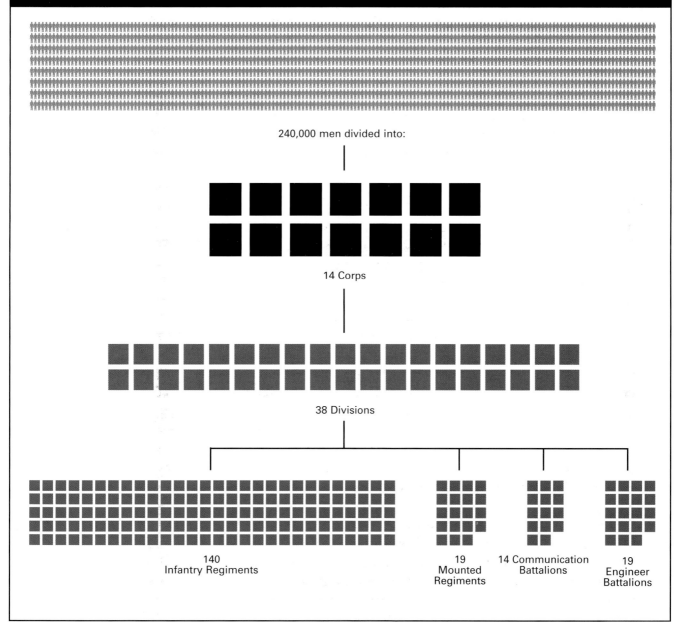

240,000 men divided into:

14 Corps

38 Divisions

140
Infantry Regiments

19
Mounted
Regiments

14 Communication
Battalions

19
Engineer
Battalions

the security, police and intelligence services of the Third Reich, studied in more detail below, but a few other departments and special interests are worth discussion.

Major administrative departments included the *SS-Hauptamt* (SS Main Office), which was essentially the bureaucratic heart of the SS, and the *Hauptamt SS-Gericht* (Main SS Legal Office). The latter was the SS legal body, and it came to establish internal courts and legal officials in every *Oberabschnitt*. An important effect of this body was that by internalizing legal processes, it effectively placed SS personnel outside the rule of civilian law, something that was important for the SS given the scale of its human rights violations.

In terms of developing Hitler's racial policies, the *SS-Rasse- und Siedlungshauptamt* (RuSHA; SS Race and Settlement Office) oversaw issues of 'racial purity' within the SS, conducting background checks into the ancestries of SS applicants and their families. During the war period, the RuSHA was also involved in resettling Germans in the eastern territories, brutally ordering the expulsion of native families to make way for the new occupiers. SS organizations similarly involved in the brutalities of resettlement and colonization included the *Hauptamt des Reichskommissars für die Festigung deutschen Volkstums* (RKFDV; Main Office of the Reich Commissioner for the Strengthening of the German Nation) and the *Hauptamt Volksdeutsche Mittelstelle* (VoMI; Main Office for the Assistance of Ethnic Germans), both of which were concerned with reintegrating ethnic Germans into the life of the Reich.

The SS came to be an organization with very extensive economic interests, and within the *Allgemeine-SS* these were the responsibility of the *SS-Wirtschafts- und Verwaltungshauptamt* (WVHA; Economics and Administrative Department). The range of its commercial activities is suggested by the five main departments into which it was ordered:

Amt A – Finance, law and
        administration
Amt B – Supply, administration
        and equipment
Amt C – Works and buildings
Amt D – Concentration camps
Amt W – Economics

By 1943, companies directly under SS ownership or authority, or private companies 'assisted' by the SS (such as the mighty IG Farben chemical conglomerate, which had a major factory at Auschwitz), were turning over millions of RM every year. The activities pursued

included publishing, mining, textile production, fishing and food production. Also, the use of slave labour in the concentration camp system went towards fulfilling Nazi racial policy and the 'Final Solution'. Not only did the personal possessions, including clothing and even gold teeth, of murdered Jews pass into SS coffers, but even human hair was utilized in cloth manufacture.

Mention of the concentration camps leads us to the most unpalatable aspect of the *Allgemeine-SS* – its provision of guards for these institutions. Known as the *SS-Totenkopfverbände* (SS-TV; SS Death's Head Formations), they were under the authority of the *Inspektion der Konzentrationslager* (Concentration Camps Inspectorate) created by the notorious Theodor Eicke, the former commandant of Dachau.

Originally the guards were known as the *SS-Wachverband* (Guard Unit), but the SS-TV took

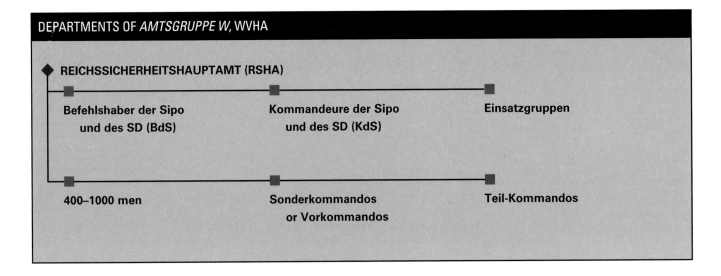

DEPARTMENTS OF *AMTSGRUPPE W,* WVHA

REICHSSICHERHEITSHAUPTAMT (RSHA)

Befehlshaber der Sipo und des SD (BdS)	Kommandeure der Sipo und des SD (KdS)	Einsatzgruppen
400–1000 men	Sonderkommandos or Vorkommandos	Teil-Kommandos

its more threatening appellation in June 1934. Although the *Totenkopfverbände* did go on to provide personnel for *Waffen-SS* combat formations, including the *SS-Division Totenkopf*, the name is forever associated with the atrocities committed in the camps.

Waffen-SS

The *Waffen-SS* was in theory Hitler's personal army, an ideologically indoctrinated military force directly loyal to him. Armed formations of the SS emerged in the early 1930s, but the main forerunner of the *Waffen-SS* was the *SS-Verfügungstruppe*

(SS-VT; SS Special Use Troops), formed in 1934 and consciously separated from the *Allgemeine-SS*. From 1935, the SS-VT was arranged into familiar battalion and regimental structures, making it evident that it was to operate as a supplementary military force to the

---

HEINRICH HIMMLER

Above: Heinrich Himmler was essentially an administrator and bureaucrat, who oversaw the Holocaust and the actions of the SS without mercy. Ironically, he was unable to stomach SS killings when he actually witnessed them, and his abilities as a military commander at the end of the war were shown to be woefully inadequate.

Birth:	*7 October 1900*
Death:	*23 May 1945 (suicide)*
Place of birth:	*Munich*
Father:	*Joseph Gebhard Himmler*
Mother:	*Anna Maria Himmler (née Heyder)*
Siblings:	*Gebhard Ludwig Himmler (b. 1898); Ernst Hermann Himmler (b. 1905)*
Personal relationships:	*Margarete Siegroth, married 3 July 1928. One daughter (Gudrun) in 1929; later adopted a son. Separated (without divorce) in 1940. Hedwig Potthast, became Himmler's mistress from 1941. Two children: son (Helge) in 1942; daughter (Nanette Dorothea) in 1944*
Military service:	*11th Infantry Regiment (Bavarian) (1917–18)*
Education:	*Munich Technical College (1919–22), where he studied agronomy*
Key pre-war positions, 1918–39:	*NSDAP member (c.1923)*
	Deputy Reichsführer-SS (1927)
	Reichsführer-SS (1929)
	Head of Gestapo (1934)
	Chief of German Police (1936)
Key wartime positions:	*Reichskommissar für die Festigung deutschen Volkstums (Reich Commissioner for the Strengthening of the German Nation) (1939)*
	German Interior Minister (1943)
	Commander-in-Chief of Ersatzheer (Replacement Army) (1944)
	Commander-in-Chief of Heeresgruppe Oberrhein (Army Group Upper Rhine) (1944)
	Commander-in-Chief of Heeresgruppe Weichsel (Army Group Vistula) (1945)

PEAK STRENGTH FIGURES OF WAFFEN-SS DIVISIONS 1–12

1st SS-Panzer Division *Leibstandarte SS Adolf Hitler*
22,100 (Dec 1944)

2nd SS-Panzer Division *Das Reich*
20,100 (Jun 1944)

3rd SS-Panzer Division *Totenkopf*
21,115 (Jun 1944)

4th SS-Police Panzergrenadier Division
16,100 (Jun 1944)

5th SS-Panzer Division *Wiking*
19,300 (Jun 1944)

6th SS-Mountain Division *Nord*
21,300 (Dec 1944)

7th SS-Volunteer Mountain Division *Prinz Eugen*
21,100 (Dec 1943)

8th SS-Cavalry Division *Florian Geyer*
12,900 (Jun 1944)

9th SS-Panzer Division *Hohenstaufen*
19,611 (Dec 1943)

10th SS-Panzer Division *Frundsberg*
19,300 (Dec 1943)

11th SS-Volunteer Panzergrenadier Division *Nordland*
11,740 (Jun 1944)

12th SS-Panzer Division *Hitlerjugend*
21,500 (Dec 1943)

regular army. Hitler made it clear to the armed forces that the SS-VT was in no way intended as a future replacement for the army, but rather as a body that would give the NSDAP the authority of a warrior organization. Nevertheless, suspicion and near hostility between *Waffen-SS* and *Wehrmacht* formations was common. The *Wehrmacht* saw the SS as political fanatics drawing away soldiers from regular military service, while the SS classed themselves as an elite force separate from the common ranks of the German Army. Note, however, that a series of directives issued in 1938 placed the *Waffen-SS* formations under the overall control of the *Wehrmacht* – even Hitler realized that in a war zone it was pointless to have the *Waffen-SS* pursuing independent objectives. The only exception to this rule was if *Waffen-SS* units were used to combat internal threats

Right: Foreign volunteers serving in the *Wehrmacht*, the *Kriegsmarine* and the *Waffen-SS* came from almost every country in occupied Europe, as well as from Allied nations and from neutrals like Sweden and Switzerland. By the end of the war over half of the *Waffen-SS* was non-German.

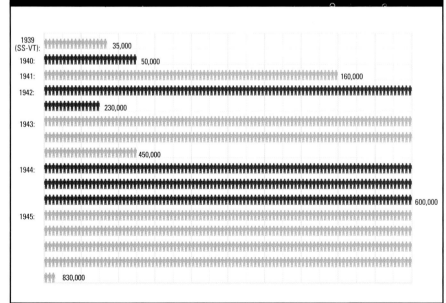

TOTAL NUMBERS IN WAFFEN-SS SERVICE, 1939–45

1939 (SS-VT): 35,000
1940: 50,000
1941: 160,000
1942: 230,000
1943: 450,000
1944: 600,000
1945: 830,000

FOREIGN RECRUITS TO WAFFEN-SS BY COUNTRY

FINLAND
c.3000

NORWAY
c.6000

ESTONIA
c.25,000

SWEDEN
c.300

LATVIA
c.80,000

DENMARK
c.10,000

SOVIET UNION
c.60,000+

GREAT BRITAIN
c.50

NETHERLANDS
c.50,000

GERMANY

BELGIUM
c.40,000

LUX.
c.2000

FRANCE
c.20,000

SWITZ.
c.300?

HUNGARY
c.20,000

ROMANIA
c.50,000

ITALY
c.15,000

YUGOSLAVIA
c.30,000

BULGARIA
c.600

SPAIN
c.1000

ALBANIA
c.7000

within Germany, in which case Himmler would take control.

Elements of the SS-VT were used in the invasion of Poland in September 1939, and the next year the combat units of the SS finally became the *Waffen-SS*. The organization would grow from a handful of regiments in 1939 to a force of 38 divisions and 830,000 men. It constituted a significant portion of German fighting strength, and its infantry, Panzer and Panzergrenadier formations (particularly those formed during the 1930s and early 1940s) generally acquired a strong fighting reputation on all fronts. Standards of training for the first three years of the war were high, with an emphasis on aggression and realism, plus the development of an extreme esprit d'corps.

At the same time, however, the *Waffen-SS*'s ideological foundations often expressed themselves in brutality and war crimes. At Wormhoudt, France, on 28 May 1940, soldiers from the *Leibstandarte SS Adolf Hitler* regiment murdered 80 British and French POWs. Far worse was to come, including the murder of 642 men, women and children in the French town of Oradour-sur-Glane on 10 June 1944 by the 2nd SS-Panzer Division *Das Reich*. During the crushing of the Warsaw Uprising in August to October 1944,

DIVISIONAL STRENGTH OF FOREIGN OR PART-FOREIGN WAFFEN-SS DIVISIONS, 1945

5th SS-Panzer Division *Wiking*	14,800
6th SS-Mountain Division *Nord*	15,000
7th SS-Volunteer Mountain Division *Prinz Eugen*	20,000
8th SS-Cavalry Division *Florian Geyer*	13,000
11th SS-Volunteer Panzergrenadier Division *Nordland*	9000
13th *Waffen* Mountain Division of the SS *Handschar* (Croatian No 1)	12,700
14th *Waffen* Grenadier Division of the SS *Galizien* (Ukrainian No 1)	22,000
15th Waffen Grenadier Division of the SS (Latvian No 1)	16,800
18th SS-Volunteer Panzergrenadier Division *Horst Wessel*	11,000
19th *Waffen* Grenadier Division of the SS (Latvian No 2)	9000
20th *Waffen* Grenadier Division of the SS (Estonian No 1)	15,500
21st Waffen-Mountain Division of the SS *Skanderberg* (Albanian No.1)	5000
22nd SS-Volunteer Cavalry Division *Maria Theresia*	8000
23rd *Waffen* Mountain Division of the SS *Kama* (Croatian No 2)	c.5000
23rd SS-Volunteer Panzergrenadier Division *Nederland* (Netherlands No 1)	6000
24th *Waffen* Mountain Division of the SS *Karstjäger*	3000
25th *Waffen* Grenadier Division of the SS *Hunyadi* (Hungarian No 1)	15,000
26th *Waffen* Grenadier Division of the SS *Hungaria* (Hungarian No 2)	13,000
27th SS-Volunteer Grenadier Division *Langemarck* (Flemish No 1)	7000
28th SS-Volunteer Grenadier Division *Wallonien* (Walloon No 1)	4000
29th *Waffen* Grenadier Division of the SS *Italien* (Italian No 1)	15,000
29th *Waffen* Grenadier Division of the SS (Russian No 1)	not known
30th *Waffen* Grenadier Division of the SS (Russian No 2)	4500
30th *Waffen* Grenadier Division of the SS *Weißruthenische*	not known
31st SS-Volunteer Grenadier Division *Böhmen-Mähren*	11,000
33rd *Waffen* Cavalry Division (Hungarian No 3)	not known
33rd *Waffen* Grenadier Division of the SS *Charlemagne* (French No 1)	7000
34th SS-Volunteer Grenadier Division *Landstorm Nederland* (N/lands No 2)	7000
36th *Waffen* Grenadier Division *Dirlewanger*	8000
37th SS-Volunteer Cavalry Division *Lützow*	not known

admittedly low-grade *Waffen-SS* units participated in the killing of an estimated 200,000 civilians, in the most appalling ways. Few SS soldiers were ever penalized for such barbarities.

Foreign servants

What is particularly interesting about the *Waffen-SS* is the way in which it illustrates the hollowness of Nazi racial theory. As the war continued, the overwhelming pressures on German manpower meant that even the SS decided to open its doors to foreign soldiers, including those from occupied nations. Some of these inclusions caused little controversy. The concept of including 'Germanic' (Scandinavian or Northern European) volunteers in the *Waffen-SS* had been discussed by Hitler and Himmler even prior to World War II. Himmler had greater dreams of Nordic unity than Hitler, and envisaged a collaborationist Nordic empire led by the SS.

There were some grounds for recruiting soldiers from Western occupied countries. Most European states had some degree of fascist political life, and Belgium, Holland, Norway and Denmark all had their own fascist parties. Following the campaigns in Western Europe in 1940, the first steps were taken to recruit willing and ideologically conformist collaborators. In 1940–41, the first SS division recruited from foreign volunteers was created, the 5th SS-Panzer Division *Wiking* (Viking), which included in its ranks Scandinavian, Finnish, Estonian, Dutch and Belgian volunteers, commanded by German officers. Indeed, Western European contributions to the *Waffen-SS* show how Hitler's ideas of a pan-Germanic empire might have seemed well founded – the Netherlands alone provided 50,000 recruits for *Waffen-SS* service, Belgium provided 40,000, France 20,000 (of 40,000 volunteers in total), Italy 15,000, Denmark 10,000 and Norway 6000. Even Spain, which was supposedly neutral, provided enough volunteers to create, in 1941, an entire division (the 250th Infantry Division, or 'Blue

FOREIGN RECRUITS TO WAFFEN-SS, BY COUNTRY

Albania	7000
Belgium	40,000
Bulgaria	600
Denmark	10,000
Estonia	25,000
Finland	3000
France	20,000
GB	50
Hungary	20,000
Italy	15,000
Latvia	80,000
Luxembourg	2000
Netherlands	50,000
Norway	6000
Romania	50,000
Soviet Union	60,000
Spain	1000
Sweden	300
Switzerland	300
Yugoslavia	30,000

Division'), although that formation dispersed in 1943.

Such foreign resources were encouraging, but from 1942 Himmler and Hitler also began to debate the merits of incorporating Eastern Europeans into the ranks of the Waffen-SS. Here was delicate ground, as the Nazis' racial views on many Eastern ethnicities were not favourable. Yet the presence of fascist elements in Eastern Europe, and anti-Stalin sentiments amongst large swathes of the Soviet population (such as the Cossacks and Kalmyks), meant that the possibilities for significant expansions in auxiliary and combat manpower were real.

The Wehrmacht was actually the first force to use Soviet manpower, creating Hilfswillige (Volunteer Assistant, or 'Hiwi') auxiliary support units made up of Soviet deserters, civilians or volunteer POWs. In the Baltic States, the SS had also discovered that many anti-Semitic locals (including police forces) had actively participated in denouncing and murdering Jews, including assisting with the Einsatzgruppen operations. Steadily the contributions of Osttruppen (East Troops) swelled, including forming entire armed battalions for anti-partisan operations, and eventually some one million Soviets would work for the Third Reich, with wildly varying degrees of willingness.

From 1943, the Waffen-SS had also come to terms with its own racial issues and began recruiting Eastern Europeans (including people from the Balkans) and Soviets to form new 'legions' and divisions. The ethnicities of the new divisions included Belorussians, Russians, Cossacks, Latvians, Croatians, Bosnian Muslims, Hungarians and Albanians.

The manpower contributions were likely to have exceeded 200,000, but the soldiers' performance in combat frequently left a lot to be desired, reflecting their mixed loyalties. In fairness, they were often poorly armed and trained, and suffered disastrous levels of casualties. The Galizien (Galicia) Division, for example, formed in 1943, was almost entirely destroyed at the battle of Brody in June 1944, with 80 per cent casualties. Such formations were also frequently involved in war crimes, using the authority of the SS to settle ethnic scores within their own territories, often under the mask of anti-partisan operations.

Although it had been Himmler's, and to a lesser degree Hitler's, plan to develop an international SS army, the reality was that loyalty to the Nazis was partial. Many foreign units fought for the Germans until the very end of the war, but only because as turncoats they faced the wrath of their home nations if Germany were defeated. Yet there remains the possibility that had Hitler's armies treated the populations of the occupied eastern territories better, the numbers of foreign volunteers, and indeed the enthusiasm with which they fought, could have been that much greater. Certainly some areas had suffered terribly under Stalin. Hence the Ukraine, for example, spawned nationalist groups such as the Ukrainian Insurgent Army, which eventually came to cooperate with the Germans from the late spring of 1944. There were also the efforts of the Russian Liberation Army (POA) under General Andrei Vlasov. Created in 1944 (largely against Hitler's wishes, it should be added), it grew to divisional strength.

Such support for the Nazis was not enough to tip the scales of the war on the Eastern Front. Yet given the scale of Stalin's crimes against his own people, it is not inconceivable that more enlightened German policies in the east could have turned even larger volumes of the Soviet populace against their leader and government.

STRUCTURE OF THE GESTAPO, 1939		
Division	Commander	Responsibility
Division I	Werner Best	Organization, administration, legal affairs
Division II	Reinhard Heydrich	Aggressive actions against opponents of the Nazi regime
Division III	Günther Palten	Counter-intelligence

Security services

The implementation of Hitler's vision for both Germany and the occupied territories depended significantly on the police and security services of the Third Reich.

In effect Hitler, via Heinrich Himmler and the SS, turned Germany into a police state, constantly monitoring its citizens for any signs of subversion. Had Germany won the war, or at least held on to some of its conquests, this system would have established itself over the lives of additional millions of people in the conquered lands for generations to come.

The two regular police forces in Germany were the *Kriminalpolizei* (Criminal Police), or *Kripo*, and the *Ordnungspolizei* (Order Police) or *Orpo*. Although they were ostensibly civil police forces, they still came under the auspices of the SS, via the person of Himmler. In July 1936, Himmler (who was already *Reichsführer-SS* and head of the *Gestapo* – see below) was appointed *Chef der Deutschen*

Below: The prisons of the Gestapo, which formed a network throughout Germany, Austria and Czechoslovakia, were insidious tools of social control. They not only served as places of incarceration and interrogation, they also acted as visible reminders of Nazi power.

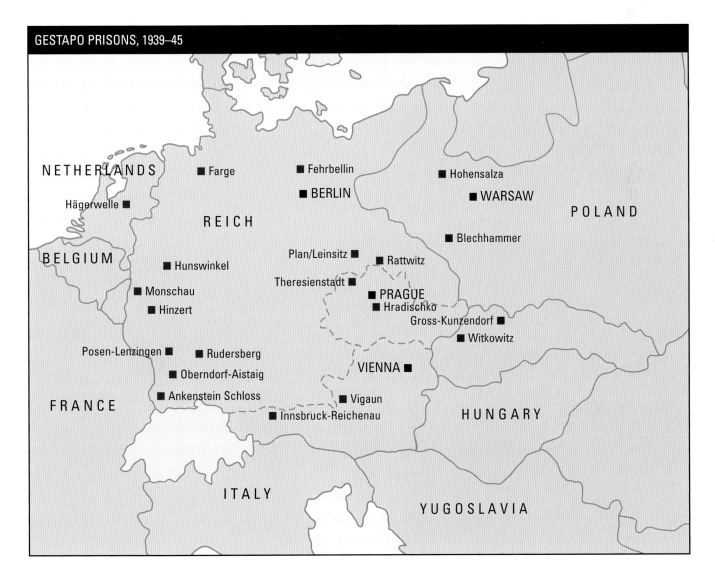

GESTAPO PRISONS, 1939–45

Polizei (Chief of the German Police). His authority now extended over all aspects of German law enforcement and security services, including the *Kripo* and *Orpo*. (In 1943 he also became Minister of the Interior, giving him the ability to interfere directly in the judicial process.) *Allgemeine-SS* members consequently infiltrated the police to a large degree, especially in the *Orpo*, which from 1936 until the end of the war was headed by the unpleasant character of *SS-Oberstgruppenführer* Kurt Daluege.

Yet while the regular police forces were certainly implicated in political policing, if only by sharing local knowledge with other Nazi agencies, the Third Reich contained far more powerful intelligence and security agencies.

The first SS security service to be set up was the *Sicherheitsdienst* (SD; Security Service), formed in 1931–32 by Himmler (but headed by Heydrich) to 'discover the enemies of the National Socialist concept and … initiate countermeasures through the official police authorities'.

Essentially it was a domestic spy organization, which took on real authority once Hitler was in power. It became extremely powerful and all-pervasive, monitoring and arresting any who were deemed a threat to the regime, from Jews and communists to Seventh-Day Adventists and homosexuals, and spreading its tentacles into Austria and Czechoslovakia during the later 1930s. During the war years, it also organized military-style operations against partisans, and tracked down, arrested and deported Jews,

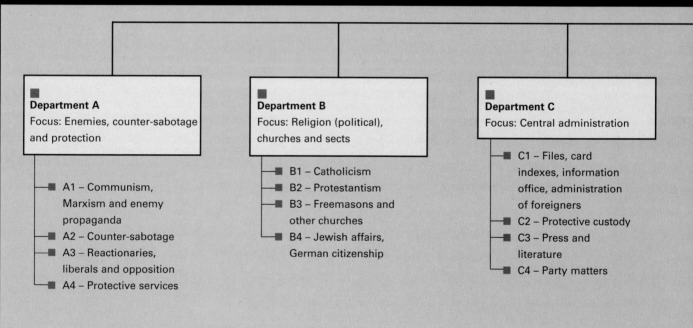

DEPARTMENTS OF THE GESTAPO, 1943

Department A
Focus: Enemies, counter-sabotage and protection

- A1 – Communism, Marxism and enemy propaganda
- A2 – Counter-sabotage
- A3 – Reactionaries, liberals and opposition
- A4 – Protective services

Department B
Focus: Religion (political), churches and sects

- B1 – Catholicism
- B2 – Protestantism
- B3 – Freemasons and other churches
- B4 – Jewish affairs, German citizenship

Department C
Focus: Central administration

- C1 – Files, card indexes, information office, administration of foreigners
- C2 – Protective custody
- C3 – Press and literature
- C4 – Party matters

sending them to the concentration camps.

The SD was not alone in such efforts. The infamous *Geheime Staatspolizei* (*Gestapo*; Secret State Police) became one of the most feared instruments of Nazi coercion during the war. It was established in 1933 by Hermann Göring (who at this time was the Prussian Interior Minister), and had similar political goals to the SD. Indeed, the overlapping responsibilities of the SD and the *Gestapo* caused much wasted energy and many inter-agency conflicts throughout the existence of the Third Reich. From June 1936, to make matters even more complex, Reinhard Heydrich was both the chief of the *Gestapo* and the head of the *Sicherheitspolizei* (Sipo; Security Police), the umbrella organization incorporating the *Gestapo* and the *Kripo*. Adding to the confusion was that both the SD and *Gestapo* involved themselves in foreign intelligence, as did the *Abwehr* intelligence organization that was, until 1944, overseen by the high command of the *Wehrmacht*. (In 1944 the *Abwehr* passed to SS authority.)

Out of the competition between the *Gestapo* and the SD, the *Gestapo* undoubtedly emerged as the more powerful of the two agencies. For example, by 1939 the SD had 3000 operatives and 50,000 informers. The *Gestapo*, by contrast, had 20,000 members and 100,000 informers. It should be noted that in September 1939 all the state and party intelligence services were brought together under the authority

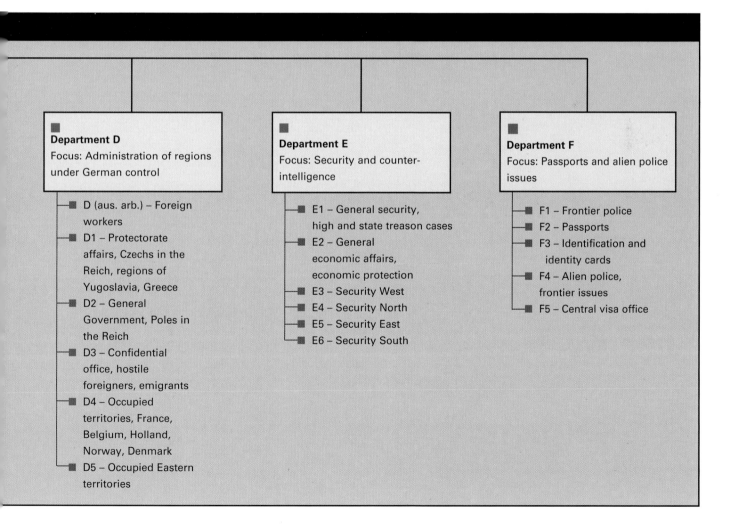

Department D
Focus: Administration of regions under German control

- D (aus. arb.) – Foreign workers
- D1 – Protectorate affairs, Czechs in the Reich, regions of Yugoslavia, Greece
- D2 – General Government, Poles in the Reich
- D3 – Confidential office, hostile foreigners, emigrants
- D4 – Occupied territories, France, Belgium, Holland, Norway, Denmark
- D5 – Occupied Eastern territories

Department E
Focus: Security and counter-intelligence

- E1 – General security, high and state treason cases
- E2 – General economic affairs, economic protection
- E3 – Security West
- E4 – Security North
- E5 – Security East
- E6 – Security South

Department F
Focus: Passports and alien police issues

- F1 – Frontier police
- F2 – Passports
- F3 – Identification and identity cards
- F4 – Alien police, frontier issues
- F5 – Central visa office

THIRD REICH POLICE UNITS, 1934–39

◆ **POLICE FORCE**

Sonderpolizei (Special Police)
- Eisenbahnpolizei (Railway Police) Ministry of Transport
- Bahnschutzpolizei (Railway Protection Police) SS
- Bergpolizei (Mines Police) Ministry of Economic Affairs
- Reichsbahnfahndungsdienst (Railway Criminal Investigation Service) Ministry of Transport
- Postschutz (Post Office Protection) Ministry of Post & Telegraph
- Zollbeamten (Customs Officials) Ministry of Finance
- Forstschutzpolizei (Forestry Police) Forestry Office
- Werkschutz (Factory Protection) Air Ministry
- Deichpolizei (Dyke & Dam Police) Ministry of Economic Affairs
- Flurschutzpolizei (Agricultural Police) Ministry of Agriculture
- Jagdpolizei (Game Conservation Police) Forestry Office
- Hafenpolizei (Harbour Police) Ministry of Transport
- Hilfspolizei (Auxiliary Police)

Sicherheitspolizei, Sipo (Security Police)
- Kriminalpolizei, Kripo (Criminal Police)
- Geheime Staatspolizei, Gestapo (Secret State Police)
- Grenzpolizei (Border Police)
- Weibliche Kriminalpolizei (Women's Branch of the Criminal Police)

Sicherheitsdienst, SD (Security Service)
- Inland SD (Domestic SD)
- Ausland SD (Foreign SD)

Ordnungspolizei, Orpo (Order Police)
- Schutzpolizei, Schupo (Protection Police)
- Schutzpolizei des Reichs
- Verkehrsbereitschaften (Traffic Police)
- Kasernierte Polizei (Barrack Police)
- Schutzpolizei der Gemeinden (Municipal Police)
- Polizei Fliegerstaffeln (Police Flying Units)
- Polizei Nachrichtenstaffeln (Police Signal Units)
- Gendarmerie (Rural Police)
- Polizei Reiterstaffeln (Mounted Police Units)
- Verkehrskompanien (mot) zbV (Motorized Special Duty Traffic Police)
- Wasserschutzpolizei (Waterways Protection Police)
- Motorisierte Gendarmerie (Motorized Traffic Gendarmerie)
- Feldjägerkorps, FJK (Auxiliary Police)
- Verwaltungspolizei (Administrative Police)
- Gesundheitspolizei (Health Police)
- Hochgebirgs Gendarmerie (Mountain Gendarmerie)
- Gewerbepolizei (Factory & Shops Police)
- Baupolizei (Buildings Police)
- Feuerschutzpolizei (Fire Protection Police)
- Feuerwehren (Fire Brigades)
- Luftschutzpolizei (Air Raid Police)
- Technische Nothilfe, TeNo (Technical Emergency Service)
- Landespolizei (Barracked Territorial Police)
- Landwacht (Rural Guards)
- Stadtwacht (City Guards)

of the *Reichssicherheitshauptamt* (RSHA; Reich Main Security Office). The RSHA was under Himmler's overall authority, but from 1939 was led by Heydrich, until his assassination by Czech resistance fighters in Prague in 1942. Its reach over the lives of Germans and conquered Europeans alike was severe, and it was also integral to delivering the deportation and murder of Jews as part of the 'Final Solution'.

The security services of the Third Reich evolved steadily rather than being the product of a Hitlerian 'masterplan', but once they were established and under SS authority they became a critical tool of Nazi policy. The fear generated by the *Gestapo* alone meant that even when Germany was staring defeat in the face, sedition there was extremely limited. Those arrested by the security services could expect no help from the judicial process, if they made it that far – torture used to extract confessions meant that many died in grim cells at the hands of merciless interrogators. In the occupied territories, citizens became used to discovering that neighbours had simply disappeared following a night-time visit from the Nazi authorities.

What is particularly chilling about the Nazi security services is that much of their power and seeming ubiquity came from large numbers of informants, foreign and domestic, who kept the agents fed with a steady stream of information and suspicions.

Indeed, it is estimated that 80 per cent of all *Gestapo* investigations originated in denunciations. Although resistance organizations did exist and fight in the occupied territories, in the west in particular their efforts were limited by the betrayals of their countrymen.

Hitler Youth

Hitler was obsessed with youth. While he often viewed the old as set in their ways, cynical and full of obsolete ideology, he saw youth as the raw material for moulding Germany's brighter future.

Yet his model of youth was not one of tenderness or indulgence, as stated clearly in a speech in 1939:

A violently active, dominating, intrepid, brutal youth – that is what I am after. Youth must be all those things. It must be indifferent to pain. There must be no weakness or tenderness in it. I want to see once more in its eyes the gleam of pride and independence of the beast of prey. Strong and handsome must my young men be. I will have them fully trained in all physical exercises. I intend to have an athletic youth – that is the first and chief thing. In this way I shall eradicate the thousands of years of human domestication. Then I shall have in front of me the pure and noble natural material. With that I can create the new order.

– Hitler, 1939

To achieve his vision of a remodelled youth, Hitler and the Nazis created a range of Nazi youth organizations run precisely to create the sort of effects outlined. There were four principal Nazi youth organizations – two for boys, two for girls – arranged by age bracket. For boys aged 10–14, the first port of call was the *Deutsches Jungvolk* (DJ; German Young People), after which they could go into the *Hitlerjugend* (HJ; Hitler Youth) until they were 18. The parallel organizations for girls were the *Jungmädelbund* (JM; League of Young Girls), then the *Bund deutscher Mädel* (BdM; League of

HITLERJUGEND – UNIT STRUCTURES	
Unit Title	*Structure*
Kameradschaft	10–15 boys
Schar	3 Kameradschaften; 50–60 boys
Gefolgschaft	3 Scharen; 150–190 boys
Unterbann	4 Gefolgschaften; 600–800 boys
Bann	5 Unterbanne; about 3000 boys
Oberbann	5 Banne; about 15,000 boys
Gebiet	About 75,000 boys; 223 Banne divided among 42 Gebiete
Obergebiet	About 375,000 boys; 42 Gebiete divided among 6 Obergebiete

German Girls). Competing non-party youth organizations were progressively banned (apart from Catholic youth leagues), and in March 1939 membership of the Hitler Youth (using the term to include all Nazi youth organizations) was made compulsory for 10- to 18-year-olds.

Looking first at the male experience, the Nazi youth organizations, but especially the HJ, were heavily focused upon physical exercises and outdoor sport, often with a competitive edge. Weakness was not tolerated, and the levels of training could be brutal, less capable boys often being subjected to bullying and intimidation. In the HJ, the instruction also became more militaristic in focus following the reintroduction of conscription in 1935 – the HJ was naturally viewed as a repository of future soldiers. Rifle practice, fieldcraft, camouflage training and lectures from serving soldiers became commonplace. Furthermore, the HJ also created three sub-branches to reflect the arms of service of the *Wehrmacht*. These were the *Motor-HJ*, *Marine-HJ* and *Flieger-HJ* for training that would later connect to Panzer/ army, navy and air force specialisms respectively. From March 1942, with the war adding extra pressure, HJ members aged 16 to 18 could also attend *Wehrtüchtigungslager der Hitlerjugend* (Military Service Competency Camps for the Hitler Youth), which were preparatory three-week infantry combat training courses.

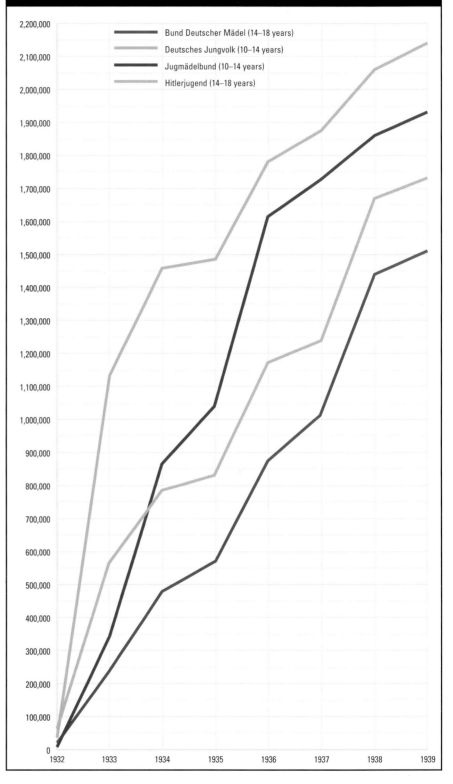

NAZI YOUTH ORGANIZATION MEMBERSHIP BY ORGANIZATION, 1932–39

- Bund Deutscher Mädel (14–18 years)
- Deutsches Jungvolk (10–14 years)
- Jugmädelbund (10–14 years)
- Hitlerjugend (14–18 years)

Female experience in the Hitler Youth was far less militaristic, although it still heavily emphasized physical training. Hitler viewed the female sphere as principally domestic and maternal, and the BdM included training in how to run a home and cook for a family. They would also receive instruction in National Socialist history and politics, ensuring that the young people were 'on message' from an early age.

Fighting youth

So were Hitler's ambitions to create a hard youth truly realized?

The Third Reich certainly found its youth extremely useful. Both boys and girls were utilized in huge numbers for a six-week period every summer by the *Landdienst* (Land Service), serving as agricultural workers by collecting harvests and performing similar duties. Also, once a German boy turned 18 he

had to perform nine months of work for the *Reichsarbeitsdienst* (RAD; Reich Labour Service), working on construction or other civic projects, before he could join the military. From 1943, however, in which year the conscription age was dropped to 17, eligible boys could join the armed services without passing

Below: The *Hitlerjugend* was organized nationally into *Gebiete* (Districts). In 1933, each of these districts would hold about 75,000 boys, and the *Gebiete* went down through multiple subdivisions until they reached the *Kameradschaft* (lit. 'Comradeship'), which comprised about 15 boys led by a *Kameradschaftsführer*. The structure of the *Hitlerjugend* was deliberately militaristic and preparatory for the armed services.

HITLERJUGEND DISTRICT LOCATIONS,1942

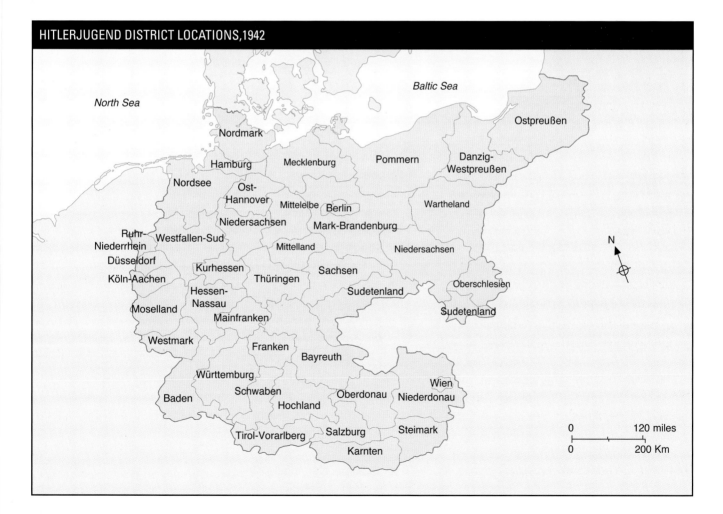

Art exhibits by themselves have shown more than 2.5 million workers the creations of true German art ... Apart from the concerts in factories and art exhibitions, the Kraft durch Freude also utilizes theatrical performances, other concerts, vocal and musical groups to introduce the manifestations of German culture to every working German. Twenty-two million citizens have attended theatrical performances, 5.6 million the KdF concerts and 17 million have found relaxation in more than 40,000 cabaret and variety performances, and so acquire new strength for their daily work.
– Das danken wir dem Führer!,
1938

Holidays

Apart from local entertainment, the greatest benefit of being a Kdf member was the organization's holiday programmes. Utilizing Germany's expanding rail network, which had reached 72,656km (45,146 miles) by 1939, KdF members were able to visit a variety of national and (by connecting to foreign rail routes) international destinations, including Portugal, Norway, Madeira, Bulgaria, Turkey

and the Baltic coast. From the latter sailed a range of KdF cruise liners, which took people out to Spanish, Norwegian and Italian coasts. The cruises, however, were generally

the preserve of the better-off middle classes, who could afford the extra costs. For example, 28 RM would purchase a week's hiking in the Harz mountains. A two-week cruise to

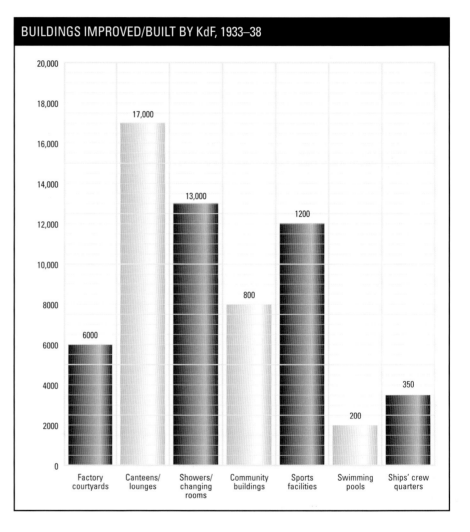

BUILDINGS IMPROVED/BUILT BY KdF, 1933–38

TOTAL VISITOR/PARTICIPANT NUMBERS TO KDF ATTRACTIONS, 1933–38

Art exhibits — 2.5 million
Theatre — 22 million
Music — 5.6 million
Cabaret — 17 million
Holidays — 20 million

Italy, by contrast, set the bar much higher at 155 RM. Note also that the cruise ships were also heavily frequented by senior party members as well as *Gestapo* agents, demanding that the holidaymakers stay on their best behaviour throughout.

Slave labour

Although Hitler found many willing servants from within the Third Reich, his regime was also supported by a vast army of unwilling slave labourers.

The conquests made between 1939 and 1942 opened up seemingly limitless human resources for exploitation by German industry and agriculture, of which the Third Reich took full advantage. Foreign labourers were placed into one of four categories by the Nazis. *Gastarbeiter* (guest workers) were actually not slaves at all, but were Germanic workers from either racially accepted occupied countries

(such as Norway) or from Axis allies. Underneath this admittedly tiny grouping were the *Militärinternierter* (military internees, or POWs), *Zivilarbeiter* (civilian workers) and *Ostarbeiter* (eastern workers). These three categories were basically slave labour, very much at the mercy of their overlords. The nationality of the worker could make a critical difference to the nature of his or her treatment – workers from Poland or the Soviet Union were often treated little better than animals, whereas those from sophisticated parts of Europe might be treated as near equals, and even provided with a wage that was on a similar level to that of native Germans. (Such salaries would also be subject to taxation.) Some *Ostarbeiter* might also receive a wage, but it would be a fraction of that earned by a German, despite longer hours and poorer working conditions.

Slave labour became particularly important to the economic life of the

GERMAN LABOUR FRONT (DAF) MEMBERSHIP, 1933–42	
Date	
December 1933	9.36 million
June 1934	about 16 million
April 1935	about 21 million
September 1939	about 22 million
September 1942	about 25 million

Reich. In fact, by 1944 Germany was using 5.3 million civilians and 1.8 million POWs as workers in industry and agriculture – a total of 24 per cent of the entire German workforce. In total, between 1939 and 1945 12 million people were used as forced labour.

Furthermore, forced labour was also an instrument of the 'Final Solution' and the ethnic destruction intended as part of *Lebensraum*. For Hitler, those he conquered were simply tools at the Reich's disposal.

FOREIGN CIVILIANS USED AS FORCED LABOUR IN GERMANY, JANUARY 1944

- Czechoslovakia 248,000
- Poland 1.4 million
- Yugoslavia 270,000
- Soviet Union 2.17 million
- France 1.1 million
- Norway 2000
- Denmark 23,000
- Netherlands 350,000
- Belgium 500,000
- Greece 20,000
- Italy 180,000

Tools of War

The Third Reich was one of the most militarily inventive regimes in history. All three of its armed services – Heer, Luftwaffe and Kriegsmarine – pushed against the boundaries of current military technology and designed weapons systems that were state-of-the-art.

Not all of these systems made it into service, or even beyond blueprint or prototype stages, but during the last desperate years of the war they gave Germany a glimmer of hope for swinging its outcome back into Hitler's favour.

In fact, most ideas were expensive distractions that took away resources from producing more fundamental weapon systems.

Left: United States Army personnel examine Heinkel He 162s on an assembly line in the Seegrotte Caves at Hinterbrühl, Austria, following the German surrender in May 1945.

Production war

World War II was to a large degree decided on matters of war production, a truth that Hitler only partially understood. By 1942 Germany was at war with the combined industrial might of the British Empire, the United States and the Soviet Union.

Between them they could dwarf the Third Reich in output of aircraft, armoured vehicles, small arms, munitions, ships and all the other tools of war. Germany had effectively mobilized its manpower, more than doubling the number of men in uniform between 1939 and 1945. Yet if it did not have the weapons and equipment to arm such men, and if losses of those items exceeded production levels, then defeat became almost a matter of mathematical certainty, despite the *Wehrmacht*'s evident tactical strengths.

War production in Germany prior to 1942 was a confused affair. Initially the overall goals of rearmament fell within the realm of the Four-Year Plan under Göring, who certainly oversaw a massive increase in both military expenditure and the percentage of the workforce (60 per cent by the summer of 1941) and industry channelled into military contracts. In reality, the production of armaments had no effective centralization, with each branch of service fighting for its share of the pie, resulting in confused priorities and wasted energy.

The appointment of engineer and committed Nazi Fritz Todt to the position of *Reichsminister für Bewaffnung und Munition* (Reich Minister for Armaments and Munitions) in early 1940 had given more of a focal point to war production, but the inefficiencies and infighting continued, often dominated by the demands of military commanders who understood little about war economies.

The result was that while war production came to dominate the economy by 1941, outputs of materials increased at only marginal levels. For example, in terms of armoured fighting vehicle (AFV) production, Germany produced 1643 tanks and self-propelled guns in 1940, increasing to 3790 in 1941. This increase sounds positive until put into contrast with the Allied powers. The Soviet Union produced 2794 AFVs in 1940, but 6590 in 1941, while beleaguered and isolated Britain even managed to increase production from 1399 in 1940 to 4841 in 1941. Adding depth to the picture was that the United States manufactured 4052 AFVs in 1941, despite not being involved in the war for much of the year. Taken cumulatively (including the 1940 figure of 331 vehicles produced in the United States), the primary Allied powers churned out more than 20,000 combat vehicles in 1940–41, against Germany's 5433.

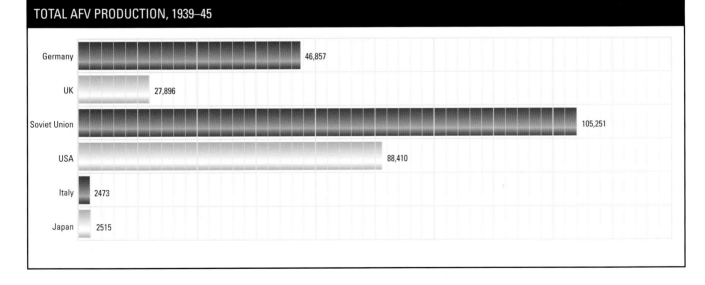

TOTAL AFV PRODUCTION, 1939–45

Germany	46,857
UK	27,896
Soviet Union	105,251
USA	88,410
Italy	2473
Japan	2515

Such differences were repeated across almost all areas of war production, from aircraft to small arms. At first the victories of 1939 and 1940 masked this reality, but the insatiable appetite of the Eastern Front for men and equipment soon threw the issue into a harsh relief. Hitler became increasingly aware of the need to rationalize his economy, and the opportunity came with the death of Fritz Todt in an air crash in February 1942. In his place he appointed Albert Speer, a man who had already built up great experience of the workings of German industry.

Speer's revolution

Under Speer, Germany's war production levels were transformed. He centralized all major decisions about military manufacturing under himself, via a central planning board that had control over raw materials allocations, and set up production departments with responsibilities for specific areas of armaments. He also liaised more closely with industrialists, rather than listening only to the shrill and frequently overlapping demands of the field commanders, and utilized the solid backing of Hitler to override those who tried to take him in different directions.

Speer's leadership revolutionized the German war economy when it needed it most. Looking back at AFV production levels, the output jumped to 6180 in 1942, then 12,063 in 1943 and 19,002 in 1944. The numbers of artillery pieces

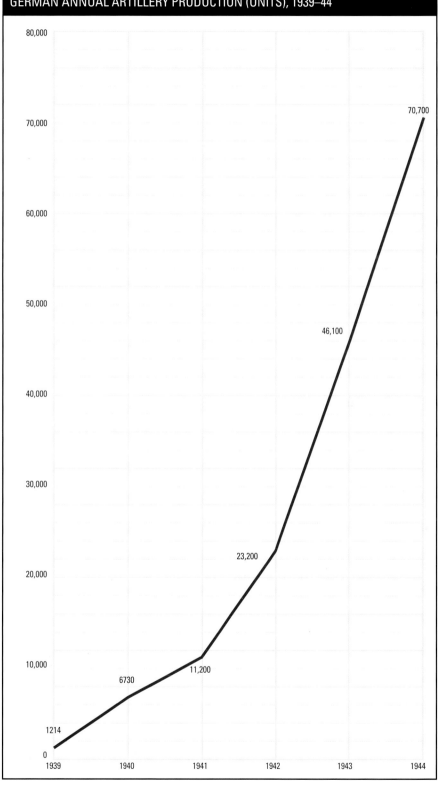

GERMAN ANNUAL ARTILLERY PRODUCTION (UNITS), 1939–44

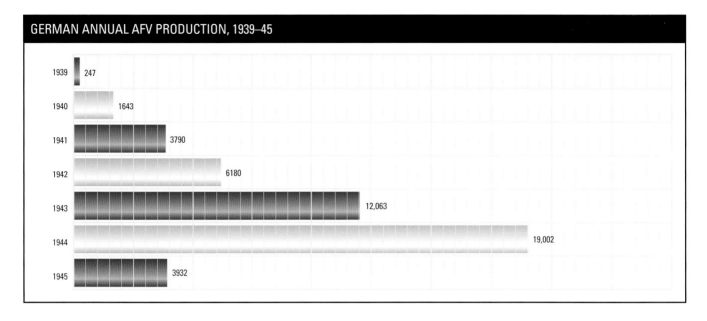

GERMAN ANNUAL AFV PRODUCTION, 1939–45

1939   247

1940   1643

1941   3790

1942   6180

1943   12,063

1944   19,002

1945   3932

rolling out of the factories went from 6730 in 1940 to 70,700 in 1944. One area outside Speer's remit until 1944 was aircraft manufacture, but once he was in charge the total jumped from 25,527 in 1943 to 39,807 in 1944.

And yet context once again puts Speer's undoubted achievements into perspective. Looking at the war in total, while Germany manufactured 46,857 tanks and self-propelled guns between 1939 and 1945, the Soviets, Britain, Canada and the United States combined made 227,235. Germany produced 674,280 machine guns compared with the Allies' 4,744,484, and 189,307 military aircraft to 633,072 Allied types. Even factoring in the additional demands of the Pacific theatre on the Allies, it was clear that however great Germany's industrial achievements, they were not enough. And losses were vast.

By 1944, the German Army was losing virtually the equivalent of a regiment every day on the Eastern Front alone. The *Luftwaffe* lost more than 116,000 aircraft in the war. These depletions were exceeded by overall production, but pilots were not so easily replaced, and manning the aircraft with quality personnel became a significant problem.

The combined effects of Allied industrial dominance, Allied bombing (which initially limited but did not bring down German industry) and political panic at military defeats led to Speer losing Hitler's confidence and his authority over war production in 1944. Thereafter, the German economy began a precipitous collapse across the board.

Taking a step back, the industrial dominance of the Allies, plus Hitler's own desire for a rapid victory, spawned much creativity within the military design community. At first,

Hitler was looking for new weapons that would give the Third Reich a decisive advantage. Later, when the war turned against Hitler, he wanted magic bullets that would draw victory from the jaws of defeat.

Creative war

The Third Reich produced a huge variety of experimental, advanced, futuristic and plain insane weapons systems prior to and during World War II, far too many to reflect upon fully here.

The status and nature of these projects varied tremendously. Some never left the conceptual stage, remaining as blueprints on a drawing board. Others not only made it into production but also went on to kill and injure thousands of people. Here we will concern ourselves principally with the Third Reich's most visionary weapons, those that Hitler hoped would be game-changing technologies on the battlefield. It should be remembered that Hitler was personally fascinated with military technology, and if a project caught his interest he would keep a close eye on its development, often interfering in the design process. His interest would quickly wane, however, and his eye flit away to something else that caught his attention.

Land warfare

In the realm of land warfare, Germany undoubtedly produced some of the most impressive pieces of technology in the entire conflict. Tanks such as the Tiger and the Panther, both in service by mid-1943, had almost no equals on the battlefield. In one engagement on the Eastern Front on 7 July 1943,

during the battle of Kursk, a single SS Tiger engaged about 50 Soviet T-34s, destroying 22 in the process and forcing the rest to retreat. On the Western Front, it would cost on average five to 10 Allied tanks for each Tiger destroyed.

The Tiger was one of the heaviest tanks on the wartime battlefield (a Tiger II weighed 68.5 tonnes/67.4 tons), but the threat from heavy Soviet tanks such as the KV-1 and the sheer numbers of T-34s led German designers to experiment with even more monstrous machines.

A fine example was the PzKpfw VIII *Maus*, a heavy tank developed by Krupp in 1942 and 1943. It was enormous – weighing in at 188 tonnes (185 tons), it was 10.1m

(33ft 1.5in) long and 3.5m (11ft 6in) tall. Hitler himself was involved in selecting the armament – a 128mm (5in) main gun was chosen, with the option of later scaling it up to 150mm (5.9in). Such weapons would have been able to outrange and destroy all enemy AFVs, while the tank's armour would have been impregnable to any known tank or anti-tank gun.

The *Maus* reached a limited prototype stage in 1943 and 1944, but by this point Hitler's enthusiasm for the project had already faded. Moreover, as a combat vehicle, it was simply too big to make practical sense – few bridges, for example, would have been able to take its weight – and its maximum speed would be a grinding

TIGER UNIT KILL-TO-LOSS RATIO, 1942–45

501st Heavy Panzer Battalion	3.75
502nd Heavy Panzer Battalion	13.08
503rd Heavy Panzer Battalion	6.75
504th Heavy Panzer Battalion	2.29
505th Heavy Panzer Battalion	7.14
506th Heavy Panzer Battalion	2.23
507th Heavy Panzer Battalion	5.77
508th Heavy Panzer Battalion	1.28
509th Heavy Panzer Battalion	4.17
510th Heavy Panzer Battalion	3.08
13th Coy, Panzer Regt *Grossdeutschland*	16.67
3rd Bn, Panzer Regt *Grossdeutschland*	5.10
13th (Heavy) Coy, 1st SS Panzer Regt	9.52
8th (Heavy) Coy, 2nd SS Panzer Regt	8.06
9th (Heavy) Coy, 3rd SS Panzer Regt	8.93
101st SS Heavy Panzer Battalion	4.67
102nd SS Heavy Panzer Battalion	7.89
103rd SS Heavy Panzer Battalion	12.82
Average	5.74

MAUS, TORTOISE AND T-29 COMPARED

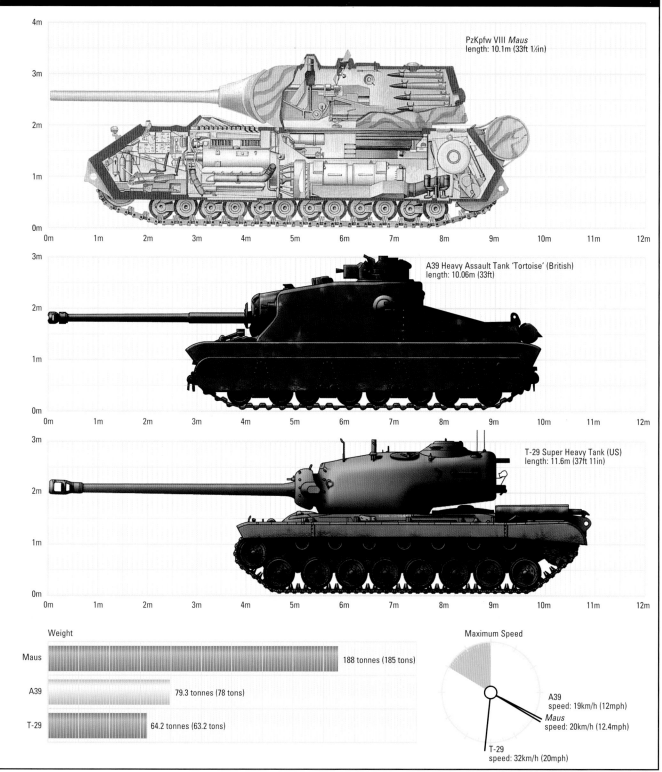

PzKpfw VIII *Maus*
length: 10.1m (33ft 1⁷⁄₈in)

A39 Heavy Assault Tank 'Tortoise' (British)
length: 10.06m (33ft)

T-29 Super Heavy Tank (US)
length: 11.6m (37ft 11in)

Weight

Maus — 188 tonnes (185 tons)

A39 — 79.3 tonnes (78 tons)

T-29 — 64.2 tonnes (63.2 tons)

Maximum Speed

A39
speed: 19km/h (12mph)

Maus
speed: 20km/h (12.4mph)

T-29
speed: 32km/h (20mph)

20km/h (12.4mph), at which point its firepower advantages would probably have been undone by mobility disadvantages.

Yet there were some even larger conceptual vehicles on the Third Reich's drawing board, ones that defied sense and credibility. One outlandish idea, first mooted in the 1930s, was that of 'land battleships', truly enormous armoured vehicles mounting firepower equivalent to that of a capital warship. The *Landkreuzer P1000 Ratte*, proposed to Hitler in June 1942 by engineer Eduard Grotte, was a tracked vehicle measuring 35m (114ft 10in) in length, towering 11m (36ft 1in) high and weighing an extraordinary 1800 tonnes (1771.6 tons). Its main gun turret was to carry two 280mm (11in) naval guns, with secondary armament including a 128mm (5in) gun in a rear turret and integral anti-aircraft weapons. At its thickest, the armour would be 360mm (14.2in) thick.

Quite how the *Ratte* would have contributed to victory is unclear. While undoubtedly an impressive weapon for relatively static heavy bombardment roles, the vehicle's limited mobility and huge size would have made the *Ratte* a prize target for Allied bombers. Hitler was actually keen on the idea, but Albert Speer saw it as nothing more than a waste of metal, and the project was cancelled in 1943 before practical work could begin.

Interestingly, Krupp proposed in 1942 an even larger development of the *Ratte*. The *Landkreuzer P1500 Monster* was, appropriate to its name, essentially an 800mm (31.5in) *Dora/schwerer Gustav K* railway gun mounted on land tracks. Had it reached beyond the idea stage, it would have weighed 2500 tonnes (2460.5 tons), again raising the question as to what it would do in a new world of manoeuvre warfare.

When it came to designs for new land warfare weapons, Hitler does seem to have had a preference for the huge. Other concepts in various stages of development included high-velocity superguns with ranges approaching 100km (62 miles). These flights of fantasy should not mask the fact that the Germans developed some truly ground-breaking land warfare technologies. Aside from its fine range of tanks, the *Heer* fielded the world's first assault rifles (the FG42 and the MP44), effective hand-held anti-tank weapons in the form of the *Panzerfaust* and *Panzerschreck*, and pushed ahead with pioneering work in range-finding and infrared technologies.

Naval warfare

Of all the three services, the *Kriegsmarine* seems to have garnered the least interest from Hitler. Germany's leader was an old infantryman, and a tactical thinker at heart, hence he was not fully engaged with the operational and strategic nature of naval resources. The fact is reflected in his under-investment in the submarine arm prior to the onset of war, even though the U-boats became one of the most influential weapons systems of the entire conflict. Nevertheless, that is not to say that Hitler did not periodically involve himself with naval projects.

When war broke out in 1939, Hitler's naval designers already had at blueprint stage a new class of battleships – the H class – to replace the *Bismarck* class, as an integral part of the 'Z-Plan' (see Chapter 2). Hitler made his own unrealistic contributions to the planning phases for these vessels, including an initial insistence that the ships be armed with unprecedented 508mm (20in) main guns – the largest naval guns at the opening of World War II were 406mm (16in) weapons. Eventually his naval designers managed to pull Hitler down to the smaller calibre, having convinced him that the increased weight and size of the new ships would lead to more problems than benefits.

U-boats

Although construction began on the H-class vessels in 1939 and 1940, the war soon changed Hitler's attitude to large surface warships. Following the sinking of the *Bismarck* in May 1941, the extreme vulnerability of battleships to air and underwater attacks became apparent. For the remainder of the war, large German warships such as *Tirpitz* and *Scharnhorst* spent much of their time skulking about in northern waters, attempting to stay safe rather than taking the fight to the enemy. For such reasons, and the need to direct raw materials in other directions, the H-class projects were all eventually postponed or abandoned.

As regards U-boats, however, there was genuine technological progress, spurred on by the escalating losses that the U-boat force inflicted on the Allies from 1941 to 1943. Yet by the end of this period, being a U-boat crewman had become an extremely dangerous occupation, the Allies having introduced an ever-more efficient range of sub-killing technologies that eventually won the battle of the Atlantic.

For this reason, the *Kriegsmarine* attempted to improve U-boat survivability by increasing the vessels' submerged endurance. A submarine's power when submerged was electrical, typically supplied by batteries that had been charged by the boat's diesel engines when running on the surface. (Diesel engines need an oxygen supply to work, hence they could not be used underwater.) The batteries would usually last just a few hours, and

GERMAN ANNUAL U-BOAT PRODUCTION, 1939–45

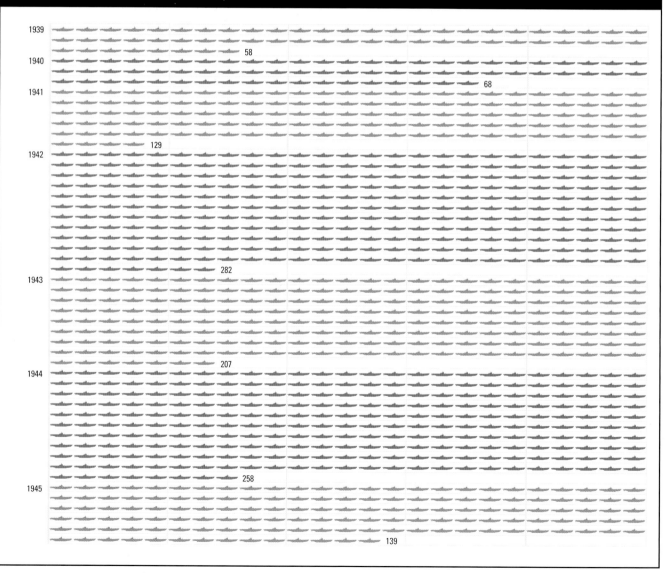

1939	58
1940	68
1941	
1942	129
1943	282
1944	207
1945	258
	139

provide limited speeds. Back in the 1920s, engineer Hellmuth Walter had pioneered an air-independent propulsion (AIP) system that derived power from a hydrogen peroxide solution called Perhydrol, used to create steam to drive a turbine motor. Interest in the design was sparked again in 1940, and three Type XVII U-boats were completed using the motors. The AIP system's problem was that it was liable to explode, and a different option was employed in the subsequent Type XXI and Type XXIII craft.

The Type XXIs and Type XXIIIs had a figure-of-eight hull cross-section, and the increased volume meant that there was space for a huge 69-cell battery bank that could keep the boats running submerged for up to 11 days. Recharging could be accomplished underwater in just a few hours by using an extended *Schnorkel* (snorkel) tube. The Type XXI was a blue-water vessel with an impressive submerged range of 630km (340 nautical miles). The Type XXIII, on the other hand, was designed for coastal duties.

H-CLASS BATTLESHIPS ON THE DRAWING BOARD

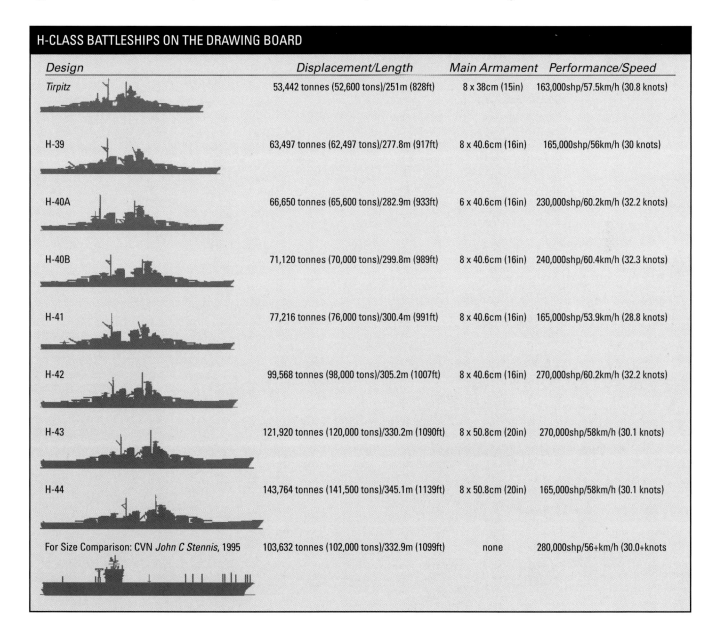

Design	Displacement/Length	Main Armament	Performance/Speed
Tirpitz	53,442 tonnes (52,600 tons)/251m (828ft)	8 x 38cm (15in)	163,000shp/57.5km/h (30.8 knots)
H-39	63,497 tonnes (62,497 tons)/277.8m (917ft)	8 x 40.6cm (16in)	165,000shp/56km/h (30 knots)
H-40A	66,650 tonnes (65,600 tons)/282.9m (933ft)	6 x 40.6cm (16in)	230,000shp/60.2km/h (32.2 knots)
H-40B	71,120 tonnes (70,000 tons)/299.8m (989ft)	8 x 40.6cm (16in)	240,000shp/60.4km/h (32.3 knots)
H-41	77,216 tonnes (76,000 tons)/300.4m (991ft)	8 x 40.6cm (16in)	165,000shp/53.9km/h (28.8 knots)
H-42	99,568 tonnes (98,000 tons)/305.2m (1007ft)	8 x 40.6cm (16in)	270,000shp/60.2km/h (32.2 knots)
H-43	121,920 tonnes (120,000 tons)/330.2m (1090ft)	8 x 50.8cm (20in)	270,000shp/58km/h (30.1 knots)
H-44	143,764 tonnes (141,500 tons)/345.1m (1139ft)	8 x 50.8cm (20in)	165,000shp/58km/h (30.1 knots)
For Size Comparison: CVN *John C Stennis*, 1995	103,632 tonnes (102,000 tons)/332.9m (1099ft)	none	280,000shp/56+km/h (30.0+knots)

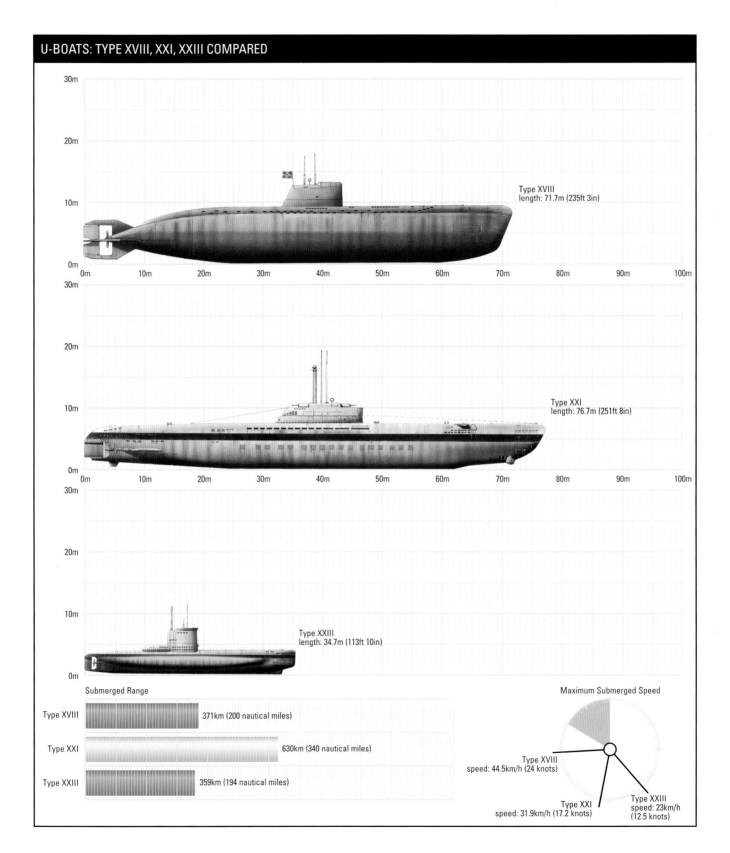

U-BOATS: TYPE XVIII, XXI, XXIII COMPARED

Type XVIII
length: 71.7m (235ft 3in)

Type XXI
length: 76.7m (251ft 8in)

Type XXIII
length: 34.7m (113ft 10in)

Submerged Range

Type XVIII — 371km (200 nautical miles)

Type XXI — 630km (340 nautical miles)

Type XXIII — 359km (194 nautical miles)

Maximum Submerged Speed

Type XVIII
speed: 44.5km/h (24 knots)

Type XXI
speed: 31.9km/h (17.2 knots)

Type XXIII
speed: 23km/h
(12.5 knots)

The *Elektro* boats, as they were known, utilized some of Germany's latest acoustic homing torpedoes – a major innovation in maritime warfare – such as the G7e T4 *Falke* (Falcon) and G7e T5 *Zaunkönig* (Wren). A total of 118 Type XXIs and 61 Type XXIIIs were commissioned, but only one (perhaps two) of the former saw service, while six Type XXIIIs went on patrol. As with so much of Germany's innovative technology, these high-tech submarines came too late in the war to make a real difference to its outcome. In addition, the frequency with which the Allies were sinking U-boats became unsustainable – whereas 86 were destroyed in 1942, 239 were sunk in 1943 and 234 in 1944, by which time the Germans had lost the underwater war.

Air warfare

It was in the field of air warfare that Hitler's regime made its most visible innovations. They had the incentive to do so. From 1942 the Allied strategic bombing campaign hammered the Reich day and night, and considerable resources were diverted into combating the US, British and Commonwealth bombers.

By 1944, Germany's need to win the air war was crushing. It could not compete in terms of aircraft production volumes, so increasingly looked to new, revolutionary aircraft types, particularly fighters. In July 1944, the Nazi government established the *Jägernotprogramm* (Emergency Fighter Programme), which essentially made fighter development and production the central priority of the *Luftwaffe*. Of the new aircraft emerging, there were some impressive piston-engined types, including the twin-fuselage Messerschmitt Me 609 and the Heinkel He 219, but it was in the field of jet and rocket fighters that the greatest innovations took place.

Jet aircraft

Jet aircraft designs had been tested in Germany since the late 1930s, with the He 178 and He 280. The defining *Luftwaffe* jet, however, was the Me 262, which began its development journey back in 1938 but did not see production and service until the summer of 1944. Powered by two Jumo turbojets, the Me 262 outperformed anything in the skies, as long as it kept its pace up (the Me 262 had a poor turning circle at low speeds). It had a maximum speed of 900km/h (559mph), and had an armament of four 30mm (1.2in) cannon and the option of 24 55mm (2.17in) R4M unguided air-to-air rockets, which were ripple-fired into Allied bomber streams. The Me 262 also came in a bomb-loaded ground-attack variant – Hitler had personally interfered in the aircraft's development, and initially decreed that it be developed as a high-speed bomber, to the detriment of pure fighter production numbers.

In action, the Me 262 inflicted a kill-to-loss ratio of 4:1 on Allied aircraft, and the jet's speed meant that there was little Allied fighters or gunners could do in response, except catch the jets on the ground or moving slowly at low altitudes. Had there been thousands of Me 262s available, they could have indeed changed the face of the air war over the Reich.

As it was, only 1430 were produced, nowhere near enough to counter the many thousands of Allied bombers and fighters streaming over Germany.

The same proved true of other late-war jet fighter projects such as the He 162, powered by a single top-mounted BMW turbojet. Only 116 of these aircraft were

FIGHTER PRODUCTION, NEW TYPES

Type	1939	1940	1941	1942	1943	1944	1945	Total
Dornier Do 335	–	–	–	–	–	23	19	42
Focke-Wulf Ta 152	–	–	–	–	–	34	46	80
Focke-Wulf Ta 154	–	–	–	–	–	8	–	8
Heinkel He 162	–	–	–	–	–	–	116	116
Heinkel He 219	–	–	–	–	11	195	62	268
Messerschmitt Me 163	–	–	–	–	–	327	37	364
Messerschmitt Me 262	–	–	–	–	–	564	730	1294
Messerschmitt Me 410	–	–	–	–	271	629	–	910

completed by the end of the war. In its desperation, Germany also explored rocket aircraft designs. One that actually saw combat was the Me 163 *Komet*, which was powered by a Walter HWK 109-509A-2 rocket motor and could reach a speed of 960km/h (596mph). Its range, however, was a mere 80km (50 miles), so it was designed to make a single high-speed pass through the enemy bomber stream, blazing away with its two 30mm (1.2in) cannon.

Later weapons options included the R4M salvo rockets and upward-firing 50mm (2in) recoilless guns. Predictably, the 300 or so Me 163s completed made little impact on the war, downing just 16 Allied aircraft. A key problem was that the aircraft travelled so fast the pilot simply did not have enough time to get a decent aim on the trundling bombers.

Furthermore, it was launched from a two-wheeled dolly jettisoned after take-off, and landing was on a retractable skid, making it a dangerous aircraft to pilot.

Another rocket design, the Bachem Ba 349 *Natter*, was even more hair-raising to fly. Made from laminated wood and powered by a Walter 109-509A-2 rocket motor, it was launched vertically using four jettisonable rocket boosters, blasted to a position above the bombers.

The intention was that it would dive onto the bomber stream, blast it with cannon and rocket fire, then the pilot would literally crash the expendable jet into an enemy aircraft, bailing out just before impact. This alarming aircraft reached operational trials in April 1945, but Allied advances put paid to any further tests.

Strategic shortage

One important absence in the *Luftwaffe*'s arsenal throughout the war was that of a true strategic bomber, in the mould of a B-17 or Lancaster. Hitler's *Wehrmacht* was very tactically orientated in outlook, and it was focused on fighting a short *Blitzkrieg*-style conflict. Furthermore, its immediate enemies in 1939 and 1940 were literally across its borders, so unlike distant Britain it did not see an overwhelming need for a long-range bomber type.

The *Luftwaffe* did, in fact, have one operational long-range strategic bomber type, the Heinkel He 177 *Greif* (Griffon). (It also possessed a small number of long-range maritime and transport types.) Only 1000 examples of this mechanically

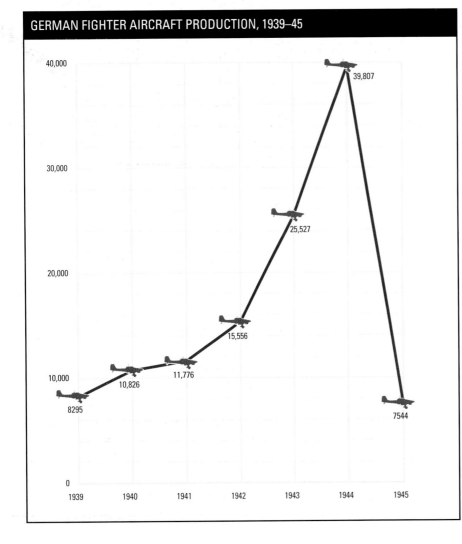

GERMAN FIGHTER AIRCRAFT PRODUCTION, 1939–45

- 1939: 8295
- 1940: 10,826
- 1941: 11,776
- 1942: 15,556
- 1943: 25,527
- 1944: 39,807
- 1945: 7544

LUFTWAFFE AND ALLIED JET FIGHTERS COMPARED

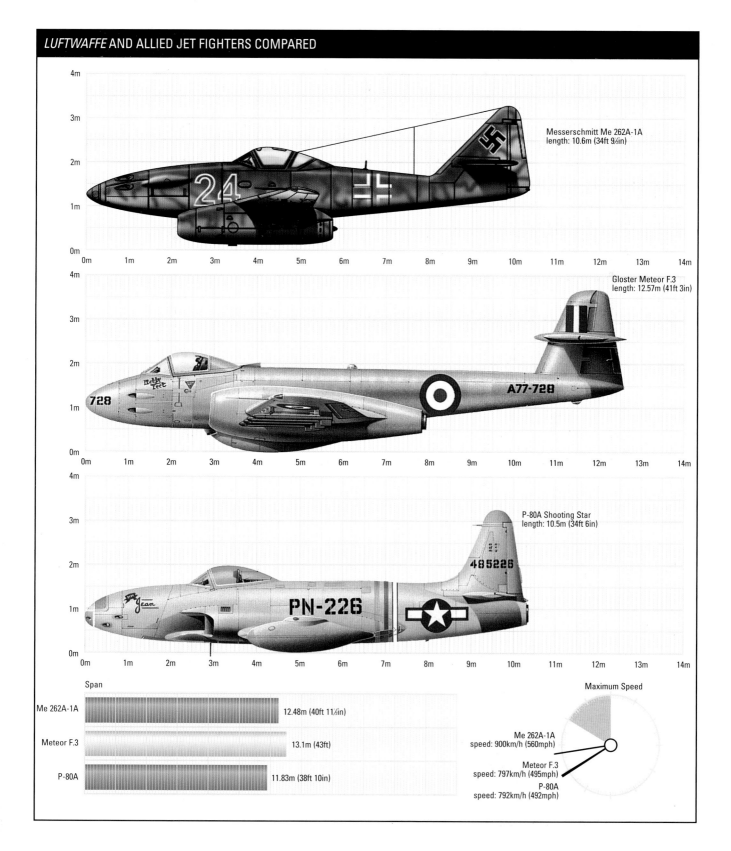

Messerschmitt Me 262A-1A
length: 10.6m (34ft 9½in)

Gloster Meteor F.3
length: 12.57m (41ft 3in)

P-80A Shooting Star
length: 10.5m (34ft 6in)

Span

Me 262A-1A — 12.48m (40ft 11½in)

Meteor F.3 — 13.1m (43ft)

P-80A — 11.83m (38ft 10in)

Maximum Speed

Me 262A-1A
speed: 900km/h (560mph)

Meteor F.3
speed: 797km/h (495mph)

P-80A
speed: 792km/h (492mph)

complex and problematic aircraft were made, and they saw only limited service on the Eastern and Western fronts, with many of the aircraft ending up as transports.

Amerika Bomber

Had this programme been brought to completion, it would have taken the war directly to the United States, but resources – and Hitler's patience – ran out too soon.

In July 1938 – more than a year before the war began and three before the United States became involved – Hermann Göring mused aloud about the need for an intercontinental bomber. The head of the *Reichsluftfahrtministerium*

Below: An *Amerika* bomber might easily have been a development of this Me 264.

(Air Ministry) had always been something of a technocrat, taking an eager interest in the details of design and development, so it was not so surprising that he should have been intrigued by such a project. It was more unexpected from a diplomatic standpoint that he should have made his thinking public: the threat to the United States, though implicit, was unmistakable.

America's reluctance to involve itself in the hostilities prior to Pearl Harbor has been a subject of much debate, many historians criticizing the country for sitting on the fence. It's easy to forget that, as the Nazis saw it, the United States had done no such thing, but had made its support for Germany's enemies very clear. The British might mutter that strings were attached (in the form of territorial concessions, mainly

island bases) when America agreed to supply the Royal Navy with 50 destroyers in September 1940, but as the Germans saw it 50 ships were 50 ships.

It was certainly soon after the signing of the Destroyers for Bases Agreement that Göring got the long-range bomber project formally under way. And there was no beating about the bush when it came to naming what he announced was to be known as the *Amerika* bomber. Germany's five leading aviation manufacturers were asked by the *Reichsmarschall* to draw up plans for a plane capable of making the round trip from Germany to the United States and back, a distance of almost 11,000km (7,000 miles). On the surface, at any rate, Germany had succeeded in opening up the Atlantic as an arena of war.

Its U-boats were wreaking havoc among the convoys. By air, though, the ocean was off-limits, while in America itself people sat safely at home, spared the kind of pounding suffered by the people of Europe.

The *Amerika* would be a big beast – there was no way to avoid that. Along with the fuel for such an epic journey, it would have to be able to carry a payload of 6.5 tons or more – heavy bombs to make the trip worthwhile. New York was identified as the target destination but if, as Hitler hoped at the outset, the Portuguese dictator António de Oliveira Salazar were to make the Azores available for bases, a plane of this kind would be able to make forays far inland.

Intercontinental range

While Junkers, Heinkel, Messerschmidt, Focke-Wulf and Horten all got to work roughing out their blueprints for the *Amerika*, Göring's staff were busy drawing up plans for its deployment. In the lengthy document they prepared for their chief's approval, one underlying assumption is clear. The project was intended to use air power to cancel out air power. Of the 19 likely US targets identified, most had some connection with the aviation industry: as well as aircraft and engine plants (including Pratt & Whitney, based in Connecticut; Wright Aeronautical, in New Jersey) there were aluminium processors, instrument makers and optics specialists. Factors to consider were not just the damage caused by long-

range bombing raids – on industry, the military and general morale – but also the costly ramping-up of air defences America would feel obliged to undertake in response.

The project was a major test of engineering ingenuity, and the different companies responded in different ways. Most, like Messerschmitt with the Me 264, Junkers with the Ju 390, and Heinkel with the He 277, came up with supersized versions of otherwise conventional aircraft. Appearances were deceptive, though: the exacting demands that were going to be made on airframes and engines required an enormous number of modifications – to engines especially, so that they could withstand the rigours of such long flights in such harsh conditions.

Careful calculations had to be made, and compromises reached, trading off speed and power against fuel efficiency – not just for economy's sake, but so that the aircraft would stand a chance of making it home after its trip. Factor in the need to maximize capacity and lifting power, and the complexity became bewildering. Focke-Wulf ended up proposing two possible designs: the Fw 300, which had four wing-mounted engines and the Focke Wulf Ta 400, which was even larger and had six.

There was clear scope for lateral thinking. The maverick Horten brothers, Reimar and Walter, produced a chevron-shaped 'all-wing' aircraft, to be powered by early jet engines, and

with something of the look of the Stealth Bomber flying today. It was indeed specially designed to slip undetected through radar fields, shielded not just by its shape but by its wooden construction, using a special glue that was high in carbon.

The brothers, both mavericks, were gratified by Göring's enthusiastic response to their design – but dismayed to find themselves asked to work with Junkers engineers. They insisted on adding extra tails and fins to enhance stability – at the expense, as the Hortens immediately recognized, of range.

Mistel bombers

One suggestion was that a composite aircraft be constructed. Basically, one plane would ride piggyback upon another. A Heinkel He 177 long-range bomber would fly out as far as it could across the Atlantic, carrying a smaller Dornier Do 217 bomber on its back. Once it reached the limit of its range, the He 177 would turn around, parting company with the Do 217. This would then continue to its target before – far out of reach of home now – ditching in the sea. Its crew would then be picked up by a waiting U-boat.

All these ideas fell foul of the Führer's interference, and his limited attention-span; Hitler insisted on being involved, but was constantly distracted by more glamorous projects. And, as the hostilities wore on, mundane practicalities intervened to spoil the project – not

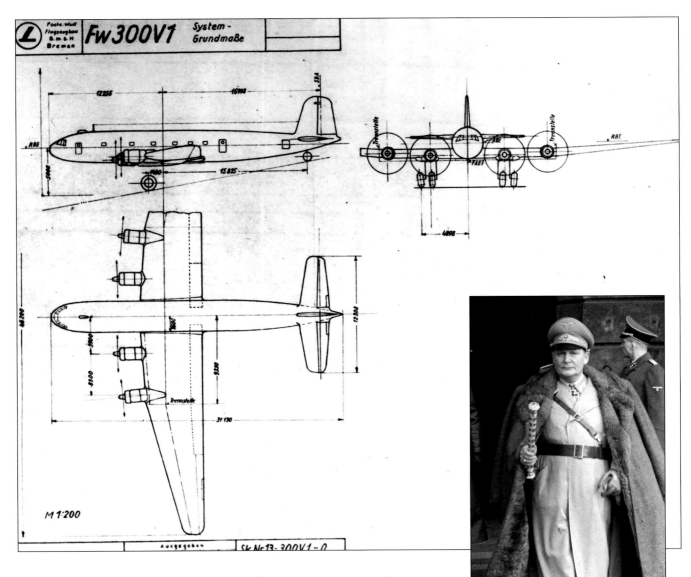

least the outrageous requirements intercontinental flights were going to make in terms of fuel.

As the numbers of aircraft that could attack the United States would necessarily be small, what would be the actual point of the attacks? The answer suggests some extreme possibilities.

Retaliation weapons
During the second half of World War II, with Germany heading for defeat,

Above: The Focke-Wulf 300 (VI version seen here) had four engines mounted on its low-set wings. Liquid-cooled, they would be designed by Daimler-Benz or Junkers. The plane was never built, not even as a prototype.

Hitler began to put increasing faith in *Vergeltungswaffen* (retaliation weapons). These were weapons supposedly of such destructive force that they would alter the balance of power purely through technological

Above: Hermann Göring took his role seriously as head of the *Reichsluftfahrtministerium* (Air Ministry).

supremacy. Hitler alluded to the advent of these weapons in several speeches and conversations, but in 1943 and 1944 he unleashed two of them against Britain and Northwestern Europe.

From V-2 to A-10

These were the infamous V-1 flying bomb and the V-2 ballistic missile. They were quite different in principle. The V-1 was a pilotless pulse-jet powered aircraft, armed with a large warhead in its nose. Launched from either a ramp or bomber aircraft, it had a range of just 240km (150 miles) and had basic gyroscopic guidance – at a pre-set distance, the V-1 would automatically go into a steep dive onto its target. By contrast, the far larger and more destructive V-2 was fired in a ballistic trajectory that literally passed through the edges of space, during which it reached a maximum

velocity of 5750km/h (3600mph). It carried a massive 2150lb (975kg) warhead to a maximum range of 400km (250 miles).

The V-1 and V-2 were capable terror weapons. Together they killed about 10,000 people and wounded many thousands more. But their general inaccuracy and entry so late into the war meant that strategically they had no decisive effect, apart from diverting hundreds of Allied bombers to attack their launch and production sites. The factors which might have radically changed that situation were exponentially more lethal warheads, combined with an extended range.

Regarding the range issue, several options were explored. One of the most promising involved fitting wings to the V-2 design, to provide a glide capability that could take the missile out to about 600km (373 miles). Two tested missile types

were produced, known as the A-4b and A-9, and there were even plans to fit an A-4b with additional rocket boosters to give a range of up to 1000km (621 miles).

Neither of these missiles went beyond the development and design stages, but that didn't stop German rocket scientists proposing even more advanced options, in this case capable of hitting the United States. Although details are sketchy, it appears that around 1943 what was effectively an intercontinental ballistic missile (ICBM) was proposed. It was a two-stage weapon, the first stage (known as A-10) driven by no less than six V-2 rockets. When these had exhausted themselves, the second stage of the missile – an A-4b or A-9 – would detach from the nose for flight to the target. What was to be known as the A-10 *Amerikarakete* had a potential range of 5000km (3107 miles). Evidence

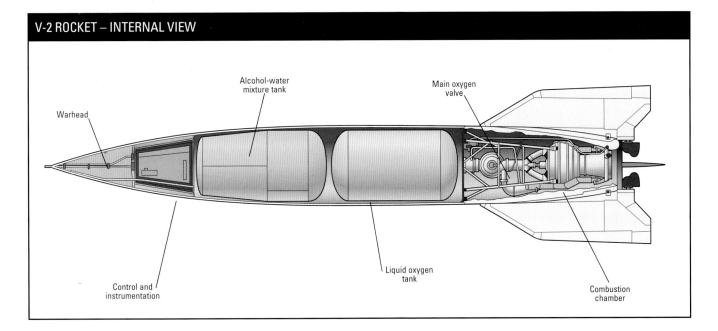

V-2 ROCKET – INTERNAL VIEW

Warhead

Alcohol-water mixture tank

Main oxygen valve

Control and instrumentation

Liquid oxygen tank

Combustion chamber

suggests that work on the missile began in earnest in 1944 but was eventually shut down when the Allies captured V-weapon sites.

Chemical and nuclear warheads

Even more terrifying than the prospect that the Nazis might have completed an ICBM before the war's end were the potential warheads it (or any other V-weapon) might have carried. For example, during the 1930s the Nazis developed two lethal nerve agents – Tabun and Sarin – and significant volumes of them were produced, but thankfully never used in anger. This was despite the fact that 500,000 chemical artillery shells and 100,000 Tabun-filled bombs had been stockpiled by the end of the war; it does not require a great leap of imagination to envisage how nerve agents could have been delivered through long-range rocket weaponry.

As the world now knows, the race to develop and deliver the atomic bomb was won by the United States. There is some evidence to suggest, however, that the Germans might have been just steps behind the Americans, and may have even pulled ahead. The story of Germany's atomic weapons programme is complicated, and masked by the fact that disinformation was commonplace. What we do know is that in the late 1930s a group of German physicists began investigations into the military applications of nuclear energy. In

A-10 *AMERIKARAKETE*

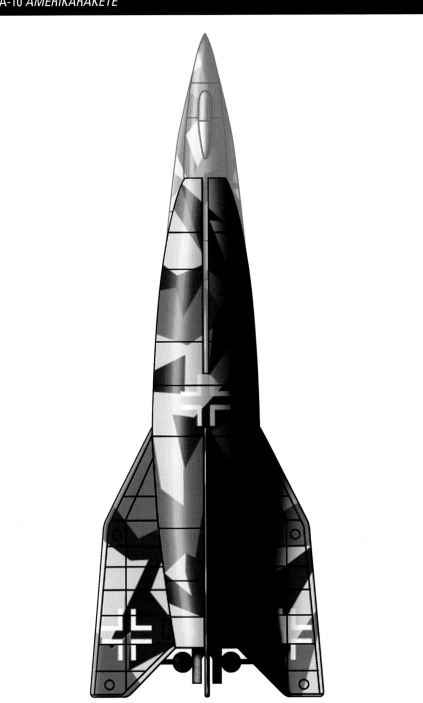

Specifications

Length: 25.8m (84ft 8in)
Max. Diameter: 4.3m (14ft 1in)
Span: 9m (29ft 6in)

Launch Weight: 101,000kg (222,200lb)
Warhead: 1000kg (2200lb)
Range: 5000km (3107 miles)

mid-1939 the *Heereswaffenamt* (HWA; Army Weapons Department) authorized and sponsored the setting up of a uranium production facility in Oranienburg; the HWA also now took over the nuclear development programme, and closely liaised with and monitored Germany's best physicists.

By 1942, during which year the HWA gave up its control of the programme to the *Reichsforschungsrat* (RFR; Reich Research Council), it appeared that Germany's attempts to develop a nuclear weapon had largely gone on the back burner. Yet the true picture is more shadowy. A patent application of 1941, submitted by physicist Carl Friedrich von Weizsäcker, shows a clear understanding of the overall workings of achieving a nuclear explosion through a fission process using the appropriate isotopes of uranium and plutonium. The same

year, the industrial giant I.G. Farben built a suspicious production plant a few kilometres from Auschwitz concentration camp, with an electricity consumption far in excess of its declared purpose of making synthetic rubber.

Anecdotal evidence at least suggests it could have been part of an atomic research programme. Even more revealing is a 1943 map prepared by a *Luftwaffe* study team. It shows New York, Manhattan Island and the surrounding areas of New Jersey and Long Island. Superimposed over the map are concentric rings radiating out from the centre, each ring labelled with a destructive effect.

Given the scale of the map and the size of the rings, the blast pattern seems similar to that of a 15- to 17-kiloton bomb. A list of key industrial targets for the *Amerika* Bomber also suggests that a nuclear weapon could have been

intended to ensure destruction from a single aircraft.

The most contentious arguments about Germany's atomic weapons programme, however, revolve around the possibility that the Nazis actually tested a device somewhere off the Baltic coast in October 1944. An apparent eyewitness, the Italian war correspondent Luigi Romersa, claimed that he saw the devastating explosion, and subsequently had to hide from 'deathly rays, of utmost toxicity'. A *Luftwaffe* officer flying in the area also gave an account to US military officers on 19 August 1945:

I noticed a strong, bright illumination of the whole atmosphere, lasting about 2 seconds. The clearly visible pressure wave escaped the approaching and following cloud formed by the explosion ... A cloud shaped like a mushroom with turbulent, billowing sections (at about 7000m

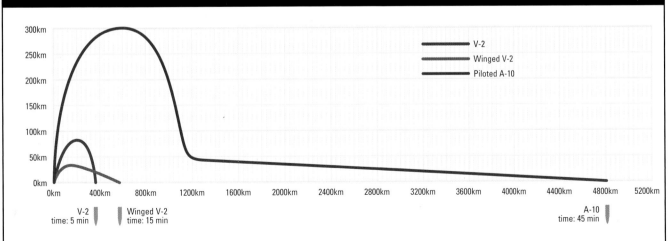

SURFACE-TO-SURFACE MISSILE RANGES

GERMAN NUCLEAR DEVICE

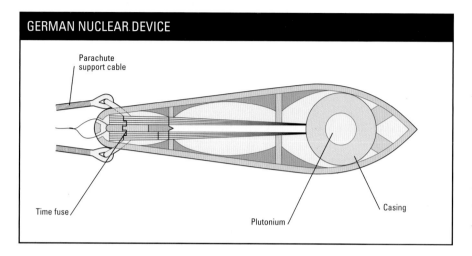

Parachute
support cable

Time fuse

Plutonium

Casing

Above: This is the only known German diagram of a nuclear weapon; it was discovered in an incomplete report compiled shortly after the war. Although the diagram is very basic and is far from being a detailed design for a nuclear bomb, the report contains an accurate assessment of the critical mass required for a plutonium bomb, which was almost certainly derived from German wartime research. The report also indicates that German scientists had carried out extensive theoretical work on hydrogen bombs.

altitude) stood without any seeming connections over the spot where the explosion took place. Strong electrical disturbances and the impossibility to continue radio communication as by lightning, turned up.

There is an authentic ring to this account, which not only accurately describes the phenomenon of an atomic explosion and subsequent mushroom cloud, but also the disruptive electro-magnetic pulse that accompanies such a powerful detonation.

Even so, there is much stacked against the credibility of such an account, including questions about why the apocalyptically minded Hitler did not use such a weapon

KEY SCIENTISTS IN THE NAZI ATOMIC WEAPONS PROGRAMME

Scientist	Position	Area of research
Walther Bothe	Director of the Institute for Physics at the Kaiser Wilhelm Institute for Medical Research	Measurement of nuclear constants
Klaus Clusius	Director of the Institute for Physical Chemistry at the Ludwig Maximilian University of Munich	Isotope separation and heavy water production
Kurt Diebner	Director of the HWA testing station in Gottow and experimental station in Stadtilm, Thuringia	Measurement of nuclear constants
Otto Hahn	Director of the Kaiser Wilhelm Institute for Chemistry	Transuranic elements, fission products, isotope separation, and measurement of nuclear constants
Paul Harteck	Director of the Physical Chemistry Department of the University of Hamburg	Heavy water production and isotope production
Werner Heisenberg	Director of the Department of Theoretical Physics at the University of Leipzig and acting director of the Kaiser Wilhelm Institute for Physics in Berlin-Dahlem	Uranium production, isotope separation, and measurement of nuclear constants
Hans Kopfermann	Director of the Second Experimental Physics Institute at the Georg-August University of Göttingen	Isotope separation
Nikolaus Riehl	Scientific Director of the Auergesellschaft factory	Uranium production
Georg Stetter	Director of the Second Physics Institute at the University of Vienna	Transuranic elements and measurement of nuclear constants

if he had one readily to hand. Ultimately, we cannot know the entire truth of what occurred, nor the true extent of Hitler's atomic programme. What we have seen in this chapter, however, is that Hitler's technological flights of fancy often latched onto the idea of delivering massive destruction upon targets as far away as the United States. Thankfully he never achieved his goals, although with purely conventional weapons he still led much of the world into ruin.

Below: A map based on a 1943 original prepared by a Luftwaffe study team identifying potential targets in the eastern United States, such as New York City. The blast pattern is remarkably similar to that of a 15- to 17-kiloton nuclear bomb.

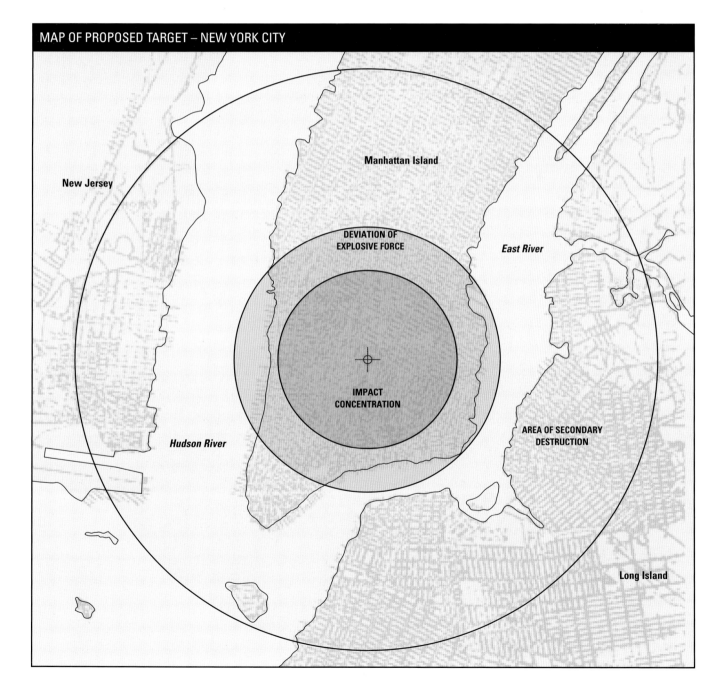

MAP OF PROPOSED TARGET – NEW YORK CITY

New Jersey

Manhattan Island

DEVIATION OF
EXPLOSIVE FORCE

East River

IMPACT
CONCENTRATION

Hudson River

AREA OF SECONDARY
DESTRUCTION

Long Island

Bibliography

Books

Bishop, Chris. *Order of Battle: Germany Infantry in WWII.* St Pauls, MN: Zenith Press, 2008.

Bishop, Chris. *Order of Battle: German Panzers in WWII.* St Pauls, MN: Zenith Press, 2008.

Burleigh, Michael. *Germany Turns Eastward.* London: Pan Books, 2002.

Carr, William. *Hitler – A Study in Personality and Politics.* London: Edward Arnold, 1986.

Dearn, Alan. *The Hitler Youth 1933–45.* Oxford: Osprey Publishing, 2006.

Deighton, Len. *Blitzkrieg – From the Rise of Hitler to the Fall of Dunkirk.* Fakenham: Book Club Associates, 1979.

Evans, Richard J. *The Third Reich in Power 1933–1939 – How the Nazis Won Over the Hearts and Minds of a Nation.* London: Penguin Books, 2006.

Grunberger, Richard. *A Social History of the Third Reich.* London: Phoenix, 2005'

Kirk, Tim. *The Longman Companion to Nazi Germany.* Harlow: Longman Group Limited, 1995.

Layton, Geoff. *Germany: The Third Reich 1933–45.* London: Hodder & Stoughton, 2000.

Lucas, James. *Germany Army Handbook 1939–1945.* Stroud: Sutton Publishing, 1998.

Overy, Richard. *The Penguin Historical Atlas of the Third Reich.* London: Penguin Books, 1996.

Quinn, Carl Underhill. *Adolf Hitler – Pictures from the Life of the Führer.* New York: Peebles Press, 1978.

Rees, Laurence. *The Nazis – A Warning From History.* London: BBC Worldwide, 2002.

Snyder, Louis L. *Encyclopedia of the Third Reich.* Ware: Wordsworth Edition Limited, 1998.

Trevor-Roper, Hugh. *Hitler's Table Talk 1941–1944.* London: Phoenix Press, 2000.

Useful websites

Axis History Factbook – http://www.axishistory.com
Feldgrau.com – http://www.feldgrau.com
United States Holocaust Memorial Museum – http://www.ushmm.org
German Police in World War II – http://www.germanpolice.org
The Nizkor Project – http://www.nizkor.org

Glossary

Arbeitlung – Battalion/Detachment
Admiral (Adm) – Admiral
Anschluss – Union with Austria, March 1938
Arbeitsgaue – Divisional Work Districts
Armee – Army
Armeegruppe – Army Group
Auftragstaktik – Mission-oriented Tactics
Ausbildungs – Training
Autobahn – Motorway

Bataillon – Battalion
Befehlshaber der Ordnungspolizei (BDO) – Chief of the Order Police
Bekenntniskirche – Confessional Church
Bergpolizei – Mountain Police
Blitzkrieg – Lightning War
Blockwart – Block Warden
Bodenständige – Static
Bund Deutscher Mädel (BDM) – League of German Girls

Chef der Deutschen Polizei im Reichsministerium des Innern – Chief of the German Police in the Reich Ministry of the Interior
Christliches Landvolk – Christian Agrarian Party

Der Stürmer – 'The Stormer' (newspaper)

Deutsche Arbeitsfront (DAF) – German Labour Front
Deutsche Glaubensbewegung – German Faith Movement
Deutsches Jungvolk – German Young People
Deutsches Nachrichtenburo (DNB) – German News Bureau
Deutschnationale Volkspartei (DNVP) – German National People's Party
Die Endlösung – 'The Final Solution'
Dienststelle Ribbentrop – Ribbentrop Bureau
Dienstverpflichtung – Compulsory service

Einsatzgruppen – Task Forces (mobile death squads)
Einsatzkommando – Sub-unit of an Einsatzgruppen
Eisenbahnpolizei – Railway Police
Entartete Kunst – Degenerate Art
Ersatz – Replacement
Ersatzheer – Replacement Army

Feldgendarmerie – Field Police
Feldgerichtsabteilung – Court-Martial Department
Feldheer – Field Army
Feldjäger – Sharpshooters
Festung – Fortress
Flakkorps – Anti-Aircraft Corps

Fliegerdivision – Air Division
Flieger-HJ – Hitler Youth Paramilitary Aviation Enthusiasts
Fliegerkorps – Air Corps
Frankfurter Zeitung – 'Frankfurt Newspaper' (newspaper)
Fregattenkapitän (Fkpt) – Captain (junior)
Freikorps – Free Corps
Fremdarbeiter – Foreign Workers
Führerbunker – Hitler's bunker
Führerkanzlei – Führer Chancellery
Führerprinzip – Leadership Principle

Gastarbeitnehmer – Guest Workers
Gau – District
Gauleiter – District Leader
Gebiet der Kriegsverwaltung – Military Administrative Zone
Gebietskommissar – Area leader
Gebirgsjäger – Mountain Light Infantry
Gefechtsgebiet – Combat Zone
Geheime Feldpolizei (GFP) – Secret Field Police
Geheime Staatspolizei (Gestapo) – Secret State Police
Generaladmiral (Gen-Adm) – General-Admiral (equivalent to an Army Colonel-General)
Generalbevollmächtigter für den Arbeitseinsatz – General Plenipotentiary for Labour Deployment

Generalbezirke – General Regions
Generalfeldmarschall – Field Marshal
Generalgouvernement
 – General Government (of Central Poland)
Generalkommissar – Commissar general
Generalmajor – Major-General
Generaloberst – Colonel-General
Germania – latin term for Germany. *Welthauptstadt* ('World Capital') Germania was the name Adolf Hitler gave to the projected renewal of the German capital Berlin, part of his vision for the future of Germany after the planned victory in World War II.
Geschwader – Group (RAF); Wing (USAAF)
Gleichschaltung – Coordination
Großadmiral – Grand Admiral
Großdeutsches Reich – Greater Germany

Hafenpolizei – Harbour Police
Hakenkreuz – 'Hook Cross', Swastika
Hauptamt Ordnungspolizei
 – Order Police Headquarters
Hauptgebiete – Main Districts
Hauptkommissar – Commissar captain
Hauptmann – Captain
Haus der deutschen Kunst
 – House of German Art (Munich)
Heeresgruppe – Army Group
Heimatsgebiet – Home Zone
Heiliges Römisches Reich deutscher Nation
 – Holy Roman Empire of the German Nation
Herrenvolk – Master Race
Hilfspolizei (Hipo) – Auxiliary Police
Hilfswillige ('Hiwis') – Voluntary Assistants
Hitlerjugend (HJ) – Hitler Youth
Hochseeflotte – High Seas Fleet
Höchste SS- und Polizeiführer (HöSSPF)
 – Supreme SS and Police Leader
Höherer SS- und Polizeiführer (HSSPF)
 – Higher SS and Police Leader

Jagdpolizei – Game Conservation Police
Jäger – Chasseur, Light (of infantry)
Jungmädelbund – League of Young Girls
Junker – landowner

Kaiserlich – Imperial
Kaiserliche Marine – Imperial Navy
Kampfgruppe – Battle Group
Kapitän zur See (KptzS) – Captain of the Sea
Kasernierte Polizei – Barrack Police
KdF-Wagen – 'KdF-Car' (later the Volkswagen)
Kommandeure der Orpo
 – Commanders of the Order Police
Kraft durch Freude (KdF) – 'Strength through Joy'
Kreis – Local Council
Kreisgebiete – Area Districts
Kreisleiter – County Leader
Kreispolizeibehörde
 – City/County Police Authority
Kriegsmarine – (German) Navy
Kriminalpolizei (Kripo) – Criminal Police
Kristallnacht – 'Night of the Broken Glass'

Landdienst – Land Service
Länder – States, Provinces
Landesinspekteur – Regional Inspector
Landspolizeibehörde – Regional Police Authority
Landtag – Provincial Parliament
Lebensborn – 'Fount of Life'

Lebensraum – 'Living Space'
Luftflotte – Air Fleet
Luftwaffe – (German) Air Force

Militärinternierte – Military Internees, POWs
Militärverwaltung – Military Administration
Minister für Kirchenfragen
 – Minister for Church Affairs
Motorisierte Infanteriedivision
 – Motorized Infantry Division

Nationalpolitische Erziehungsanstalten (NAPOLA)
 – National Political Education Institutes
Nationalsozialistische Deutsche Arbeiterpartei (NSDAP) – National Socialist German Workers Party
Nationalsozialistischer Deutscher Dozentenbund (NSDDB) – National Socialist Germany University Lecturers League
Nationalsozialistischer Deutscher Studentenbund (NSDSB) – National Socialist German Students League
Nationalsozialistischer Lehrbund (NSLB)
 – National Socialist Teachers League
NS Rechtswahrerbund – Nazi Lawyers Association

Oberkommando der Luftwaffe (OKL)
 – Luftwaffe High Command
Oberkommando der Marine (OKM)
 – Naval High Command
Oberkommando der Wehrmacht (OKW)
 – Armed Forces High Command
Oberkommando des Heeres (OKH)
 – Army High Command
Olympiastadion – Olympic Stadium, Berlin
Operationsgebiet – Operations Zone
Ordnungspolizei (Orpo) – Order Police
Ortsgruppenleiter – Local Group Leader
Ortspolizeibehörde – Local Police Authority
Ostarbeiter – Eastern Workers
Osthilfe – 'Help for the East'

Panzerschiff – Armoured Ship, Pocket Battleship
Parteikanzlei – Party Chancellery
Parteitage – Party Days (Rallies)
Pflichtjahr – Duty Year (BDM)
Polizei Abschnitt – Police Sector
Polizei Gruppe – Police Group
Polizeiverwaltungsbeamten – Administrative Police
Polizeivollzugsbeamten – Uniformed Police

Raum – Space
Regierungspräsident – Government President
Reichsarbeitsdienst (RAD) – Reich Labour Service
Reichsbank – Reich Bank
Reichsbevollmächtiger – Reich Plenipotentiary
Reichsfilmkammer – Reich Chamber for Film
Reichsgau – Administrative district created in areas annexed by Nazi Germany
Reichsheer – Reich Army
Reichsjugendführer – Reich Youth Leader
Reichskammer der bildenden Künste
 – Reich Chamber for Fine Arts
Reichskommissariat – Reich Commission
Reichsleiter – Reich Leader
Reichsleitung der NSDAP
 – Reich Leadership of the NSDAP
Reichsministerium für die besetzen Ostgebiete
 – Reich Ministry for the Occupied Eastern Territories

Reichsmusikkammer – Reich Chamber for Music
Reichspressekammer
 – Reich Chamber for the Press
Reichsrundfunkkammer
 – Reich Chamber for Radio
Reichsschriftumskammer
 – Reich Chamber for Literature
Reichssicherheitshauptamt (RSHA)
 – Reich Main Security Office
Reichstag – German parliament in Berlin
Reichsstatthalter – Reich Governors
Reichstheaterkammer – Reich Chamber for Theatre
Reichswehr – Reich Defence Forces
Reviere Polizei – Precinct Police
Rückwartiges Gebiet – Rear Area

Schnellboot – Fast Boat
Schutzmannschaften der Ordnungspolizei
 – Detachments of Order Police
Schutzstaffel (SS) – Security Squad
Schwarze Reichswehr – Black Reichswehr
Sicherheitsdienst (SD) – Security Service
Sicherheitspolizei (Sipo) – Security Police
Sonderkommando – Special Unit
Sonderpolizei – Special Police
Sportpalast – Winter sports stadium in Berlin
SS- und Polizeiführer (SSPF)
 – SS and Police Leader
SS-Oberabschnitt Führer
 – SS Leader of the Main Districts
SS-Polizei Regiment – SS Police Regiment
Staffel – Squadron
Sturmabteilung (SA) – Assault Detachment/Storm Detachment

Technische Nothilfe – Technical Emergency Service
Thule Gesellschaft – Thule Society
Truppenamt – Troop Office (Schwarze Reichswehr)

Untermenschen – Sub-humans

Vizeadmiral (VAdm) – Vice-Admiral
Volk – People
Völkischer Beobachter
 – 'People's Times' (newspaper)
Volksdeutsche – Ethnic Germans
Volksgemeinschaft – People's Community
Volksgerichtshof – People's Court
Volksgrenadier – People's Grenadier
Volkssturm – People's Militia
Volkswagen – People's Car
Vorläufige Reichsheer – Provisional Army
Vorläufige Reichsmarine – Provisional Navy
Vorläufige Reichswehr
 – Provisional Defence Forces

Waffen-SS – Armed SS
Wehrertüchtigungslager der Hitlerjugend
 – Military Service Competency Camps for the Hitler Youth
Wehrkreis – Military District
Wehrmacht – (German) Armed Forces
Wehrwirtschaft – War Economy
Welthauptstadt Germania
 – 'World Capital Germania'

Zellenleiter – Cell Leader
Zeppelinwiese – Zeppelin Field (Nuremberg)
Zivilarbeiter – Civilian Workers

Index